THE APPALACHIAN TRAIL:
ONWARD TO KATAHDIN

by
Jan D. Curran

RAINBOW BOOKS, INC.

Library of Congress Cataloging-In-Publication Data

Curran, Jan D., 1934-
    The Appalachian Trail -- onward to Katahdin / Jan D. Curran.
        p.   cm.
    Includes index.
    ISBN 1-56825-072-X
    1. Appalachian Trail—Description and travel. 2. Middle Atlantic States—
Description and travel.   3. New England—Description and travel.   4. Hik-
ing—Appalachian Trail. 6. Curran, Jan D., 1934—Journeys—Appalachain Trial.
I. Title.
F106.C87   1999   99-18373
917.404'43—dc21   CIP

The Appalachian Trail:
Onward To Katahdin
by Jan D. Curran

ISBN 1-56825-072-X / softcover / $14.95

Publishing industry inquiries (reviewers, retailers, libraries, wholesalers, dis-
tributors/media) should be addressed to:

Rainbow Books, Inc.
P.O. Box 430, Highland City, FL 33846-0430
Editorial Offices—
Telephone: (888) 613-BOOK; Fax: (941) 648-4420; Email: RBIbooks@aol.com

Individuals' Orders: (800) 356-9315; Fax: (800) 242-0036; Online: (http://www.)
upperaccess.com, amazon.com, barnesandnoble.com

Printed in the United States of America.

CONTENTS

DEDICATION

This book is dedicated to all those who assisted me in making this journey of a lifetime possible — whose support, both physical and psychological, was crucial to the successful conclusion of my adventure. Their positive focus helped carry me through those times when fatigue and my frailties threatened to drag me down, when my negative inclinations seemed to dominate, when I was struggling to prevail through miserable weather conditions that created equally miserable rages in my inner weather.

I have already mentioned many to whom I am indebted. But I particularly want to thank Cathy Morris who, when the going was the toughest, reached down in her reservoir of effervescence to offer encouragement: "You can do it, Old Soldier, you can do it." I still hear those words when I encounter a vexing obstacle and know that the AT Medic still works her magic.

Other Rainbow Books in our highly acclaimed

The Appalachian Trail
Series

by Jan D. Curran

The Appalachian Trail:
How To Prepare For & Hike It

The Appalachian Trail:
Journey Of Discovery

FOREWORD

My hike of the Appalachian Trail was different from other journeys and adventures in my life, primarily because it took place in the Appalachian Mountains where I became more directly exposed to the reality and order of life in the natural world. In essence, it stripped away my veneer of psychologically civilized comfort and forced me to look in a dispassionate way at the fundamental importance of the gift of life. It gave me an opportunity to consider my part in the natural world, to see how the natural world functioned and, by extension, how I functioned.

I came to learn that I was involved in a continuing evolution where change was the dominant factor in life, that the very essence of life was the process of change and that it was ultimately the source of all growth. I learned that for real spiritual and psychological growth to occur, I had to more fully participate in the process than I had in the past. Clearly, I had not only to be open to, but embrace change as the engine that powered my spiritual development. It required me to understand that real spiritual growth cannot occur in any other way. I had a responsibility, not only to understand that, but also to actively participate in this natural progression of life.

Some call it aging or maturing, and view matters of life with beginnings and endings, complete with goals or fulfillment of some sort. At least, that was how I envisioned spiritual growth which I considered would be complete as soon as I could arrive at the point where I could face death without fear and with spiritual confidence. I viewed the world and myself as a finite little universe where everything had their clearly defined dimensions. I expected that when I reached a certain goal or objective, the future, as far as it was concerned, would thereafter and forevermore be secured.

In the tradition of human consciousness, and particularly our Western trained consciousness with its goal and result oriented philosophy, it was difficult for me to comprehend that life is a continuous process and that my participation in the process could not be measured in finite, quantifiable terms. By extension, I knew we were all interrelated and a part of the process and that none of us fully understands the forces that shape our existence or guide the process. We know only that comprehension of that force is beyond our cognitive or sensory powers. And because our culture basically discounts anything that cannot be rationally explained or perceived or understood from sensate sources, it becomes difficult for us to accept our spiritual dimension. Therefore, we often ignore it and its importance, or seek approaches to the concepts that are more compatible with our culture and our sensory focus.

I also realized for the first time that anyone who has set foot on a spiritual path has begun a journey for life. A journey not just in the traditional meaning of the term as it relates to one's life- span, but also in the sense that it is a journey to learn about the fundamental essence of life for all time.

Of course, I also looked forward to again becoming "one with the Trail." There is something alluring, almost hypnotically enticing, about the concept of bonding with the Trail. I had found this bonding to be very pleasant and useful in overcoming times of difficulty on the Trail during the preceding summer when I had hiked the southern half of it. I think it was because such bonding forces the hiker to participate in the natural order of things in the mountains. It was almost like a kinship had developed between me, the hiker, and my mountains and that kinship was the glue that held me on the Trail. It allowed me to dominate the negative impulses arising from the elements and the grinding physical demands of hiking long distances.

Then, too, I still thought in terms of campfires and starry nights and walking on the soft carpets of needles in the fresh forests of firs and pines. Meanwhile, sun-dappled forest floors with wild flowers and birds kept appearing in my reveries. Perhaps it was these thoughts that most heightened my sense of anticipation as the time to return to the Trail drew closer.

Whatever propelled me, I welcomed the opportunity to again test my will against the elements and my own frailties. Perhaps that is a slightly unfair assessment; I now knew I would finish the Trail. The only question that remained in my mind was the spiritual and personal growth aspect. It was now mostly a matter of what I would learn and how I would learn it. I now knew that the real focus of my journey was internal, and I really wanted to get on with evaluating the process of my change.

CHAPTER 1

I exhort you also to take part in the great combat, which is the combat of life, and greater than every other earthly conflict.
— *Plato*

Starting Again
"You can do it, Old Soldier . . . You can DO it!"

It was a classic late spring day in Turner Gap. The fierce blue sky contrasted color-to-color with the intensity of the mid-morning sun. The hills and valleys of central Maryland were swathed in the lush greens of a land embraced by the promise of growth. New generations of wildflowers were coming on stage. Life exploded into the yearly spectacle that humbles those who think about life's beginnings. A perfect day to resume one's hike to Maine. My anticipation, fashioned from a winter's worth of dreams, fairly pumped the adrenaline into my blood, and my breathing increased as I surveyed the scene.

I searched for the point where the AT emerged from the forest. I had departed from the Trail at that spot the previous September. It seemed like such a long time ago. Everything should have been familiar, but I could recall only the Gothic stone chapel and rustic old South Mountain Inn. One of the oldest public houses on the AT, the inn still offers meals and drinks. (Some say it dates back to as early as 1732. Others put it at 1780.)

White blazes, indicating the trace of the Trail, followed a narrow asphalt lane from the main highway up the mountain. After a couple of hundred yards, the blazes turned left into the forest and followed the crest of South Mountain to the north.

This was not a steep climb, and I anticipated a relatively easy walk. I was mistaken.

The heat reflecting in shimmering waves from the pavement played optical tricks with objects in the distance and made breathing difficult from the outset. Progress was slowed; not only by the heat, but also by the frequent stops the body demanded to accommodate the requirements newly placed on it. After only a few yards, the shoulder and waist straps on my backpack began to pinch and rub in places familiar with pain from a year ago. My lungs gasped for additional air. Legs rubbery from the fatigue, induced by the stress of unaccustomed weight, betrayed my initial confidence. An unintentional comparison recalled with irony the excellent conditioning I had achieved the previous summer. Had I been in that kind of shape now, I would have breezed up to the ridge crest. Twenty agonizing minutes later, my hiking companion Cathy and I removed our packs and sat on a rock to savor the refreshing coolness of the forest.

Dr. Cathy Morris from Coral Gables, Florida, was the Director of Research at Dade County Community College. I had met her briefly during my hike of the Southern Appalachians the previous summer. We had maintained contact over the winter and talked intermittently about her joining me on the Trail in the spring. She was enthusiastic about adding a few hundred more miles to her AT "experience," and she had saved about six weeks of vacation time with the intention of accompanying me from Maryland to wherever we found ourselves at the end of that time.

Cathy had worked hard to prepare for the hike, devoting most of her leisure time to walking and jogging with weights and aerobics. As fit as she was, she was also experienced enough to know that nothing prepares hikers to hike long distances in the mountains — other than hiking long distances in the mountains.

That was evidenced by her naturally talkative mood becoming increasingly quieter the farther up the ridge we progressed. Her lips pressed tightly against her teeth and a look of determination replaced her usually jovial expression. One could tell an inner struggle was taking place, that she was involved in serious business. Later, she laughed, when I mentioned that I was having problems getting acclimated to carrying a pack again, "Yeah, tell me about it."

The Trail Guide pertaining to Maryland indicated we were at the site of an old battlefield. The battle of South Mountain on September 14, 1862 had been a precursor to the battle of Antietam, one of the bloodiest campaigns of the Civil War. In fact, the Confederate command post for the battle had been located in Turner Gap.

Once on the ridge crest, the Trail was fairly level and easy to walk; and we soon covered the two miles to Washington Monument State Park where we stopped for lunch. We watched a group of children, 12-to-13-year-olds on a class outing playing softball or badminton, or swooping down a long curving slide. They laughed and ran in the full enjoyment of life that only children are allowed. Certainly they were oblivious to the knowledge that they were playing on a field, where scarcely more than a century before, soldiers, many not much older than they, were killing and dying for reasons they only vaguely understood.

The main attraction in the park is, as the name implies, the Washington Monument, the first public monument to President George Washington. Built in 1827, it is rather unimposing as monuments go. Constructed from native field rocks, it rises to a height of about 30 feet in a shape that reminded me of the milk bottles the milkman used to leave at our door when I was a child. An interior stairway spiraled to a narrow observation platform, where a panorama of lush spring fields and forests-draped hills rewarded the ambitious.

South Mountain reverberated with the sound of cicadas; a swelling natural buzz or high-pitched humming that changed in volume with the wind and the arrival of new members. It was the cicadas' turn to be on nature's stage, and they would be the loudest and best of all. Although mostly incessant and slightly overwhelming, occasionally the noise would subside. Then some male, seeking an advantage, would issue his strident invitation to the females, and the mountain would swell with the urgent chorus of his competitors.

I was ignorant of cicadas. In fact, I had no idea about what was making the noise until I asked Cathy.

"They remain dormant in the ground for 17 years," she explained.

"How's that?"

"Those suckers burrow into the ground and live there for 17 years. Then, they come out, mate and die."

I had noticed that the forest floor was pockmarked with millions of tiny holes like some giant aerator had rolled over it. "You think these holes are where they come from?"

"You got it!"

The pathway was littered with the carcasses of the blunt-faced insects, their cellophane-like wings folded back against their stout bodies. I looked up, trying to catch a glimpse of one in flight, but saw only occasional twinkling when the wind gently swayed the treetops and the sun reflected from the wings of those attached to the branches. Once every 17 years . . . Remarkable!

It was late afternoon when we reached Annapolis Rocks and set up camp. After supper we walked down to the rocks to view the sunset. Even the cicadas ceased their humming as the sun began to disappear; it was as if they too were awed by the display of golden streaks across the flame-red backdrop with violet mountains, undulating in waves, seemingly headed over the edge.

Sometime around midnight, I was abruptly awakened by a group of men stumbling around the forest, trying to set up camp by flashlight. Oblivious to our presence, they called loudly back and forth among themselves and hissed or uttered profanities while tripping over roots or rocks. Eventually, though, they pitched their tents, and the forest again became quiet.

I tried to go back to sleep, but I drifted in and out of consciousness for the remainder of the night. My mind ambled all over the intellectual and psychological landscape. It was an intriguing journey, one filled with dissonance. Despite the enormous physical challenges involved, I truly desired to return to the Trail. The paradox was striking. I was a creature of comfort, yet I wanted desperately to become immersed in the wilderness, to feel again the surge of primeval emotion that attends one's presence in the power and majesty of nature. I wanted to again draw into my soul the incomparable vistas from the mountain tops, views that reached across green and gold patchwork quilt valleys, decorated by sun glistening ponds, across rolling blue hills and skies, where clouds lazed about or sometimes scudded across a storm blown horizon. I wanted to again smell the earth and the forest fresh with rain, hear water tumbling down laurel-framed brooks and admire the riot of blooming wildflowers spattered about mountain meadows. In short, I wanted to again become a part of these old hills, and I was willing to sacrifice the comfort of civilization and the predictable; and, of course, my control over the elements in life.

In between those thoughts, I wrestled with issues that companionship raised. I was pleased to have Cathy accompany me. But I was concerned about the impact on my spiritual development. I sensed that solitude was a necessary medium to induce growth. In the past I had used solitude as an avenue to meditation, and that in turn had greatly aided in my development. Now I was unsure how company would affect my ability to concentrate. Would I be able to achieve the degree necessary for meditation? I was still struggling with these issues when the sun came up.

As we were climbing back to the Trail from Annapolis Rocks, I thought about the story I had read somewhere about a young female physician who had become addicted to narcotics. She had traveled the now familiar journey into drug abuse, going from one substance to another, trying different remedies to combat her addiction, and failing every cure, only to return again to drugs as an escape from her demons. Finally, filled with despair, she acknowledged her lack of power in controlling her addiction and decided to place her fate in God's hands. She recounted that she prayed and that when she finished praying it felt like a huge weight had been lifted from her shoulders; and she never again felt the need to use drugs. She had, as she described it, turned control of her problem and her life over to God, and He had responded. Maybe there's a message there for me, I thought. Maybe I need to give up some control!

Two men heading towards us broke my concentration. One was tall, about six feet, the other about five-and-a-half feet tall. Both wore ragged jeans, had scruffy beards, disheveled long hair and bloodshot eyes. As we neared, the tall one smiled broadly, saying, "Y'all stay at Annapolis Rocks?"

We nodded.

"We're headed back there now to get our stuff. Ain't supposed to camp there."

"We were wondering about that," Cathy said. "There's a sign on the way down from the Trail, but it's so beat up we didn't take it seriously,"

"That's 'cause they been havin' trouble there. People partyin' and trashin' the place. Last ones were some Viet Nam Vets. They really messed it up. Sign went up right after that. Someone even started a forest fire. Drunk most likely."

"Then, how come you're goin' back?" asked Cathy.

"There's a State Ranger headed this way, and we figure we best be outta there!" he laughed.

The Ranger was not far behind the men. He was a young man in his early 20s with a powerful physique that accentuated his nicely tailored uniform. We learned that he hiked only the Maryland section of the Trail - going from end-to-end, back-and-forth, helping hikers and keeping attuned to events. He described in some detail what to expect from the Trail ahead. And shortly after that, we encountered several groups of people, carrying brightly-colored rappelling ropes and heading for Annapolis Rocks.

At noon we stopped at the Hemlock Hill Trail Shelter for lunch and were joined a short time later by end-to-end thru-hikers Bill and Laurie Foot from Lynchburg, Virginia, and Randy Moore from Macon, Georgia.

Bill and Laurie were tall handsome people, enjoying the adventure of a lifetime. Bill had been a purchasing executive for a large firm, and Laurie was a school psychologist. They had been considering doing the Trail on and off for several years; and, then, seemingly all at once, they decided to just do it. Laurie quit her job, and Bill took a leave of absence. Now here they were. A courageous decision. People don't often sacrifice financial security to follow a dream . . .

Their children had totally different responses to their parents' decision. Their 20-year-old son was positively excited about it. Their 11-year-old daughter was aghast that her parents were acting like a couple of adolescent scouts. Bill and Laurie had taken the Trail Name: "The Happy Feet." They had started from Springer Mountain in the early spring and planned to thru-hike to Maine by the end of summer. The 24th of September was the target date for their climb up Katahdin.

Randy was short and thin in stature, but he was wiry and

tough, a real power hiker. A shock of red hair, a beard and an impish grin complemented the intensity of his spirit. He had a dry sense of humor and peppered his remarks with rich and original descriptions and phraseology. He had slowed his pace to accompany the Happy Feet — he enjoyed their company — and the Happy Feet in turn welcomed his positive and good-natured riposte.

I mentioned how I'd hiked the southern portion of the AT the previous summer. I intended my comment for Bill, but he didn't respond, and it hung there in the air, looking for someone to acknowledge it.

Laurie picked it up. "Why did you come off the Trail?"

"Got started too late to do it all in one season," I responded defensively. "Couldn't get away from my job any sooner."

"What do you do?"

"I was an Army Officer. I'm retired now."

"Oh." End of conversation

I was persistent. "You all look to be in great shape. How far you hiking on average in a day?"

"About 18 miles," Bill said.

"That's impressive." I anticipated some response, but none was forthcoming. Awkwardness prevailed, until Randy broke the silence.

"That's for sissies. Power hikers do a lot better'n that," he said with mock seriousness. Everyone laughed. A conversation ensued between Randy, who had adopted the Trail name, "Macon Tracks" and the "Happy Feet." Cathy and I became their audience.

The terrain we covered during the afternoon was basically easy, the path mostly level, well-worn, with only a few rocks to trip the inattentive. Although it was only our second day on the Trail, we easily covered 11 miles before stopping at Devils Racecourse Shelter for the night. We were surprised to find Randy and the Happy Feet at the shelter. I had assumed they would be far ahead us, given their edge in fitness. They also had not expected us, and it took a few minutes for them to rearrange their gear to make room for us in the shelter.

The evening flowed in a convivial atmosphere with Randy assuming the unintentional role of entertainer-in-chief, steering the conversation, while directing a series of good-natured barbs at the Happy Feet and Yankees. Occasionally one or the other of the Feet team would respond to defend or counterattack, but they were hopelessly outclassed, as I would have been in repartee with the quick-witted Randy. He referred to himself as a true "power hiker," expressing mock contempt for those like the "Feet" who he derided as too slow to be worthy of membership in the fraternity of "power hikers."

There followed more spirited conversation, but Cathy and I mainly listened. Not for long, though. We were both exhausted. At least, I was; and I was soon overwhelmed by sleep.

CHAPTER 2

If a person is to get the meaning of life he must learn to like the facts about himself — ugly, as they may seem to his senti-mental vanity — before he can learn the truth behind the facts. And the truth is never ugly.

— *Eugene O'Neill*

Devils Racecourse to the Iron Masters Mansion

Before heading back to the Trail the next morning, Cathy and I decided to explore the natural phenomenon known as Devils Racecourse. It was raining lightly as we stepped out from the forest onto the ancient stream bed covered by layers of steamer trunk-sized boulders. The jumble stretched for about a hundred yards across to the forest on the far side and for several hundred yards up the mountain before disappearing into intermittent stands of trees in the distance. A sense of desolation pervaded the scene mirroring images of what I had perceived a barren earth to look like before the onset of life. We hopped aimlessly from boulder to boulder intrigued by the strange shapes and the surreal quality of the landscape.

About 15 uneventful minutes later, satisfied that we had sufficiently explored the Devil's Domain, we headed back to the Trail. (I suspected our boulder trip was a subconscious ploy to delay the inevitable tough little climb back to the ridge crest.) We climbed steadily for about an hour, until reaching the 2000-foot high point of the Trail in Maryland. Just north of the high point, the Trail descended to High Rock, a popular hang gliding site with superb views to the west. From there it was just under two-and-a-half downhill miles to Pen Mar County Park, and we covered the distance in time for lunch.

The park, a former resort owned by the Western Maryland Railroad, encompasses a grove of old shade trees with a large, 19th Century style, wooden dance pavilion tucked into one corner. One could almost picture ladies in Victorian dress with lace gloves and parasols strolling the paths with beau's wearing spats and bowler hats. Numerous picnic tables and benches were sprinkled among the trees, and centrally positioned were a couple of concession buildings, where PTAs and Firemen's Auxiliaries sold cakes or cookies or grilled their barbecues.

It was Saturday and a dance had been scheduled for the afternoon. The pavilion was already occupied by bustling musicians setting up amplifiers and other sound equipment. The atmosphere was decidedly festive. Eager families streamed into the park with excited children racing ahead to lay claim to the choicest picnic tables near the pavilion. Most everyone carried large baskets or boxes filled with foods of every description from basic ham sandwiches to roasted chickens; black forest cakes; and gallons of sodas and Kool-Aid to wash it all down.

Cathy and I selected an unoccupied picnic table away from the pavilion. We didn't want not to attract too much attention; neither did we want to be in anyone's way. But as fate would have it, we landed next to a table, which an older couple had selected for a banquet. Their preparations were deliberate — probably the result of many visits. First came a long white paper table covering, held in place with bowls of potato salad. There followed assorted platters of sandwiches, jars of pickles and relish, cartons of fried chicken pieces and soft drinks. The spread was crowned by a large, homemade cinnamon cake which, at the appropriate time, was set in the center of the table on the one space left conspicuously vacant. Then, the activity ceased as everyone stopped to admire the horn of plenty that spilled across the table.

We watched mesmerized as the food surfaced from the seemingly bottomless baskets, and when it was apparent that the table was fully set and no more food was forthcoming we turned our attention to our table. Two pathetic cans, tuna fish and liverwurst, sat beside two equally pathetic peanut butter cracker packets and our water bottles. Cathy looked up to see me watching; she rolled her eyes toward the sky and shrugged her shoulders. When I asked if we should try to strike up an acquaintance with those of more distinguished means, she groaned and made a beeline for the ladies room, having ordered me to guard our food.

As I was sitting there, a thin little girl with large front teeth, big blue eyes and blond pigtails spied me. She looked alternately at the packs and me. Finally, after several seconds, she could no longer contain her curiosity. "What are you doing?" she asked, pointing to the packs.

"I'm hiking the Appalachian Trail."

"What's that?"

"It's a foot trail through the Appalachian Mountains. It goes all the way from Georgia to Maine."

"Where are you going?"

"I'm headed for Maine." I expected she would run off and tell her family about this weird guy walking to Maine.

She sensed instinctively that she had a captive. "How much does that weigh?" She pointed again to my pack.

"About 45 pounds. Do you know how much 45 pounds is?"

She nodded, her face serious. Then, came the most basic question of all. This was one very honest and bright little girl. "Why are you doing it?"

"Because I like to hike, and I want to see America."

"Wouldn't it be easier to do it in a car?"

"Yes, but you miss a lot of stuff in a car. You know, the animals and flowers and people like yourself."

"Do you sleep alone in the woods?"

"Yes, but mostly at shelters with other people."

"Aren't you scared of bears an' stuff?"

"Nope."

She was quiet for a moment. "I'm in the 6th grade."

"You must be very smart to be in the 6th grade."

She nodded her head. "My mommy is in the fire department auxiliary." She motioned toward the concession stand area.

At that moment Cathy arrived. She quickly sized up the situation. "Let's get some ice cream." Without the hint of hesitation, the girl followed, dancing around Cathy as they headed for the concession stand. Cathy returned about five minutes later minus the girl. "No ice cream, no candy and no potato chips!

Some concession stand!"

We opened our cans of tuna fish and liverwurst, and began conversing with our neighbors. It was not by any cold calculation that we entered the conversation, but clearly there was unconscious skullduggery at work. They offered almost immediately to share their bounty. Of course, we refused to hear of depriving them of any fried chicken or potato salad. Then, they offered some potato chips. Crisp, greasy, salty, insatiable potato chips. The temptation was nothing short of overwhelming.

Cathy was the first to crack. After that first breech in our dietary defenses, it took very little time before a pitiful and complete surrender took place. When one of the ladies offered cinnamon cake, we barely hesitated. In fact, we ate two pieces each and probably would have gone for thirds except for our consciences.

After leaving the park, we tried to find a stone marker, dating from 1776; the Trail Guide indicated marker designated a point on the Mason-Dixon line. We searched around in vain. Twenty minutes later we gave up and continued on our way, dropping easily down the mountainside to Falls Creek, which we crossed on a rustic little foot bridge. Climbing back to the ridge on a full stomach was a little more difficult, a fact reflected in our longer break at Mackey Run Shelter. The remainder of the Trail in the afternoon was a pleasure. The forest was open, and cool breezes wafted gently across the ridge. We made several short detours to unusual rock formations, where we stopped to admire panoramic views of lowland forests and farms. My Trail journal reflected my appreciation for the beauty of the Maryland and southern Pennsylvania countryside, not the wild spectacular beauty of peaks and canyons and raging waters, but the rustic beauty of a tended land with fields of grain and cattle and well-kept tidy farms.

Antietem Shelter sat on a small, lush island, reached by a bridge across one side of Antietem Creek. The upstream portion of the island consisted of multi-colored stones and pebbles worn smooth by years of water flow. Farther downstream, the rocks gave way to a layer of fertile soil, and at the water's edge, rich long grass trailed downstream with the flow. In front of the shelter, a giant old tree with only tatters of bark remaining had fallen across the creek. Its trunk had been trimmed and shaped to provide level footing for those wanting to venture out over the water. I walked halfway across the creek and nearly fell in when I turned to come back. Branches near the bank provided good handholds for anyone wanting to brave the water. After a hot day on the Trail, the temptation was just too great; and I slid down the bank with great anticipation, which cooled almost immediately after hitting the water. I didn't stay long.

In the morning we headed up toward Buzzard Peak and Snowy Mountain, stopping occasionally to admire stands of ox-eye daises, sunflowers and Asiatic day flowers interspersed with fleabane, bladder campions and evening lynchnis. Then, around mid-morning, we slipped off the Trail for the village of South Mountain and ice cream.

South Mountain is a travel guide photographer's model for rural Pennsylvania. Freshly-painted houses, spotless yards with orderly gardens - populated with brightly-hued dwarfs and animal figures, and cutouts of well-fed ladies in polka dot patterns bending over in a permanent pose — lined the road into town. The people were as colorful and lively as their homes.

As we were leaving the convenience store with our ice cream, we almost knocked over a bearded old man seated beside the door. His wide smile induced me to stop.

A large, brick, institutional building had attracted my attention. "What's that?" I asked, pointing to the huge building.

"Used to be a tuberculosis sanatorium," he replied.

"What's there now?"

He shrugged his shoulders.

"Hospital?"

"Yeah."

"A VA or government hospital?"

"Used to be a tuberculosis hospital."

"Is it still a tuberculosis hospital?"

He shrugged his shoulders.

"How long you lived here?" I asked.

"All my life."

"Could be an old folk's home."

He looked up and smiled again — a large gap toothed smile surrounded by a froth of flowing whiskers.

We bid him a good day and went our way.

The twin Raccoon Run shelters, small, low-built structures

together, could probably hold a total of about eight people, maybe ten if everyone liked coziness. They sat almost directly on the Trail in a well-maintained grassy opening in the thickets that covered the ridge. The shelter register contained a number of verses created by the Happy Feet to be sung to the contemporary tune containing the refrain, "Every day, getting a little closer." An entry by Macon Tracks said something about the North not showing him much.

After a short stop for soft drinks at the Caledonia State Park swimming pool, we headed for Quarry Gap twin shelters. On the way we passed the Locked Antlers Camp, an abandoned hunting cabin which the Trail Guide indicated had a spring. We rummaged through the refuse-strewn forest for about half an hour in a vain attempt to locate the spring. Our efforts succeeded only in unearthing or tripping over discarded tin cans, an oil stove, sheets of metal, assorted pots and an unseemly collection of trash. I was appalled at the "desecration" of the environment and was not timid about voicing my displeasure with man's insensitivity toward natural beauty.

"Cut it out!" Cathy said, after one of my particularly nasty tirades. She was not hesitant about letting me know when my negativity was overreaching. But on after thought, she said, "Really is pretty bad, though. Let's get outta here! Hunters!" She spat the word out like a bad tasting flavor. Her vision of Judgment Day had all the critters killed by hunters lined up, their beady little eyes focused accusingly on their malefactors so as to influence the Almighty to sentence them to their just rewards. For Cathy eternal damnation was probably sufficient.

The twin Quarry Gap shelters stood only a few hundred yards up the ridge from the Locked Antlers Camp. The setting was idyllic with large stands of mountain laurel in full and frothy blossom and rhododendron bursting with promise, waiting their turn for the floral stage. On the far side of the shelter clearing, a crystalline stream flowed easily down the gently sloping ridge. The air perfumed by the scent of the flowers and the quiet rush of water created an atmosphere of tranquility.

My thoughts, as though inspired by the scenery, turned inward. I dwelt at some length on the concept of God being an essential presence in my existence and concentrated on trying to solve the ages old question: for what purpose did I exist? My life, indeed, everyone's life had to have a significance other than procreation or something greater than that which could be determined from the corporeal values we assign ourselves — but how to find, to identify that significance?

Perhaps another level of consciousness was the answer. My reflection came not as a flash of pure insight, but rather as an extension of the experience gained from listening to sermons and reading books about spirituality and mysticism during the winter. I had learned the importance of going within to find my answers, of giving my inner consciousness the opportunity to guide me in my searches for answers to questions of the spirit.

I believed I already knew instinctively some of the requirements for spiritual growth. But I had to combat the need to be in control at the conscious level. The fact that I was totally incapable of dealing with matters of the spirit through my sensory or rational consciousness seemed not to make the least bit of difference to my ego. It would will what it wanted, and no matter how intently I tried to sit back and let go, my consciousness simply would not accept that it couldn't be in charge. I was in for some very challenging personal battles. Clearly much meditation and work stood before me. But of extreme importance was that for the first time I fully recognized I was dealing with a situation where my sensory, rational cognitive powers were utterly useless. It was a small step, but it was absolutely vital to the process.

The next morning, radiant stands of white and pink mountain laurel along with representatives from the spruce family, Norway, blue and red, as well as white and pitch pines accompanied our climb to the ridge. Farther on, we encountered some spectacular saucer magnolias on the hillside.

Just after passing Toms Run Cabin we came upon an abandoned homestead; several of its fieldstone walls were still standing. The wooden portions, roofs, etcetera, had long since disappeared. Although lacking human presence, it was far from uninhabited. Clinging to the side of one wall at a height of about eight feet, a large black snake observed our approach. Satisfied that we meant no harm, it continued its climb even before we had departed.

It was five o'clock by the time we reached Pine Grove Furnace — after a sixteen-mile day. We stopped initially at the small store down the hill from the Iron Masters Mansion to buy provisions. We didn't buy much. First, the stock was definitely limited. Second, the prices were just short of outrageous.

The Iron Masters Mansion is a pre-Revolutionary War structure built, as the name indicated, for the Iron Master, the man in charge of the furnaces and the iron-making operation. The building was enormous, beautifully constructed and tastefully appointed. The floors, all hardwood, were polished to a soft amber glow, which, along with colonial style, solid, natural-colored wood furniture, gave the rooms a warm aura of age and tradition. On the outside, the old fired, red brick walls were accentuated by white-framed windows and eaves, and a porch with massive white wooden columns that ran the length of the building. Standing on a large grassy knoll surrounded by an impressively large, manicured lawn, it overlooked ground that sloped gently down toward the furnaces.

The iron-making operations have long since departed to more efficient venues, and along with the operations, the Iron Master. The building has since evolved into a youth hostel, and the Iron Master has become a caretaker/hostel manager.

The other guests at the mansion included two physicians and a patent attorney from RCA. Mary Lee Howell, an obstetrician, was doing her internship at her alma mater, Duke University. She was accompanied by David Lorbach, also doing his internship at Duke. The patent attorney was newly un-retired LeRoy Greenspan from Lancaster, Pennsylvania.

LeRoy Greenspan told me he had decided to return to work after becoming bored and negative in retirement. It "rejuvenated" him, as he described it.

I explained why I had come on the Trail and suggested it might be a good idea for selected executives to periodically leave the work environment for a slightly extended period to help put their private and business lives in balance, if not in perspective. I was convinced such a period would be beneficial to many senior military officers by allowing them to get away from the self-warping intensity of focus on career enhancement and progression.

LeRoy agreed, saying he occasionally needed to get away from everything, family included. A couple of weeks day-hiking or something similar helped him "refresh" his "mental outlook."

Our conversation drifted, engaging everything from the Three Mile Island nuclear power incident to nuclear power generation of electricity, to the impact on the environment of continuing use of fossil fuels. After more than an hour discussing the dangers associated with air pollutants and the greenhouse effect, my brain experienced its own mini-meltdown from ecological/ nuclear overload, and I headed for the bedroom to repair the damage.

CHAPTER 3

That day she put our heads together,
Fate had her imagination about her,
Your head so much concerned with outer,
Mine with inner, weather.

— *Robert Frost*

Iron Masters Mansion to Shikellamy YMCA Camp

We departed the hostel at about 7:30 a. m., planning to hike some nine miles to Moyer's Campground to spend the night. The weather was ideal, cool and clear, and the Trail well maintained with only a few gradual changes in elevation. Walking was easy, and we made good time, arriving at the side trail leading to the campground at 3:00 p. m., much earlier than planned. Since the hiking had been relatively easy to this point, we thought it would remain so and decided to press on to Campbell Shelter some seven miles farther down the Trail. That may have been a mistake.

We didn't anticipate the difficulty of the climb up Rock Ridge or the energy-draining rock scramble on the ridge crest that followed, where a maze-like Trail snaked in, out and around a series of house-size boulders. We didn't reach Campbell Shelter.

The climb up Rock Ridge and the boulder maze had taken its toll. We had covered some 15.8 miles by the time we reached Little Dogwood Run, and an inviting campsite nestled in a draw beside a gently bubbling stream, was irresistible.

Cathy and I had stumbled upon an agreeable arrangement

when it came to making camp. We set up camp first; put up the tent, laid out sleeping gear, collected water, et cetera. Then, Cathy cooked supper, while I wrote my Trail notes. She liked to cook but wasn't especially excited about cleaning up. That became my chore. And during that time, Cathy worked on her Trail notes.

The Trail the next day began with a climb up Colon Hill. There followed a short descent into a draw, then a climb to White Rocks Ridge. White Rocks was an outcropping of 500-million-year-old quartzite rock that formed the northern terminus of the Blue Ridge chain. The Trail was very rough and rocky but not without merit; several short side trails led to overlooks with excellent views, and the knowledge that I was walking over rock with a 500-million-year history inspired a sense of reflection.

It was mid-morning by the time we came to Campbell shelter. We filled our water bottles and drank as much spring water as we could hold. After a short, well-earned rest, we headed down the mountain to the picturesque Cumberland Valley.

The Trail followed roads across the valley, and the walking was easy. We encountered flourishing stands of wild flowers: whorled loose strife, celandine, chicory, black-eyed susans, daisies and many more. Flickers and goldfinches flew around us, and once a magnificent scarlet tanager watched us from a lone tree by the roadside.

The farms were impressive. Most buildings were freshly painted, fences all mended, and the fields were clean and lush. The livestock was similarly cared for. Horses, their coats glistening in the sun, their tails and manes combed and trimmed, stood in small groups among the cattle. Fat, clean cows chewed contentedly on rich grass beside ponds that sparkled in the sun. Occasionally a cow near the road would raise its head to watch as we passed.

A grassy road embankment under a luxuriant old maple tree, near the junction of Kiner Boulevard and Middlesex Road, became our sidewalk cafe for lunch. Across the road from us stood the home of Bonnie and Michael Shaffer, a white frame house with gray trim that fit in perfectly with the surroundings — almost like it grew there. Of course, we didn't know the Shaffer's lived there, until young son Phil arrived carrying a pitcher of fresh, cold well water. And shortly after — we'd just finished lunch — Bonnie came over with a broad smile and two

bowls of freshly picked strawberries. It was a spontaneous friendliness; we came to appreciate and admire in the people of the
Cumberland Valley in particular and in the state of Pennsylvania generally.

During the ensuing conversation, we learned of the plan to
re-locate the Trail from the roads through the valley to more
remote terrain to the west. Bonnie told us that she and other
people along the Trail in the valley liked the hikers and were
disappointed that the Trail was being relocated.

Cathy and I nodded as she talked, trying to accommodate
our own feelings in the matter as we compared the special beauty
of the farms and the people, with the unknowable that a relocation would present. We understood the need to get the Trail off
the roads. Still, we felt the family farms of the Cumberland Valley represented a steadily fading part of Americana and that it
was a treasured experience to have walked the countryside. In
the final analysis, though, the Trail was a wilderness experience, and the farms were certainly not wilderness. A visit to
them could be very rewarding, but you couldn't have both.

A county road crew was refueling an asphalt laying machine and had pulled the tanker along side the asphalt layer
thereby blocking traffic in both directions for the duration of
the refueling process. The result was a mini-traffic jam. Five
members of the road crew all clad in grease and oil stained cov-
eralls clustered around the man doing the refueling. Two of the
workers, probably bored by the operation, looked around for
other amusement at just the time we approached. They came
over to the side of the machine.

"This the Appalachian Trail?" the questioner yelled to make
himself heard above the clattering of diesel engines in the background.

"It surely is." I responded.

"See, I told you it was," he called back to someone in the
refueling cluster.

"How far does it go?" asked the other man.

"From Georgia to Maine."

"How far you goin'?"

"Up to Maine."

My response created a stir and everyone but the fuel han-
dler came to look us over. Long blond hair cascading incongru-

ously down the back of one crewmember testified to the quality of the county's equal opportunity program. She was markedly cleaner than the others, and it was my guess that she didn't actually work with asphalt. Either that or she had been blessed with the feminine knack for grooming that males are genetically unable to master.

"How far you come?" came from somewhere in the group.

"From Georgia," I responded.

"Christ, you been hikin' all the way from Georgia?" came the incredulous response.

"I started in Georgia last summer. Got off in Maryland at the end of the summer and started back on again about a week ago."

"Oh," said the voice, disappointment clearly registering.

Suddenly our notoriety dissipated. The asphalt crew watched as we walked up the sidewalk to the Shipe house. They had no idea that the "Ice Cream Lady" lived there, and that hikers would kill for ice cream. No one was home, though; it was with considerable disappointment that we returned to the sidewalk and headed past the line of cars still jammed by the refueling operation.

We had not passed more than five cars when the driver of one honked the horn and motioned vigorously to us to come over. She opened the passenger side window and asked if we were looking for the "Ice Cream Lady." We both nodded. "That's me. Go back and sit on the porch. I'll be with you soon's I get outta this damn tie-up."

Bonnie Shipe was a vivacious and gregarious person with a great deal of knowledge about the Trail, its history and traditions as well as the people who walked it. We visited for more than an hour with her drinking large containers of Kool-Aid and eating large double cones of chocolate swirl ice cream. Bonnie had, over the years, amassed an impressive collection of photos of thru-hikers and showed us albums crammed with pictures of hikers waving in jubilation from the summit of Katahdin. It was a pleasant and interesting visit, and I felt a sense of regret as we departed and headed once again up the hill.

It was 4:00 p. m. when we reached US Route 11 and the motel recommended by Bonnie. It had been a long day but a rewarding one, and I was put in reflective mood by my experience with the people.

These were people with a positive outlook. I sensed no negative undercurrents in their expression or demeanor. Their inner
spark seemed different. Certainly they were subject to the same
concerns of everyday life — jobs, money, family problems, et
cetera, that others worried about. Yet, they exhibited an infectious enthusiasm that I came to admire in those who were generally excited about life. There was an aura of joy about them.

It occurred to me in that moment that personal happiness
is largely the product of personal selection; that people chose to
be happy or unhappy by the focus they applied to their lives. It
was much like the lesson I had learned about hiking in the rain.
The weather was neutral. How I responded to it was my responsibility. I could accept it and find beauty, or I could reject it and
find misery. Similarly life presents us with many negative and
positive situations and circumstances. We have the freedom to
focus on the negative or the positive and in so doing to choose
the perspectives that govern our outlooks, either happiness or
unhappiness.

I could accept that all is not perfect, but I also understand
that happiness has to do, not with perfection, but with acceptance. If I could accept that, I am a valuable, loving creature of
God. I need only experience the inner joy such acceptance brings
— and that is the stuff of real happiness.

In the morning we stopped at the truck stop where the AT
crossed US Route 11. We stuffed ourselves with ham, sausage,
eggs, pancakes, toast, jelly, orange juice and coffee, and read
the Trail register. Entries by the Happy Feet and Macon Tracks
referred to the "half gallon club" at Pine Grove Furnace. Membership can be gained only by eating half a gallon of ice cream.
I think Bill Foot joined twice — rather unfortunate financially,
since the ice cream is not free.

The Happy Feet were not too happy with the planned relocation across the Cumberland Valley. Laurie volunteered that
she thought hikers in the future would ignore the relocation
and continue to walk the roads as we had done. I doubted that
would happen. Most hikers only follow the blazes and consequently wherever the Trail takes them. It would certainly depend on how the Trail approached the new location. If it goes
only to Mt. Holly and does not swing east, then no one will take

the roads. I was sure the usage would follow the relocation.

Climbing out of the valley, we crossed in succession Blue Mountain, Little Mountain and Cove Mountain, the last being the toughest. It was fairly early when we arrived at the trail leading to the Thelma Marks Memorial shelter. The shelter was some distance down the mountain, and the spring was even farther away; we decided to continue on to Duncannon, which was only three miles farther on.

We stopped for a minute at Hawk Rock to admire the view of the confluence of the Juniata River, Sherman Creek and the Susquehanna River. From there, the Trail dropped precipitously to the Susquehanna River Valley. In places, the descent was treacherous, primarily because of wet earth and rocks, and we proceeded with great caution.

Several animals scampered off the Trail as we approached. Most were squirrels, but we encountered a pair of ground hogs, and strangely enough, a box turtle lumbering up the hill. Cutest, though, was a baby rabbit that simply crouched and watched as we passed by. Farther down the mountain, we encountered a weasel, obviously on the hunt, sniffing the ground as it loped across rock deposits. I wondered if it was on the trail of the baby rabbit we had just seen. If so, the rabbit was in big trouble.

Duncannon is a long, ribbon-thin settlement close on the banks of the Susquehanna. It is only a few hundred yards wide at its widest point, but it stretches on for about two miles, so that when hiking through it after a long day, it seems to go on forever.

The Trail Guide indicated that Duncannon offered accommodations. I suspected it meant the Doyle Hotel, but the run-down brick building with soot blackened windows didn't exactly inspire confidence on my part. A peek through the front door revealed a bar dimly lit by neon beer signs. A figure at the bar came to life as the jukebox began wailing a country western lament. We continued on. Later I was informed by other thru-hikers that we should have stayed at the Doyle Hotel, that the people were friendly to hikers.

We had hiked more than 20 miles by the time we finally crossed Clarks Ferry Bridge over the Juniata River. We were both exhausted, and although the truckstop was less inviting than Doyle's Hotel, several run-down motel buildings behind the truckstop looked for all the world like mini-mansions.

Actually the place was filthy. The electric baseboard heat was on high as was a window air conditioner. The bathroom was dirty, and the commode did not work. Still, it had a roof, beds and running water; certainly it was no worse than most of the shelters we had slept in. We unpacked our gear and laid out our sleeping bags, then headed for the restaurant. The food was about as bad as the rooms, but after downing several beers, it really didn't matter. The half-cooked chicken even tasted half-way good.

It was 8:30 the following morning when we crossed the bridge over the Susquehanna and headed for Shikellamy YMCA Camp some 14 miles away. I wasn't feeling particularly good (the beers may have had something to do with that), but the weather was pleasant and hiking not too demanding. We arrived at the camp at about 5:00 p. m. and were surprised that we were not welcomed with open arms. The camp director informed us that hikers were usually not allowed to use the facility, since there normally wasn't any room. But due to the fact that they were barely into the process of opening the camp and because there were many empty bunks, he decided to make an exception. "Just don't advertise it," he pleaded.

Shortly after midnight, I was jolted awake by a series of palpitations. It took a few seconds to focus my thoughts and realize that my heart was beating irregularly. I bolted upright and hit my head on the overhead bunk.

"Dammit," I hissed.

Cathy was immediately alert to my discomfort. "You all right?"

"My heart's gone bananas again. Nothing serious, at least I don't think it's serious."

"Not serious?" The concern in her voice knifed through the darkness.

"Well, it's not dangerous. I ain't gonna die is what I mean. But it sure is aggravating."

"What're you gonna do?"

"Beat's me. Just lie here 'til it goes away, I guess. Not much else I can do."

"We need to get you to a doctor?"

"No use in that. They'd only put me in a hospital and charge me an arm and a leg. Anyway, if it's like the other times, it'll convert in a couple of hours. Go back to sleep, and we'll work it out in the morning."

End of conversation.

I rolled onto my right side, propped my head up with my arm and slipped into a fitful sleep. I awoke at 7:00 a. m., expecting to find my heart beating normally. It wasn't. The effect was psychologically devastating. I lay in my sleeping bag for a few minutes and assessed my situation. During previous episodes, I had converted back to my normal rhythm after five hours. I had already passed that time by two hours.

Cathy stirred. "How you feeling?"

"Still got problems."

"That's not good."

"Yeah, tell me about it."

"What're we gonna do?"

"Really haven't sorted that out yet. First thing is to get this damn thing beating regularly again." As I said it, I rolled out of my sleeping bag and stood up. Initially I staggered a little. Then, with my improved balance, I wobbled down the steps toward the bathhouse.

My heart converted to its normal beat at about the time my feet hit the bottom step. I brushed my teeth and washed up going through the motions with mechanical indifference. I was exhausted by the time I returned to the bunkhouse. Clearly I was in no condition to strap 45 pounds on my back and spend the day climbing mountains. After a few minutes discussion, during which I railed against arrhythmias and age in general, I confided to Cathy that the time had come, once and for all, to deal with the problem.

Much as I hated it, I had to face reality. I needed to interrupt the hike, I had decided to return to Berryville and get an appointment with my mother's cardiologist.

"What about me?" Cathy asked when I informed her of my decision.

I had been totally absorbed in my own dilemma; the question took me by surprise. I became irritated with myself for not having brought Cathy into my deliberations. An instant appraisal followed. There seemed to be only three alternatives for her.

"Good question, I responded. "Looks like you go on alone,

you can go back to Coral Gables, or you can come with me to Berryville and hang around 'til I get this thing sorted out." My response came out with the clinical objectivity that I had learned to dislike in dealing with "experts" in positions of authority in the bureaucracy. The lack of sensitivity in my reply reflected my negative mind set.

If I had hurt her feelings, Cathy didn't let it show. "Well, I'm not going on by myself. That's for sure. I still have five weeks of vacation left, and I don't plan to spend it in Miami. That seems to leave me with one choice. How do we get back to Berryville?"

That was the easy part. The hard part was getting to see a cardiologist. That was the first reaction from the secretary in a local doctor's office. A call directly to the office of my mother's cardiologist, Dr. James Laidlaw, resulted in the same response. My mother came to the rescue by demanding to speak to Laidlaw directly. She explained my situation, and I had an appointment for two days hence when he would be on emergency room duty.

The farm my father had bought when he retired from the Army lay squarely in the horse and apple country of the Shenandoah Valley, Clarke County, in northern Virginia. I could understand why my father had chosen this spot to live his life. Besides a beautiful view of the valley leading to the Blue Ridge to the east, there was a soothing atmosphere about the valley and the farm. A sense of serenity lay across the land. Here the soul had the feeling that it could take refuge from the constant battering of the challenges in every day life.

The gradual flow of spring into summer reflected in the forests, and the pastures hinted at a concept of time where the need to hurry did not exist and was therefore unknown. I spent hours walking the pastures and breathing the serenity into my soul. In the afternoons, I rested under the canopies of 500-year-old oaks and gazed across the valley to the Blue Ridge, cloaked as always in a haze that hints of mystery.

Although it was a place of quiet and tranquility, the farm teemed with life. Cardinals, orioles, bob white quail and robins seemed to be everywhere, and high up in the hollow of a dead limb, a pair of red-breasted woodpeckers occasionally peeked out to insure that all was right with the world. Rabbits and squirrels cavorted in the glen behind the house, while the cats slept by the barn or on the front porch. Occasionally a groundhog could be seen moving about in the large pasture below the house. There was a time when I would have shot them. Their burrows in the middle of the field presented the danger of a horse stepping in one and breaking or otherwise injuring a leg, and a racehorse without four good legs is useless. Sadly the horses were gone along with my father, and so, the ground hogs lived in peace.

The visit with Dr. Jim Laidlaw was the answer to a prayer. I had expected a cold clinical evaluation of my problem. What I got was a concerned physician who looked upon his job as one of getting me back on the Trail. Certainly he had to satisfy himself that I had no life-threatening condition, but once he established that, I had the feeling that we were embarked on a joint effort.

After describing my medical history, I mentioned something about wanting desperately to "climb that last God damn mountain." I was surprised by the emotional charge in the statement. I was surprised also that I swore and felt a little embarrassed.

Laidlaw nodded knowingly, saying I was involved in the "adventure of a life-time." He looked directly into my eyes and said he was going to try and work it out, so that if it were at all possible, he would get me back on the Trail. He ordered several tests, including an echocardiogram administered by a tall attractive woman named Rhonda.

The echocardiogram was an interesting experience. Rhonda moved the probe-like device across my chest saying something into a recorder to indicate which part of the heart she was observing. Occasionally she placed me in a position where I could watch the monitor and also stopped the machine and re-ran some of the images for my benefit. Viewing my heart in action created a surreal feeling. At first glance, the screen seemed to show an amorphous mass of matter resembling something from an old grade B movie where a great glob of swamp began pulsating with life and eventually formed a bizarre monster who proceeded to terrorize the landscape and the theater patrons too. But, then, as Rhonda described the shape, I could make out the outlines of an organ. In fact, I could see my very life beating and pulsing. I felt oddly detached as I watched, desperately hoping it was doing the right thing. It looked so fragile and vulnerable. Then, the realization hit me. If that thing stops moving — you're dead.

The following day I was hooked up to a halter monitor, a portable cassette recorder, which operated at extremely slow speed and recorded heart pulses in the same manner as an EKG. The electrodes were pasted to my chest just like in a normal EKG, except that at the point where the electrodes were pasted, the chest hair was shaved and the area sanded to insure good adhesion. Then, all the leads were taped in place and connected to the recorder that I carried over my shoulder like a large purse.

I was to carry the monitor around with me for a 24-hour period, which was to include hiking with my pack to get a picture of my heart under the stress of hiking. The area I elected to hike was just south of Snickers Gap on the Trail itself. There the path crossed over several ridge arms and draws that required a good deal of exertion. Cathy joined me, but without pack, and we walked almost all day.

Early in the afternoon, we stopped at the Bears Den Hostel, a large field stone structure that sat directly on the ridge crest. In addition to accommodations, water and toilets, it offered a variety of aids to hikers — field guides and maps and limited food supplies. After drinking sodas, we headed back toward the Trail, where we encountered Stephen and Debbie Helber and their daughter.

Stephen, a photographer for the Associated Press out of Newport News, Virginia, was there to get some photographs of hikers for a story on the 50th anniversary of the Trail opening. He took several pictures of Cathy and me walking down the trail from Bear's Den Hostel, then took a picture of me alone, walking Bear's Den Rocks with the Shenandoah Valley in the background. That picture subsequently found its way into numerous papers across the east and even into the Naples Daily News in Naples, Florida, the town where I lived.

After turning in the monitor the next morning, I went to the waiting room and waited for Dr. Laidlaw to appear. Instead I received a message that I was to proceed to the cardio-pulmonary laboratory. I entered a small dark room where Laidlaw was reviewing tapes of my echocardiogram.

Panic hit. He's found something! I thought.

Actually he hadn't found anything. His prognosis was that I had no heart defects or arterial blockage. Since he had satisfied himself that structural abnormalities or blockages were not a problem, he had to look elsewhere, and that elsewhere was the electrical impulses that caused the heart to react. He compared the electrical conduction system of the heart to the electrical system of an automobile engine. It depends on electrical impulses to be delivered to the spark plugs in a certain sequence and at a certain time. If this sequence is interrupted, the engine does not function properly. That, in a simple way, described the problem with my heart.

To counter the problem, he proposed using a fleccainide medication called Tambocor and prescribed dosages that were to be increased should my adrenaline level begin to override the medication.

I was euphoric when I left the hospital. I was going back on the Trail, and not only that, I had a real solution to my problem.

CHAPTER 4

One is happy as a result of one's own efforts, once he knows the ingredients of happiness — simple tastes, a certain degree of courage, self denial to a point, love or work, and above all, a clear conscious. Happiness is no vague dream, of that I now feel certain.

— *George Sands*

Stoney Mountain to Port Clinton

Our return to the Trail began at 10:00 a. m. with the ascent up Stoney Mountain. We quickly reached the ridge top and came upon the remnants of Yellow Springs, a coal mining settlement from the previous century. The area once occupied by the village is now a soft grassy forest floor, dotted with vestiges of buildings that once populated the landscape. A contemplative silence, broken only by a soft wind murmuring through the trees and shafts of sunlight punctuating the shadows, created a timelessness that teased the intellect to search for some significance.

The Trail followed an old street past a maze of stone foundations, where the moldering shapes of long-vacated houses, their outlines still clearly traceable, lay muted under moss and other growth. No other indications of human habitation still exist, and were it not for the rocks, one would ever have sensed that a thriving settlement had once existed there. But another presence seemed to have settled in, and it reminded one of history, not in the textbook sense but of a visceral kind like one feels while viewing ancient crypts in the cathedrals of Europe. I jotted something in the Trail Register to validate my presence here and moved on.

The Trail from the ridgeline down to Rausch Gap followed an abandoned railroad bed used by trains long ago to haul coal out of the mountains to the various iron furnaces that had sprouted up across the countryside. Small pieces of coal and cinders from the steam engines that labored there still cover the path. Nearby was an old strip mine, where occasional saplings bravely trying to survive, would have one believe that healing had taken place. But barren crevices in the earth, separated by streaks of rust and ochre clay, reminded one of a cancer that refused to heal.

Two barking dogs belonging to a man who had established a homestead there greeted our arrival at the Rausch Gap shelter. His dogs had staked territorial claim to the place and had to be convinced by their owner that it was all right for us to be there.

Three other people were also at the shelter: Slim Jim (Jim Pielow) from Whitewater, Florida; Daddy Long Legs (Randall Barnes) from Nashville, Tennessee; and Doug Brown. Slim Jim and Daddy Long Legs were young thru-hikers. Doug Brown, an older gentleman, was hiking a short section of the Trail.

The man with the dogs was not a hiker. I suspected he was a homeless person. He had made a mess of the place. Dirty cooking utensils and camping paraphernalia were strewn all over. In the clearing in front of the shelter he had strung a clothesline between two trees, and from it hung an unseemly collection of grimy, gray-streaked underwear. A box constructed beneath a piped spring to collect water for cooking and drinking had been appropriated for a cooler and contained a six pack of beer. In the corner, between a retaining wall and the front of the shelter, was a sleeping platform. He had scraped together a pile of dead leaves over which was draped a filthy sleeping bag.

I asked about a set of rattlesnake rattles dangling from a nylon cord attached to the man's hiking stick. He recounted proudly how his dogs had discovered the snake. He also said the dogs had tracked down a fawn with a severe cut on its leg, and that he had sutured the wound with monofilament fishing line. I looked up to see Jim roll his eyes skyward.

The man wore jogging shoes but limped around the shelter clearly in some pain. When asked about it he said that he had stepped on a piece of glass, and the glass was still embedded in his foot. Someone suggested that he remove the glass and clean the wound. At that point, he removed his right shoe, and with a large, thick-bladed hunting knife, set about trying to pry the glass fragment from his dirt-encrusted foot. After a short period of painful and unsuccessful effort, he dropped the idea and spent the remainder of the evening hobbling around the clearing on the side of his bare foot.

Slim Jim and Daddy Long Legs exhibited enough bodily similarities to their names to make it unnecessary to ask who was who. They had started together from Springer Mountain but would finish individually. Daddy Long Legs wanted to include the Vermont Long Trail in his adventure and planned to separate from Slim Jim at the junction of the Long Trail and the AT by Sherburne Pass in Vermont. Slim Jim would continue on alone from that point to Katahdin. After doing the Long Trail, Daddy Long Legs would return to the junction of the AT and the Long Trail, then complete his trek to Katahdin.

We were the last to leave the shelter in the morning. Slim Jim and Daddy Long Legs departed around 5:30 a. m. That was the last we saw of them, although we were able to follow their progress from their entries in the shelter journals along the way. They must have slowed to enjoy their adventure, since they remained only a couple of days ahead of us, until they were well into Vermont. It was raining lightly, and the temperature was comfortably cool, when we departed.

We soon came to the ruins of Rausch Gap village. The Trail passed a cemetery containing the gravestones of three members of the Jon Proud family. One of the stones marked the grave of a baby girl who had died at one year and one month. The other graves were identified as "Englishmen," one of whom passed on at age thirty, the other at age 57.

We encountered two thunderstorms during the day, not the type with lightning crashing down all around, but they were wet and reasonably uncomfortable. During the first storm we took refuge under our ponchos which did little to keep us dry, but it did protect us from the wind. Some hail also arrived with the storm, making it very chilly, but it passed quickly, and with it the chill; then abruptly the sun reappeared, and it was warm again.

We arrived at the site where we planned to camp for the night in the downpour from the second storm. The "Philosopher's

Guide" indicated that in this area several hikers had lost packs stolen while their owners slept. To protect ours, Cathy rigged both packs into an "A" configuration in an upright position and tied them together with a rope running to the tent. She then placed our ponchos over the packs in such a way as to create a small breezeway in front of the tent, which also made the packs appear to be part of the tent. No sooner had she completed her construction, than a third storm rolled over us. It was not as benign as the first two. The wind blew with vengeance, and lightning crashed down all along the ridge. Tent fabric flapped furiously as did the ponchos, but despite all the furor, everything held up, and we were no wetter than when we first erected the tent.

We awoke the next day to blue sky and sunshine. The Trail followed a grassy ridge top road through open forest with splendid views to the south, then crossed a mini-Devils Race course.

In the vicinity of PA Route 501, the Trail became decidedly more difficult. There the path was sited over several steep and slippery rock formations, which required considerable energy and caution to cross. It was troubling, since only a few yards away, a fairly level forest floor paralleled the rocks. We overtook two men taking a break on the rocks. One man appeared to be in his 60s; he looked completely exhausted. The other much younger man was waiting patiently for his partner to catch his breath. As we passed, I mentioned something sarcastic about the siting of the Trail.

"Trails supposed to be a challenge," came the rejoinder from the older gentlemen draped over a rock.

I couldn't help myself. "Looks like the challenge won."

As we climbed farther up the Trail, I heard the older man ask his partner if we "expected the Trail to be asphalt with handrails."

At noon we stopped for lunch in a sunny opening in the forest; we laid our clothes and equipment out to dry. The two men we had passed earlier soon joined us. Merle Heckman and Bob Tormo were from Elizabethtown, Pennsylvania. Bob, the older, more talkative of the two, told us he had been caribou hunting in Alaska and had a beautiful set of antlers to prove it. Out of the corner of my eye I could see Cathy squirm. She looked at me darkly but said nothing. Bob said he also had done some fishing in Alaska and had caught some Arctic char and salmon. Merle, the younger man, mentioned that he had just married off his daughter and that his new son-in-law liked to hike; he hoped the two of them could do some hiking in the future.

Bob's pack was very large; all the food he carried for the six-day hike was canned. I asked how much his pack weighed. "About 35 pounds," he replied. I bit my tongue. I suspected it was almost twice that. While we were talking, Bob produced a huge hunting knife and began opening cans of food, puncturing the top with the tip, and then cutting the metal next to the rim. He mentioned that he had suffered a recent heart attack and that his wife was concerned about his hiking. He had persuaded her that he would be all right, and so — there he was. After leaving Bob and Merle, Cathy exploded. "Imagine killing a poor animal for its horns."

The weather turned hot, and we stopped early in the afternoon by Hertline Spring in the shade of some large trees to cool off and rest. While we were relaxing, a shirtless hiker with a red bandana tied around his neck came loping up the Trail behind us.

Doug Wilcox explained that he was trying to keep cool by hiking in just his shorts. A raw, angry-looking, bleeding spot on his back, where the skin was rubbed by his pack, brought into question the wisdom of his decision. But if he was perturbed by the pain, it was not evident. He shrugged it off when Cathy mentioned it. But he didn't object when she offered to clean and bandage the wound.

"Don't have any bandages," he admitted.

Cathy said she had some, and I also offered some from my first aid pack. Doug talked incessantly, while Cathy bathed and bandaged the spot.

"What's your Trail name?" he asked me.

"Old Soldier. What's yours?"

"Mine's AT Believer. You got a journal?"

I removed my notebook from my pack, and he signed his name, his Trail name, wrote, "fly fishing all the way," then drew his logo with a fishing fly character. Next he asked, "What's your Trail name, Cathy?"

"Don't have one."

"Well, you'll always be AT Medic to me."

At first, Cathy was not too receptive to the name. She had hiked from Springer Mountain to this point without one and saw no need for one now. Nevertheless, I started calling her "AT Medic," and after a time, she became used to it — eventually signing off in the shelter registers as "AT Medic."

In addition to his Trail name, his logo and his fly fishing quote, Doug also added the acronym HELLLP in every register. HELLLP stood for: Help Every Least Lost Lonely Person. He also wrote in every register: "The challenge before us is never so great as the Power behind us."

Merle and Bob passed us, while we were talking with Doug, and we followed shortly afterwards. Doug remained at the spring to wait for his hiking companions, Mark and Glenn Van Vliet, aka, "The Blaze Brothers." We soon caught up to and passed Bob and Merle who were still climbing to the ridge crest. Bob was leaning against a rock trying to gather strength, and Merle was waiting patiently as before beside the Trail.

Later in the afternoon, we arrived at a rough stone monument that marked the site of old Fort Dietrich Snyder, one of a chain of fortifications that defended the area from Indians during the French and Indian War. The date 1755 was inscribed on the stone.

The campsite above Black Swatara Spring sat in a beautiful open, grassy-floored forest directly on the ridge crest. It was a welcome sight after 12 miles struggling along the rocky Trail in the heat. Numerous fly poison plants, their conical white flowered heads bobbing in the evening breeze, populated the campsite. Despite their foreboding name, the flowers provided a delightful contrast to the dark green forest.

Glenn Van Vliet came by and stopped to talk. During our conversation, he talked about hiking in the White Mountains of New Hampshire and in Maine. I asked him to compare the mountains, and he said the Whites were steeper, and in a way, more difficult but also more beautiful. Most of the Trail was sited above the tree line. That made the mountains more rugged looking but also provided spectacular vistas. The mountains in Maine he characterized as just tough. The Trail just went straight up and straight down with few contours or switchbacks.

"How come you're hiking alone?" Cathy asked.

"Everybody hikes his own hike," Glenn replied. We learned

that Doug, Glen and Mark all got up at different times in the morning, left camp at different times and agreed only to meet at a specific point to camp for the night and even that seemed somewhat tentative. We learned that their goal for that day was 31 miles. After Glenn left, Cathy and I wondered aloud, almost simultaneously, what sort of Trail experience they were getting from the hike. They had to be almost running to make that many miles in a day. They also had to be in fantastic physical condition.

Although this was the first time I had heard the idea that "everybody hikes his own hike," I didn't really understand the significance of the phrase. It was later that I realized it was a cardinal rule in hiking that may not be broken with impunity. It was almost mandatory for hikers wishing to maintain good partnerships.

Just as dusk was descending, another shirtless hiker came by. "Hi, Mark," I called. He stopped and came over to where Cathy and I were camped. There was no question that he and Glenn were brothers. At first, I thought they might be twins, but that was not the case.

"How long ago did Doug and Glenn go by?" he asked.

"About an hour or two ago for Glenn. Doug passed us on the Trail quite a while back."

"How far is it to Neys shelter?"

I got out my guidebook. "About seven miles."

"Where's the spring?"

"About 300 yards down that blue blazed trail," Cathy said, bobbing her head to the rear and over her right shoulder.

"Think I'll just go on."

"You can have some of our water," Cathy offered.

"No thanks. I don't want to take you folks' water. I'll get some farther down the Trail."

"It's getting late. You're welcome to water. We can't use it all," I told him. "You gonna make it all the way to Neys Gap?"

"Probably going to camp out along the Trail, and meet Glenn and Doug in Port Clinton tomorrow. Well, gotta go. Good luck. Maybe I'll see you down the Trail." We watched as he disappeared into the forest.

Later, as I lay in my sleeping bag, I thought about Doug Wilcox, The AT Believer, and contemplated the innate happiness and joy that he exuded. At first, I suspected his upbeat happy demeanor was some sort of hail-fellow-well-met facade. Nobody on planet earth could possibly be so totally upbeat, I thought. Nobody I knew or had ever met exhibited such natural exuberance or such an unabashed interest in and concern for people.

After coming to know him, it was evident that Doug's happy approach to life wasn't a show or the facade of a happy idiot. Doug Wilcox was a genuinely happy, positive human being who cared for his fellow man. His concern for people who were less fortunate, physically or spiritually, showed throughout in all that he did and in all the messages he left in registers along the Trail.

Doug's focus was on the joy of life, of the thrill of being alive and on the Appalachian Trail fully participating in life. He would not let fatigue or pack strap wounds or insects or any of the discomforts that perplexed the negative mind deprive him of that joy. His strength lay in the love and strength of the Power behind, and no challenge or difficulty could stand against his joy and the infectious enthusiasm that it generated.

Before sleep overwhelmed me, I said a prayer to the Power behind me; I asked to be favored with the power of love and joy I sensed in the AT Believer.

The hike from Black Swatara Spring to Port Clinton was beautiful in every way; the weather sunny with cool breezes on the ridge crest, the landscape green and ripening, and even the rocks, for which Pennsylvania is famous, seemed a little less sharp.

Pennsylvania is a wildlife watcher's heaven, and nowhere was that more true than the AT in the eastern part of the state. The Trail paralleled State game lands for several miles east of Black Swatara Spring, and Cathy and I saw a large number of white tail deer and once a flock of wild turkeys with many young among them. We watched the progress of the birds as they sneaked through the underbrush to evade us. The tops of the blueberry and other low bushes moved as the birds brushed against them; and, thus, their locations could be pinpointed. When they reached the area of taller bushes, however, their movement could not be detected, and we lost them.

One of the deer we saw, a gray-tan doe, in an open meadow

next to the tree line, was feeding on grass and bushes. It wiggled its tail contentedly, looking over its back to the rear from time to time. Cathy and I watched quietly from about 50 yards away. Finally we moved on, and in so doing, moved upwind of the deer which caught our scent and bounded off effortlessly and into the forest and out of sight. I don't think it ever saw us.

We also passed a baby cottontail rabbit hiding under a clump of grass that was just too sparse for real concealment. The rabbit did not so much as quiver, though we were only a few feet away and had stopped to watch it. Farther on, we encountered the largest squirrel I had ever seen. It must have weighed three pounds. It bounded easily across the forest floor, its bushy tail snaking through the air behind it, then disappeared behind a tree.

We arrived to find Bob sitting alone on the Port Clinton Hotel steps; his yellow hunting hat perched jauntily to the side of his head. The hat was deceiving. An incongruously doleful expression clouded his face, leaving no doubt that he was deeply disappointed. As soon as he spied us, he called out —greeting us like long lost friends, as if we could somehow ease his pain. He went to great lengths to explain that his feet had given out. It was his heels to be exact. He said he could have continued on by going slower but to do so would have held Merle back and would have been unfair to Merle. Cathy and I nodded gravely in sympathy and muttered something about it being a wise decision and that there were other challenges in life. At that point, Bob decided he needed to go inside the building for something.

We ate supper at the bar along with another hiker, Bill Caldwell, from Memphis, Tennessee. He had started his hike at Harpers Ferry, West Virginia, and fallen in with Doug and the Van Vliets. He was not as well conditioned physically as the others and had trouble keeping up, but he said that lately his stamina had improved, and he found the going somewhat easier, although the down hill's were "killing his knees."

"What's your Trail name?" asked Cathy.

"Shiloh. I didn't have one, until I met Doug Wilcox. You know him? The AT Believer? He gave it to me." Evidently Doug felt everyone on the Trail should participate in the tradition. And if you didn't have a name, he would supply it.

At that point, the Blaze Brothers came into the hotel. They had been visiting the home of the local fire chief, swimming in his pool, drinking beer and devouring pretzels. "We seen you go by while we were swimming. Weren't sure it was you, though. Only saw backpacks and figured it musta been you." Mark was addressing Cathy and me.

"I don't know how these guys have all the luck," sighed Shiloh to no one in particular.

"Hell, he even took us into Hamburg and back," Mark said, just to rub it in a little.

"Didn't have any daughters, did he?" asked Shiloh.

"Yeah, but she was too young," lamented Mark.

"Yeah," piped in Glenn who had been watching us through slightly bloodshot eyes and with a silly grin on his face.

In the meantime, a 40-year-old dropout by the name of Seattle Joe came in, sat next to Shiloh and started talking. We learned that he had been on the road for the last three years, hiking and hitchhiking. He was walking only the part of the Trail in Pennsylvania. He had just hitchhiked in from the west, was planning to stay only one day at the hotel, then move on. He indicated that he was just about out of money and would have to drop off the Trail relatively soon to get a job. After he got financially healthy, he planned to hike across Canada. When pressed how he managed to support himself, Joe said he lived mostly from unsold food that McDonald's discarded in their garbage. Cathy sort of gulped, but Shiloh said he could see doing that. A general discussion followed about how McDonald's discarded perfectly edible food to conform to the company policy of freshness, and how it was not really like scrounging through garbage to get a meal. Everyone agreed that the Trail tended to dull one's dietary sensitivities.

Just before we finished eating, Doug Wilcox arrived to a greeting that approached acclamation. The result was a festive atmosphere that resembled a family reunion with everyone talking at the same time and everyone buying everyone else beer. The Blaze Brothers, having had a head start on the beer drinking, were in great form. Soon a young couple joined the group at the bar. The man, Kevin Krauter, had hiked the Trail end-to-end with a partner in 1983 under the Trail name, "The Stroh Brothers." Kevin said he often came to the hotel to visit with hikers. It sort of re-validated his membership in the fraternity of long distance hikers.

Everyone in the place was an original character, and Cathy and I enjoyed listening to the conversations and the interaction between hikers, former hikers, hitchhikers and novices in a free flowing atmosphere where each was accorded respect and dignity by everyone else. Even Seattle Joe, who existed from McDonald's leftovers, was accorded his share.

CHAPTER 5

Faith is the function of the heart. It must be reinforced by reason. The two are not antagonistic as some think. The more intense one's faith is, the more it whets one's reason. When faith becomes blind it dies.

— *Mahatma Ghandi*

Port Clinton to Delaware Water Gap

The following morning, after feasting on bacon and eggs, pancakes, toast and jelly, as if expecting trial by starvation, Cathy and I set out on the old Trail for Pocahontas Spring and the Windsor Furnace shelter. Helen, the hotel proprietress, had told us about the old Trail, saying it was "easy hiking;" so easy, she said, that people other than hikers had been using it as a route to the shelter.

The old Trail followed a gently climbing old logging road that snaked along the ridge side above Rattling Run. Although it had become slightly overgrown, the walking was easy. Our attempt to avoid arduous walking soon came to an end, however. After about a mile, the old road deteriorated into a well-defined footpath that soon became less than defined, and after a few yards, ceased altogether. It was then a matter of going back down the trail and heading for the relocation, and wasting the time and progress we had already made — or bushwhacking up to the ridge crest to pick up the Trail there. I knew pretty well where we were in relation to the terrain and told Cathy that if we climbed straight up the ridge for about 200 yards, we'd come to the Trail about a mile from Pocahontas Spring.

Cathy was less than enthusiastic about the prospect of crashing through the brush. "I sure hope you know what you're doin'." Her raised eyebrows displayed a skepticism that words could not sufficiently describe.

The bushwhacking was not easy. An accumulation of many seasons of fallen leaves had covered the boulder and rock-strewn mountainside. The abundance of leaves was enough to hide the rocks but not enough to fill the spaces between them, and the walking was treacherous. After about 200 torturous yards and some exasperating detours, caused by fallen trees and thick underbrush, we reached the ridge crest and the Trail at approximately the place I told Cathy we would. She was as impressed as I was smug.

We soon reached Pocahontas Spring, and finding it dry, continued without stopping, to Windsor Furnace shelter which sat in an open forest on land criss-crossed by several severely eroded logging roads. We arrived to find Shiloh stretched out on the shelter floor beside a large, blue, new-looking hexagonal tent; he was talking with its occupant, a young man named Mike. Although the tent took up over half the floor space, no one bothered to ask Mike why he had erected it inside the shelter. I suspected he didn't want to get it dirty.

Cathy was less than pleased with the tent in the shelter. "What if somebody comes?" she asked, nodding toward the tent.

"They can sleep over there," Mike replied.

"What if it's taken? You gonna take your tent down?" Cathy's irritation was clearly reflected in her tone of voice.

"They'll just have to ask me," Mike said with a hint of defensiveness.

Cathy harrumphed once, opened her mouth like she was going to say something, then, probably thinking better of it, remained silent.

I gave Mike more benefit of the doubt than Cathy did. I suspected that when faced with the realization that his tent was depriving someone of a place to sleep, he would fold the tent.

We had originally planned to spend the night at the shelter, but because we had reached it so early and because of Mike's presence, we decided to move on to one of the campsites near Pulpit Rock. "That's not very considerate of that Bozo," Cathy said, after we were out of earshot. "That shelter's for everyone, not just him. I'd tell him to get his damn tent outta there."

Situations like the one we had just encountered with Mike and previously at Rausch Gap shelter were typical of some we faced along the Trail in more populated areas like New York and New Jersey, where ease of access to shelters had attracted some peculiar visitors. Consequently we became nervous about staying in shelters; most had easy access, so we usually moved on and set up our tent off the Trail, or, if convenient, headed into town and rented a room.

Mike had mentioned that he had hiked to the shelter from Pulpit Rock and Pinnacle Rock. I asked him about the condition and the difficulty of the Trail. We found his information to be less than accurate. Not surprising. Impressions about the Trail are subjective and personal to the extreme. Most people, even experienced hikers, are unable to accurately estimate distances, but most can relate to tough climbs. Mike was an exception to even that rule of thumb.

The Trail up to the ridge crest and Pulpit Rock was nicely graded and the climb fairly easy. An observatory belonging to a local astronomy club from Lehigh Valley sat amid the trees on the ridge top just off the Trail. Although small in comparison, it had a rounded dome, reminiscent of the observatory on Mt. Palomar.

We joined a family of four for the last few hundred yards' climb up the ridge. The two children, a boy and a girl, pre-adolescents, were immediately taken with the observatory and ran off to explore it, We adults did likewise at a pace more befitting our maturity. There really wasn't much to see: basically a small, square building with silver dome sitting by itself in a small clearing. What made it interesting was its incongruity. A silver dome in the middle of a dark green forest certainly was striking.

To me, even more interesting were the nearby rock ledges known as Pulpit Rock; they provided overlooks of the emerald valleys to the south and east, where white specks of farmhouses and barns dotted the countryside. Peace and tranquility flowed naturally from the pasture and cropland with streams and ponds sparkling intermittently like sequins sewn on a flowing green gown. Occasional roads, looking for all the world like black ribbons, tied the scenery together. Considering the innately pastoral character of the landscape, it seemed that the name Pulpit

Rock was singularly appropriate for a place with such a sweeping view of this corner of God's handiwork.

After Pulpit Rock, we embarked on a rock scramble across some very large boulders which I was sure providence had placed there to test Cathy's mettle. I was able to negotiate the rocks with only minor difficulty, but for Cathy's short legs, they were more like an ordeal. But she didn't once complained. At Pinnacle Rocks, we again ran into Shiloh who, looking for company to spend the evening with, had stopped to wait for us. While we were talking and admiring the views, a large raccoon ambled out of the woods behind us and came to within about five feet. I suspected it might have been looking for food. It stopped, sniffed the air momentarily, then decided that we possessed nothing edible, or deemed us untrustworthy, and disappeared into a deep crevice between some boulders. We then realized that it was the entrance to a cave of sorts and thought immediately of exploring it. The sun was losing altitude quickly, however, and we needed urgently to move on to Gold Spring, if we planned to set up camp while daylight remained.

Shiloh planned to hike as far as he could before the date he was scheduled to participate in a history workshop in St. Johnsbury, Vermont. We learned that Shiloh was a history teacher at Hutchinson High School in Memphis, Tennessee. He was a graduate of Vanderbilt University and knew Professor Chris Hassell, the Shakespearean scholar whom Cathy and I had met the previous summer at Matts Creek shelter along the Blue Ridge in Virginia. Shiloh talked incessantly about the Trail, about his job, about his plans and just about anything that popped into his head. My participation in the conversation was reduced to nodding and minor remarks, while Cathy remained silent.

"Which state had more steel mills than the entire Confederacy during the Civil War?"

"Huh?"

"Pennsylvania," proclaimed Shiloh proudly, oblivious to my stupid response.

Even though the conversation was one sided, Shiloh was unpretentious and I enjoyed "talking" to him.

I wrote in my Trail journal that it had been a very good day. The weather had been cool, the sky sunny, and we had seen several deer and grouse as well as the usual rabbits, squirrels and chipmunks, and strangely, few wild flowers. The vistas from Pulpit and Pinnacle Rocks had been special. It was one of those times at the end of the day when the presence of other people was a comfort, but not an intrusion, and I felt really peaceful in the company of Cathy and Shiloh.

The next day was dreary in comparison to the bright sunshine of the previous couple of days. But it was still cool and the hiking was pleasant. The forest had a captivating silence, lacking the sound of crisp leaves underfoot or the wind rustling the tree branches. Cathy was unusually subdued, apparently deep in concentration. We walked in silence. Shiloh had left camp about an hour before us, and no one interrupted the quiet or intruded on our intensely private thoughts.

It was mostly down hill from Gold Spring to Eckville Road. The Trail followed a remote wooded road for almost the entire distance. On the other side of Eckville Road, we crossed a stream and a ravine on two rustic but sturdy wooden bridges. As we neared the stream, a large white tailed deer, surprised by our silent approach, launched into flight, its white tail held high like a flag, as it bounded over the ridge and out of sight.

The Trail gained some 1500 feet in elevation as it climb Blue Mountain, but the path was nicely graded and the walking enjoyable. We soon reached Dan's Pulpit, a rock promontory with views of the valley that rivaled those of Pulpit Rock. We stopped for lunch to let the beauty nourish our souls as the food nourished our bodies. According to the Trail Guide, Dan's Pulpit was named for Daniel L. Koch, one of the founders of the Blue Mountain Eagle Climbing Club. It referred to him as "Hiking's Grand Old Man" and indicated that he conducted Sunday services at that point.

In my reveries after lunch, I pictured Koch as a tall slender man with long white hair, flowing white beard, a sharp nose and flashing black eyes under bushy eyebrows. He's standing resolutely against a raging sky, his long black coat blowing in the wind as he preached hellfire and damnation for those who failed to heed the Word of God. Further reflection defined my impressions as too stark and out of character with the beauty and serenity of the land. Old Dan became a much friendlier personality in my second creation, devoted, loving and caring for the people to whom he had chosen to bring the message of brotherly love and sacrifice.

The rocks that comprise the Trail in Pennsylvania are famous for their ability to create agony as well as irritation for hikers, and the section in the vicinity of Dan's Pulpit provided ample testimony to that reality. Cathy and I were totally focused on the pathway as we picked our way across the rocks after lunch. So intent were we on not making a misstep we literally "ran" into a bear.

I was leading with Cathy close on my heels. Sensing movement ahead with my peripheral vision, I stopped abruptly to focus on who might be approaching. The approaching "someone" was a black bear. To describe it as large is simply inadequate. When one meets a full-grown bear in the middle of a wilderness its size is multiplied by its proximity and the viewer's panic. In this case, the bear was gigantic, but later, upon dispassionate assessment, I guessed it to be at about 400 pounds and about as tall at the shoulder as my hip. It was only about 15 yards away and totally ignorant of our presence. I froze instantly. Cathy, watching her footing on the rocks, did not see me stop and nearly knocked me down.

"What're you stopping for?" she grunted.

The bear stopped and raised its head at the sound of the collision.

"Shhh," I whispered. "There's a bear."

It took Cathy a split second to focus in on the animal that was now about 20 feet away. It looked directly at us. "A bear!" she squealed.

"Be quiet," I hissed.

"It's a bear! It's a bear!" she tried to whisper, but the excitement created a volume in her voice that could have been heard in Philadelphia.

The bear, as close as it was, could still not see us, but it certainly heard Cathy. It could also now smell us. It raised its nose in the air, trying to get a better sensing. Then, with some haste, it launched off the Trail to the north side into a small clearing that contained short brush and the dead branches left from some harvested trees. It then entered some thick underbrush before being swallowed by the forest. Until it reached the thick underbrush, it was never more than 20 yards away.

The bear's fur was very black, except around the muzzle

where it had a tawny coloration. As big as it was, it moved with amazing agility and grace. Most surprising was how quietly it moved through the forest. It made some noise going through the dried leaves and other vegetation, but it was much quieter than I had expected from such a large creature.

"I thought you said it was a deer," Cathy said, after getting over her excitement. I tried to respond, but she cut me off. "My first bear! Oh, boy! Wait'll I tell everybody I saw a bear!"

Pennsylvania is a land of abundant wildlife. Besides the bear, I saw more deer in Pennsylvania than any other state except perhaps Virginia. I had still not seen any rattlesnakes, although I had read an entry in a shelter journal by the "Brits" a pair of English hikers preceding us, saying they had encountered one. They went on to mention that they couldn't understand the "compulsion to kill" such a pretty little creature, going on to conjecture that it might be for some "macho" reason.

We had originally intended to stay at the Allentown shelter, but during a conversation with a southbound hiker, we learned of a "fantastic" German restaurant right on the Trail where it crossed Route 309. We had reached the shelter cut off early; there was no hesitation in our decision to press on to the restaurant. We were again to learn a basic lesson in Trail cuisine. That lesson is: dining recommendations from hikers are to be totally ignored. The reason — all hikers and most certainly thru-hikers are ravenous to the point of killing for food, and anything that offers a respite from the steady diet of trail food automatically qualifies for a three-star rating. Still, despite what I thought was mediocre fare and a somewhat difficult waitress, the respite from the daily grind of tuna and noodles was welcome. Most enjoyable was the salad bar and, of course, several bottles of Beck's dark beer produced a euphoria which more than made up for the shortcomings in the bratwurst.

As do most establishments along the Trail, this one had a Trail register, and we noted that Doug Wilcox had eaten there commenting with glowing praise on the food and the staff. There was even a greeting from Shiloh, saying we were the rear doors of the group of thru-hikers headed north. I wondered if that was a subtle way of saying we were the hikers' behind.

We didn't go very far after dinner — barely 500 yards before we found a level spot in the woods and set up the tent. Just before I climbed into the tent, a rabbit materialized from no-where, to sit up on a nearby rock, as if it was posing for a pic-ture. I fumbled around for my camera before remembering that it was out of film. The rabbit, sensing that I didn't have it all together, hopped down and disappeared into the underbrush.

We had hiked 16 miles for the day, and I was really tired. In a way I welcomed the fatigue; I wanted to see how my heart with the new medication would hold up, especially in light of the increased adrenaline flow. It was doing well — no palpitations, no suggestions of arrhythmia. The result was an aura of relief and confidence.

I noted that I had tried to meditate when I began the day by starting off with a prayer of thanksgiving, as I acknowledged the good fortune I was experiencing with my heart and asking for it to continue. I also asked for assistance in developing a stronger faith. I realized that faith is not automatically bestowed, that it, like other aspects of value in life, requires effort, and that the amount of the benefit correlates to the intensity of ef-fort devoted towards its attainment.

I realized I was still in the "give me" stage of my spiritual development. But how else does one begin when embarking on a spiritual quest? Perhaps the answer is solitude and the ability to go within for answers. Does that depend on the intensity of concentration during meditation? The questions were coming at least. And they must precede any answers. Understanding one's limitations and acknowledging them is a starting point, at least in hiking the Trail. It is no different in a spiritual journey. Of course, to this point, my inability to sustain concentration concerned me most. I vowed to continue the effort, hoping with perseverance I would be able to master the ability to look in-wardly for my answers. Perhaps in New Hampshire or Maine, I thought with some irony.

The "Knife Edge" is a rock formation with a nearly vertical slant to one side and a sheer drop-off of 15-to-20 feet on the other. It was created during a movement of tectonic plates in the earth's crust millions of years ago by one rock layer riding over another rock layer. Naturally the Trail was sited right along the very narrowest top edge to provide maximum challenge or maximum fun, or maximum fear — as the case might be.

Cathy was apprehensive when negotiating rocks of any type,

but in this instance, apprehension was replaced by low-grade terror. She looked up at the blazes, gulped once, mumbled, "Christ," clenched her jaw and followed on as close as she could, watching carefully where I had stepped, so that she could step in the same spot. Occasionally, concentrating on my own footing, I would move too far or too fast, and she would call for me to slow down.

Once she stopped after I had hopped across a small space between rocks. "That's okay for you, Bozo!" she yelled in frustration. "But these short little Polish legs weren't meant to take such big steps." Then, she hopped across too.

Fortunately the top rocks were dry. Lower down, however, and particularly the rocks near vegetation, were still wet, and the moisture, combined with fungus or algae, created a surface that could be as slick as ice and downright dangerous. The problem was that it was impossible to tell by sight which rocks were slippery and which were not. I crossed the high rocks without incident. Then, when I had almost reached the forest floor I stepped on a rock that appeared clear of growth. When my weight shifted, both feet slipped out from under me, and with a resounding thud I landed on my back. The pack probably saved me from serious injury. As it was, I landed with such force that I felt my neck snap and both arms went numb. Initially I thought I might have broken an arm or maybe my neck or back.

After the stars stopped spinning, I looked up to see Cathy standing on the rock above; she was looking down with an expression that had concern written all over it. "You all right?" asked the upside down face.

"Don't know." I didn't move. I was afraid to. My right arm hurt like hell and the left only less so. "Hope nothing's broken!"

"Hope what isn't broken?"

"Anything, dammit. My neck, my back, my arm — they all hurt."

After what seemed like several minutes, I felt gingerly around the rock below where my feet had come to rest. I got back on my feet in stages, sitting up first, checking my arms and back, then standing up. Everything seemed to be in place. Her concern abated; Cathy passed me and reached the forest floor. I climbed the rest of the way down on all fours.

A check of the Trail Guide indicated that the Trail crossed

several more rock ledges. That wasn't exactly the kind of information I had been hoping for. Continuing to hike across wet rock ledges was not worth the risk of serious injury; I decided to head for safer ground as swiftly as possible. We soon encountered an improved dirt road that we followed down the mountain to an old railroad bed that led us into Palmerton.

The nearer we got to Palmerton, the more depressing became the landscape. A zinc company is the only industry in town, and its operations have apparently had an enormous impact on the environment. Plant life on the hills, surrounding the town, is all but non-existent. The hillside approaches to the town resemble moonscapes or recent battlegrounds with occasional blackened tree skeletons etched grotesquely against the tired gray land or frozen eerily against the horizon at higher elevations. The color green had been reduced to a word in a dictionary or a shade on a color chart. An ecological nightmare had come to town.

With all the natural beauty sucked from their immediate environment, I subconsciously expected the people of Palmerton to reflect a similar psychological desolation. I could not have been more mistaken. The friendliness and cheerfulness of the people of Palmerton contrasted sharply to their ecological situation. It was, in my experience, a great testament to the endurance and vibrancy of the human spirit, and of the marvelous resiliency of people. They were like a rainbow emanating from the middle of land without color.

The large hotel across the street from the police station in Palmerton offered the promise of a civilized evening, but there were no vacancies. We crossed the street to the police station which the "Philosopher's Guide" indicated often hosted hikers for the night. The door was locked. I banged on it. No response. I went around the building to a side entrance. It too was locked. I then circled the entire building, pulling on any door I could find. As I pulled on the last one, the thought occurred that an observant citizen might notify the police that someone was trying to break into their station. The irony was inescapable. Just when you need a cop, there's none around, popped into my mind.

Fortunately, the "Philosopher's Guide" also listed the number of the police dispatcher. A quick call resulted in a policeman being dispatched to let us into the station. I wondered if he would put us up in a cell. No luck. We followed him to the basement to the "community center." We were admonished to "keep the door locked." On the way to our "quarters," we passed through the police gymnasium where a sign informed all users that the court could not be used, until the person who had stolen the basketball returned it.

Our choice of sleeping accommodations was a couple of large tables or the cement floor. Even at the risk of rolling off the tables, we chose them over the floor, and rolled out our mattresses and sleeping bags. I would have preferred to sleep in a cell. They at least had bunks.

On the way back to the Trail the next morning, we met a couple bicycling the roads in Pennsylvania. The man, an electrical engineer with AT&T, had worked most recently on a project in England. He was very knowledgeable about hiking Trails in England and proceeded to tell us about a Mr. Wainwright who had written a number of guides for trails in that country. Wainwright sought to engage publishing firms to print his guides but was refused because the firms decided there was no market for that type of book. So, he published them himself.

The books became very popular, selling into the millions, and in the process, a small industry grew up around them. And along with his guides, Mr. Wainwright became a celebrity of sorts, with people writing that they had seen him walking a trail in a specific location, reporting it like birders would report seeing a bird of some rare species. Interestingly, Wainwright, refusing to profit financially from his guides, donated all the proceeds to the English Society for the Prevention of Cruelty to Animals.

The Trail from Lehigh Gap to Wind Gap was rocky but dry; and we made good time despite stopping occasionally to admire the views. We had planned to stop at the Leroy Smith shelter, but the lure of a motel bed with sheets at Wind Gap was too much to resist. We should have stopped at the shelter; the additional four and a half miles made for a 20-mile day. We were exhausted.

We began the next day at 7:15 a.m., planning to arrive at Delaware Water Gap in time for supper. I started off with misgivings immediately. My feet hurt, my legs were rubbery, and I felt exhausted. Cathy was in a similar condition. After about 30 minutes, we stopped and headed back to the motel. The 20-

miler had proven to be too much.

We then conceived of a plan. We'd rent a car in Wind Gap, providing there was a car rental facility, drive to Delaware Water Gap, deposit our packs at the Presbyterian Church of the Mountain or a motel, head back to Wind Gap, spend the night, then slack pack the following day to Delaware Water Gap.

The plan worked. We left our packs at the HOJO's in Delaware Water Gap and headed for East Stroudsburg to re-provision and buy me a new pair of boots. The Pennsylvania rocks had eaten my Sears Specials to the point that I was walking on the sides.

I was surprised by the difficulty I had finding a pair of soft fabric boots that fit. Most of the boots were manufactured in Korea or Taiwan or somewhere outside of the States where, I suspected, experience with large shoe sizes tended to be limited and sizing decisions were rough approximations. And the boots that did conform to my foot size had other shortcomings. Either the heel of the boot was too shallow and it rubbed against my heel, or the toes were too narrow, or both. Finally I tried on a pair that fit. I wear a size 10 regular, but found that a size 12 in a pair of Hi-Tech boots was made for me.

The local Presbyterian Church had furnished a basement for hikers, and we stopped there, hoping to see Shiloh or the Blaze Brothers or AT Believer. They weren't there, but we did meet Mark Bachelor from Alabama who went by the name, "Screamin' Night Hog." He told us the others had already left, that they had waited around until the morning (it was a Monday) only to pick up their mail. Screamin' Night Hog was taking a layover day. He told us he had started from Springer Mountain on April 1st and by his estimate had passed about 150 hikers along the way. He announced proudly that he had done one 40-mile day in Virginia, starting at 4:30 a.m. and finishing at 11:30 p.m.

I learned he had just finished serving in the Marines, after a tour of duty as a platoon leader in a Marine Infantry unit. I automatically wondered about his motivation for doing the Trail. Was it similar to mine? I considered the difference in age and experience, and didn't ask.

The next morning we were surprised to see Shiloh at breakfast. He said he was laying over a day to keep away from the

Blaze Brothers and AT Believer; they were going too fast for him. He also mentioned that he had done a 37-miler the "other day."

The Trail out of Wind Gap was very rocky for the first six or seven miles, but crossing notorious Wolf Rocks without packs was not nearly as difficult as it had been over the Knife Edge, and we handled them easily. The Trail down from Mini's Mountain was easy, and some of the overlooks had nice views. On the edge of the town at Delaware Water Gap, we passed the charred remains of the Mountain Inn that had burned down on the first of June. An elderly couple sitting on the porch of the house next door told us they had once owned the inn but had sold it. The fire was so intense it was all the firemen could do to keep the flames from spreading to adjacent buildings. Considering how close their house was to the inn it must have been a terrifying experience for them.

CHAPTER 6

Everything here, but the soul of man, is a passing shadow. The only enduring substance is within. When shall awake to the sublime greatness, the perils, the accountableness and the glorious destinies of the immortal soul?

— *William E. Channing*

Delaware Water Gap to Bear Mountain

Crossing the Interstate 80 Highway bridge over the Delaware River was exciting and, to a degree, terrifying. The AT follows a narrow sidewalk next to the interstate, where the distance between the pedestrian and the interstate is a matter of feet. The roar and engine whine of 18-wheelers pushing 70 miles per hour can be intimidating to someone in an auto. To someone on foot, the noise is deafening, and the mind produces a sense of numbness as a defense. But the air turbulence was even worse.

Those who ride in cars also know how an automobile is buffeted by air turbulence from passing trucks. The impact of such turbulence on a couple of hikers, top heavy with backpacks and walking unprotected only a few feet away, was just short of savage. The gusts from frontal wind surges and currents following the trucks often staggered us and blew everything not securely fastened to the firmament like sheets of paper and plastic out over the gorge - where they then drifted down on the air currents to the water below. We clutched our hats, rather than have them accompany the paper and plastic.

Each passing truck caused the bridge to bounce and sway

underfoot. That was equally unsettling. The result was a sense of giddiness that accompanies crossing small suspension foot-bridges. Walking across them produces a sway and bounce which is natural and expected with that type of construction. But this was a different type of bridge altogether — a steel and concrete fixed bridge. I did not expect to feel it bouncing and swaying, and although it certainly did not sway and bounce like those suspension footbridges, it moved more than enough to get my attention.

When I thought about it, I realized that there had to be a certain amount of give in any such structure. Therefore, I assumed the engineers had purposely designed it with a certain range of flexibility to withstand the huge stresses and weights it was carrying.

Shortly after crossing under the Interstate, we met a young man who had hiked from Springer Mountain to Damascus the previous year and was there to just "look at the Trail." He had wanted to continue his adventure this summer but was over-taken by an opportunity he simply couldn't refuse. He was preparing for medical school under the Navy's physician acquisition program. He vowed to one day finish the Trail, even if it took him until age 60 to do it.

I found it odd that he should be there "looking" at the Trail, but on later reflection, I determined it to be a perfectly natural reaction. There is a magnetism about the Trail; particularly for those who have invested significant time and sweat on it that makes one want to go look at it. I know from personal experience that whenever I am in the vicinity of the Trail, I am struck by an almost irresistible urge to go to a crossing point, (or if I am in a car, I am constantly on the lookout for where the Trail crosses or parallels the road), just to get a glimpse of the hallowed pathway. Perhaps it is to capture in a vicarious sense some prior euphoria or perhaps it's merely to reminisce.

The Trail then followed a number of testy little climbs. As in Pennsylvania, the pathway was strewn with small rocks that made walking slow. The highlight of the day was Sunfish Pond, a glacial lake and a national landmark. We went to the water's edge via a huge rock and sat momentarily to catch our breath, listen to the sound of the wavelets lapping against the rock and admire the serene beauty in the harmony of water, forest and sky.

We continued on to a nearby spring mentioned in the Guidebook. It was dry. Cathy and I had already emptied our water bottles in anticipation of fresh water. We returned to Sunfish Pond. We filled only my bottle and threw in a couple of iodine tablets for purification purposes. After several minutes shaking and waiting, we each drank our fill. Afterwards I noticed the iodine tablets had not dissolved, and there was sediment in the bottom of bottle. (Whatever bugs were in the water were not very vicious; neither of us became ill.) We then detoured to the Mohican Outdoor Resource Center, a cooperative effort by the University of Trenton and the National Park Service, where we tanked up on water.

Shortly after passing Rattlesnake Spring (it had water), we found a nice campsite in an open, mature forest with a grass floor and set up the tent. It had only been a 13.4-mile day, but it was tiring. My trail notes indicated only 869 miles to go!

The meeting with the young doctor-to-be, for some reason, energized my long dormant focus on spirituality, and I spent much of the day thinking on and off of the spiritual awakening I had experienced the previous year. I had come off the Trail seemingly at an impasse and spent the winter in a state of periodic reflection, but I could point to no identifiable progress. Now, however, ideas began bubbling. I began again to meditate, especially on the theme that I was an innately spiritual being participating in an earthly journey. The question kept arising: Why the dichotomy between my spiritual essence and my earthly state of consciousness? Why did my humanity make recognition of and access to my essential nature such a hindrance?

Because I was human, all my previous awareness resulted from reasoning or through material effects or my senses. I had recognized that during my pervious meditation. But it became increasingly clearer that I needed to effect some sort of transition, that I could not access my spiritual reality by physical or sensory terms. The spiritual resides solely in an inner state of consciousness, which can be accessed only by "going within." It was there that all the great mystics met God and experienced the aura of truth and love that forever changed them. It was from those episodes that their great strength of purpose came and ultimately communication of the revelations that changed the course of history.

Spirituality is a completely private and intense individual experience that cannot be shared, no matter how close another person might be to you. It can also not in any way be communicated; it is essential in nature — like life. We cannot recreate it or pass it along like a possession. It is our very own essence. It belongs totally and solely to us, and no one may violate it. But it is also a charter, one that includes our birthright as a creature of God and as such necessarily includes our Father for validation.

We can go within ourselves at any time to experience it. It is our place to meet God, where God exists for us 24-hours every day of our lives. And to do that requires practice. Nothing of real value comes without effort, and in this case — this most priceless gift — the effort is life long.

I tried to relax and allow my mind to be receptive, but the drumming of rain on the tent fabric broke the spell, and I fell asleep. It rained the whole night through and all the next day.

The downpour abated when we first got up, but as soon as we took down the tent and picked up our packs, it came down in a torrent. After several hours, my thighs began to chap, and I developed blisters on my feet, which eventually broke. No amount of Vaseline could ease the friction on my thighs, and my feet were too wet for adhesive to stick. But I just continued hiking and hurting.

Despite repeated vows to maintain a positive outlook, I was totally unsuccessful. To make matters worse, the pages started to tear off the guidebook, and the map fell apart at the fold creases. Cathy fell once on some slippery rocks and barely was able to negotiate some of the steeper climbs up sheer escarpments that were made extremely difficult by slippery earth, roots and rocks.

It was 5:30 p. m. when we reached Culver Gap and NJ Highway 206, and headed for the restaurant just down the road from the Trail crossing. After a spaghetti dinner, we hiked another two miles to a motel. In reviewing the events of the day, after we had showered, put on dry clothes and attained a reasonably objective distance from the Trail, Doctor Catharine Morris, mustering the considerable intellectual power bestowed by a Ph.D., pronounced that it had been "damned miserable."

The one bright spot of the day was the wildlife. Twice we saw does, each with two spotted fawns, and later a flock of wild turkeys ran across the Trail in front of us.

Now Cathy left the room to find a telephone and returned almost immediately. "There's a deer in the front yard," she exclaimed excitedly. Sure enough, standing like a lawn statue out front was a deer — looking straight at us. It stayed motionless for a few more seconds, then bounded off.

Breakfast was a treat. A pint of orange juice, a pint of milk, six fresh cinnamon rolls, two blueberry pies and a small container of blueberry yogurt made the start of the hike an occasion for optimism. We stopped in a small oak grove to eat our food and became the main course for swarms of mosquitoes that the rain had made particularly ravenous. We ate quickly and departed, even before the last mouthful.

Though rain had been forecast, the weather was dry, mostly sunny and quite humid, a welcome departure from the rain. The Mashipacong shelter journal contained entries by Macon Tracks, Happy Feet, Blaze Brothers, Screamin' Night Hog, Shiloh, Slim Jim and Daddy Long Legs. I was surprised to learn that if we subtracted the time spent in Berryville, attending to my heart, Happy Feet was only two days ahead of us. Slim Jim and Daddy Long Legs were only a day ahead. The Blaze Brothers were way ahead, having passed through on the 29th of June. Strangely there was no entry by the AT Believer.

We reached the headquarters for High Top State Park at about 5:00 p. m. and decided to spend the night at a motel down the hill from the park. Unfortunately the place had reverted to long-term occupancy and, I suspected, the center of the local drug scene. We ended up at the Port Jervis Holiday Inn.

Upon arriving at the motel, I noticed a small car with a North Carolina license plate that read, BAK PAKR, parked next to the entrance. I think it belonged to a tall, very thin, red-bearded man whose left hand was wrapped around an "old fashioned" glass, and who, upon seeing our packs, lost control and pounced on us like long lost relatives. In a voice loud enough to be heard at High Top, he announced that he was a hiker and that he had "led" a Sierra Club expedition into the Smokies and on the AT. He emphasized the part about "leading" expeditions. A few minutes were proof enough that the glass in his hand was only the latest in a series.

Among the tidbits he offered was that he was an expert in wilderness survival and that he was downright miffed at the Rangers who were forced to go looking for him when he didn't come out of the Great Smoky National Park at the appointed time. He mentioned that his ex-wife and ex-girlfriend, concerned about his well being after a snowstorm, had called the Park Rangers. The Rangers had then initiated a search, and when he was found they had apparently delivered a pointed lecture. Cathy extricated us from the conversation by telling me loudly that we needed to get to the room and clean up. End of conversation!

"That guy's a screaming alcoholic," Cathy said, wrinkling her nose as we headed for the stairway.

The next day we hiked to the base of Pochuck Mountain. We stopped for the night in an open field just west of Liberty Corner's Road, after a strange detour around a sod farm.

It was only 8:00 p. m. when we turned in, but I fell asleep as soon as I climbed into my sleeping bag. Around 1:00 a. m., a deer snorting close by awakened me. I peeked out of the tent in an attempt to see it, and as I did, an owl issued a plaintive cry. There was no deer to be seen, but the night air was crystalline, and the sky was ablaze with stars. It was one of those moments when God was in the heavens and all was right with the world. I slipped back into the bag, and it was daylight when I awoke.

The hike to the top of Pochuck was not difficult, and we made good time. Both of us were out of water and had been, even before camping the previous night. We shortly came to dog kennels, where the owners allowed us to camel up and fill our water bottles.

On the way back to the Trail, we met a man walking with his daughter and his dog. The dog was the best-trained dog I had ever seen, outside of the professional dogs, police dogs and Seeing Eye dogs. We stopped to chat and talked a little about the Trail and ourselves. The man said his father had managed to destroy any desire he had for camping at an early age, but that he was an avid birder. As if to prove the point, he went on to described some beautiful yellow warblers he had just seen on some telephone lines down the road.

The intensity of his description — the luminescent green

body and black wings of the female and the yellow body of the male — testified to his passion. "It just comes out and asks you what you're doing in its territory," he said. He then mentioned that such birds were almost impossible to spot in the trees, but these birds were in a field "guarding their territory" and were easily spotted.

So tempting was his description that we had to see them for ourselves. Sure enough, they were still there, flying back and forth between a large field and the telephone lines.

Seven-tenths of a mile north of where the Trail crosses the Warwick Turnpike is the Willow Brook Inn, a large, wood-frame house set on gently undulating farm acreage with a small pond across the road. The gardens and lawn were trimmed with care as was the ground on which the glass-like pond sat, and the whole scene was reminiscent of a Currier and Ives print.

Cathy and I took turns paying for support services, and this was her turn. She went to make the arrangements and returned shortly followed by a man whom I took to be the owner.

"You ought to take a look," she said.

The cost of a bare room without a shower or a toilet was $20 per person. We could get a room with shower and toilet with air conditioning in the nearby town of Warwick, New York, for the same amount of money, and we would also have access to a restaurant and groceries. Another, more serious disadvantage, was the attitude of the woman who ran the place. She was suspicious of us to the point of hostility, and her refusal to be helpful or accommodating was blatantly purposeful. It was apparent that she really didn't want us there and was going to make us pay dearly for the privilege of enduring her disdain. "Don't really like to rent to hikers. They're dirty and bring in insects and fleas in their stuff," she said testily.

"Then I suggest you have your place removed from the Appalachian Trail Guide books," I replied.

I made the decision right then that we were not going to spend the night. "I don't think we'll stay. Your rooms are nice, but they don't offer a shower or a toilet, and you don't offer meals. We really would like to go to a restaurant and to shop for groceries.

"Sorry if our rooms are too plain for you," she sniffed. She then mentioned something to the man who was trying to keep a low profile about how much trouble hikers were. You could feel the woman's anger. It permeated the entire atmosphere. She was like a booby trap; in a sense, she was spring-loaded in the pissed-off position, ready to go off at any moment, and everyone around her was trying very hard not to be the cause of the explosion.

"How can we get to Warwick? Are there any cabs?"

"Look in the phone book," she snapped.

"How much is a cab? Can I use your phone. I'll pay for the call."

"I could give you a lift," a young woman sitting unobtrusively next to the rear door offered. "I got nothing to do."

I instantly accepted, then glanced back at the older woman. She looked like she was going into apoplexy.

We wasted no time getting our gear and ourselves into the car. During the ride, we learned the young woman was the owner's ex-daughter-in-law. I really couldn't imagine a more unhappy circumstance than the situation the woman was living under. I gave her $5.00 for gas and thanked her profusely for the ride. I also wished her good luck. She would need it when she returned to Willow Brook Inn.

The motel was adequate, but it was clear we had left the friendly demeanor of the people in Pennsylvania. The motel had no lobby, only a sheltered causeway, where the customer was completely isolated from the clerk who handled the transaction. It felt like I was revisiting the bare cubicle I had waited in, while driving through the Soviet checkpoint on the Autobahn to Berlin. When going through the checkpoint the visitor was required to get out of the car and go inside a cubicle, completely surrounded by bare white walls with only a small half-moon aperture through which paperwork was passed. There was no furniture. Except for the guard with his hand on his pistol, I never saw or talked to anyone. It was a perfect manifestation of the mentality of distrust and suspicion that permeated the Soviet Security consciousness which I found totally inappropriate in Warwick, New York. But in this case it was for the protection of the motel clerk from robbers. That people have to resort to such measures says volumes about the psychological environment in which we live, and just how far we have come in the destruction of the quality of life we once proudly proclaimed as a standard for the world.

That night as I reviewed the day's events for my journal, I thought back to the statement the birder had made - about his father destroying any desire he might have had for camping. It set in motion a series of thoughts about the relationship of fathers to sons and how important these often ignored, or worse, maligned, masculine bonding processes are to sons.

This gentleman appeared, on the surface, to be the victim of a father struggling to promote his concept of masculinity. Many men try to deal with their sons in the warrior way, much like the way a drill sergeant handles his charges, exaggerating discipline and physical prowess, forgetting that they are dealing with children. It doesn't work for children. The focus is not on breaking down in order to build up.

The focus should be on building up, on love and reinforcing the positive. Men should recognize that the father is the role model after which the son will fashion his particular brand of masculinity. Whatever does or does not go on between a father and his son has a profound impact in that regard. Too often it is what does not go on that becomes the determining factor in how a boy creates his personal masculinity. He is left to create his own version without guidance and therein lies the seeds for the distorted concepts that produce the anti-social abnormalities for many of us.

If men could somehow shatter the concept among many that intimacy between a father and his son is somehow unmasculine, we could improve the lives of generations of males. Until it becomes all right for men to nurture, I suspect we will continue to live in a society of men searching for their fathers with all the sociopathic behaviors that entails.

The next morning, following a short taxi ride back to the Trail, we proceeded down a soft grassy road that eventually led up the hill to the ridge top. A couple of short steep climbs to some rock ledges rewarded us with outstanding views across Surprise Lake and Greenwood Lake. I took several photographs of the rock on which had been painted NY/NJ, indicating we were crossing state lines. From there, the Trail led through an open hardwood forest on the ridgeline, and the walking was easy.

We soon encountered a thin, sandy-haired man who I took to be in his mid-thirties. He sat on a large boulder eating a peanut butter and jelly sandwich. I noticed he had a duffel bag arrangement with a bedroll attached. That immediately told me he was not a thru-hiker. But he had the lean, gaunt look of a thru-hiker who had paid his Trail dues in lost poundage.

As we approached, he called out, "See you're wearin' long pants. A bit hot, ain't it?"

"Not bad. I like the protection," I responded.

"Don't need no protection here," he observed.

"Where you headed," asked Cathy.

"Florida."

"When you expect to get there?"

"Late October or November. No rush. Just takin' in the sights along the way."

"What do you do when you're not bummin' the Trail?" Cathy asked.

The man rolled his head backwards and looked skyward with his eyes closed, as if he were asking God for strength. "I resent that."

"Resent what?" Cathy was totally startled by the response.

"I'm a very religious person," he replied angrily. "I'm not a bum."

"I didn't mean you're a bum. I only used the term bummin' as a figure of speech," Cathy explained quietly, after realizing he was deadly serious.

He shook his head, refusing to accept her explanation or in any way to be appeased. "It is very offensive to me. You called me a bum, and I resent that very much."

"She intended no harm." I sensed the need to butt in. "We apologize — if you feel offended. There really was no intent to offend you."

He shook his head again. You could tell his agitation was building. "You called me a bum, and I resent that. Resent that very much. I'm religious and find it very offensive."

"Well, I'm sorry you feel that way; no insult was intended. Then, while still watching him, I said with urgency in my voice, "Cathy, we gotta get on our way." I started off so quickly that Cathy had to almost run to keep up with me. "See ya," I said as I passed him.

"Just you remember, I'm not a bum," he said, scowling.

After a few minutes, I stepped to the side and told Cathy to lead and to keep up the pace. "He's not dealing from a full deck,"

I said as she went by. "Just keep goin' 'til I tell you to stop. I'll keep an eye on the rear." I even pushed us through our scheduled break to put as much distance as possible between him and us, and when we did stop I took the revolver from my pack and put it in my pocket for easy access should the need arise.

Cathy was clearly rattled by the event; her lips were drawn tight against her teeth; she looked much like she did when she faced the Knife Edge or some other scary aspect of the hike. Fortunately we never saw him again; neither did any other hikers behind us whom I talked to later.

During the next hour, we climbed Montvale Mountain, not a long climb, but a rock scramble nevertheless. The hike was very pretty, and along the ridges, it was sometimes exciting. There were a number of tricky little climbs and descents that required caution. The weather was sunny and warm, but the pathway stayed in the woods, and the shade helped enormously in the afternoon heat. Toward the end of the day we climbed the escarpment beside Fitzgerald Falls, a beautiful 25-foot waterfall splashing down a rocky cliff.

I was pretty tired when we stopped, although we had done only 13.6 miles, all of them had to a degree been difficult and that, added to the stress of dealing with the "bum," had taken its toll. I realized, as I climbed into my sleeping bag, that it was the 7th of July, my father's birthday. I remembered selected snatches of times with my father but fell asleep before coming to grips with anything of substance in my childhood.

We spent the next day in wet clothes caused by an early morning shower that soaked the pathway and us. Thankfully it had waited, until we had struck camp before coming down in earnest. The first seven miles consisted of a series of fairly steep climbs and descents, some of which seemed almost vertical. One particular stretch was aptly named, Agony Grind. It started off with a five-foot drop-off from a rock ledge and went almost vertically straight down. With the episode on the Knife Edge still fresh in our minds, we elected to bypass the possibility of injury and road-walked through Harriman State Park past Lake Cohasset, Upper Lake Cohasset and Toriati Lake. We set up camp in the tall grass, just off a wooded road that led to Big Stone shelter.

It rained the whole night. In fact, a thunderstorm rolled

through on top of the shower we were already experiencing. I went out like a light as soon as I got into the sleeping bag. We awoke to the sound of rain still pelting the tent the next morning. We decided to forego breakfast, to just pack it up and head for the shelter, where we expected to find relief from the water coming from above and hoped to find some coming from below. Our water bottles were running on empty.

The roof of the shelter was connected to a huge rock formation that served also as the shelter's rear wall. However, the junction of the shelter roof and the rock was less than water tight. As a result, the shelter floor was a little sloshy. A comment in the shelter journal by Craig Upshaw, "Lone Angler," indicated that he had gotten wet. He also said the spring-fed well was dry. I wished the Trail maintainers would focus more on improving water sources. All through New Jersey and New York, we found getting water to be a problem.

We ate breakfast and started off at 9:00 a. m., making another climb over the rock mound directly behind the shelter. There were some nice views to the west and one good view of Bear Mountain and the Hudson River. The climbs up Black and West Mountains were not bad but nothing spectacular. We then passed the ski jump at Bear Mountain. It didn't look all that impressive as a structure in the summer time — until I looked down the hill. The slope was awesome, and I could imagine the psychological impact of the view on the jumpers as they dove down the ramp. The term "exciting" would be understatement.

We arrived at the Bear Mountain Inn at 3:15 p. m. and took a break.

CHAPTER 7

Duty, honor, country: Those three hallowed words reverently dictate what you ought to be, what you can be what you will be. They are your rallying points to build courage when courage seems to fail, to regain faith when there seems to be little cause for faith, to create hope when hope becomes forlorn.
— *Douglas MacArthur*

Bear Mountain to Kent, CT

The Bear Mountain Inn, an aging wooden structure complete with rustic wooden room balconies and ivy covered walls, had an English manor home quality about it that clashed with its Bavarian gingerbread wood decorations. The facade was clearly past its prime. It reminded me of an aristocratic lady grown old. The pride was evident, the bearing regal; and in the symmetry of her lines, one could discern the classic beauty of her youth. I could picture the rich and the famous in formal attire, silks and furs, arriving in elegant limousines for the weekend, the uniformed doorman attending them, as they swept through the ornate wooden doors beneath the entrance canopy.

The Inn dominated the landscape like the manor homes of Europe. The grounds, although heroically maintained, appeared worn, not so much from age as from over use. Several groups of people were playing softball or throwing Frisbees on the broad estate-like lawns, and a larger number were walking the pathways. I was impressed by the crowd, because it was a weekday, and I could only imagine the mob scene that must have prevailed during weekends.

The scene, which followed my entrance into the building, completely destroyed my romantic impression of grandeur. Three uniformed young women hostesses were valiantly trying to handle the press of business forced on them by a continuing stream of people with questions or demands. One hostess was totally occupied in a dispute with a barely fluent, swarthy foreign customer over the number of persons allowed in a room. Another hostess was constantly occupied with the telephone and the computer, and she was unable to deal with people lined up three deep at the counter. The remaining hostess appeared to have been given the job yesterday. After several minutes, I was able to get her attention. She tried to be helpful. "No, no rooms are available."

I did learn that Highland Falls had a auto rental company, and I arranged with them to bring a rental car to the Inn. Then, Cathy went outside to wait, while I went in search of ice cream.

The ice cream vendor was a concessionaire as was the popcorn man and the hot dog man. A list of their specialties was tacked to the wall. I selected my favorite and called out to the young girl behind the counter. "How 'bout two nutty buddies?"

"None left."

"Okay, two ice cream sandwiches."

"We're outta sandwiches."

"Okay, got any fudge twirls?" I was ready for the answer.

"Nope," she responded, shaking her head. The girl had been flirting with a young boy, and it was obvious that I was disrupting much more important matters.

"Okay," I said with some exasperation. "What do you have?"

"Only got three things." She listed them, and I selected two popsicles and returned to the entrance.

A bus had arrived at the entrance during my absence and people were milling about in general confusion. Cathy and I sat in the middle of the people, resting against our packs — which were propped against an awning support pole — and ate our popsicles. No one paid much attention to us except for a short, plainly dressed middle-aged woman. She walked around us a couple of times, sizing us up as if we were something for sale. She looked at us from one angle, then moved to get another perspective. Finally she asked, "Are youse hikers?"

"We're walking the Appalachian Trail," Cathy responded

brightly.

"What's that?"

"The Appalachian Trail is a foot path that runs from Georgia to Maine," she explained.

"How far youse goin'?"

I cut in, "Well, I started at Springer Mountain, Georgia, last summer, and I plan to make it to Maine by summer's end."

"I wouldn't give two cents for what you're doing," she pronounced with disdain made more disagreeable by its abruptness. "Did that kinda stuff when I was younger. I usta hunt. My father forced me to go huntin' wit him."

"What're you doin' here?" asked Cathy.

"We're goin' tuh West Point."

"So are we. We're going tomorrow."

"They probably won't let youse in," the woman responded immediately.

"No problem for us. He's a colonel," Cathy said brightly.

"I come from a military family. My father was a colonel general. Died in the war when I was four years old."

I was tempted to ask what war and what army, and if she hunted at four years of age, but just then the tour guide called all the passengers to board the bus, and the woman turned away without further comment. Then arrival of the rental car broke the spell of that somewhat unlikely conversation.

It was a 1983 Pontiac Le Grand with 76,000 miles on the odometer, all of them tough. The car slowed steadily as it climbed the hill north of West Point, and I had to turn off the air conditioning to retain enough power to make it to the top. It was a mechanical disaster. The engine was not firing on all cylinders, and it wandered all over the road — especially when it hit a bump. Then, it would take off in a different trajectory like it had a mind of its own. I had agreed not to drive the thing more than a hundred miles from Highland Falls, "Just in case we need to tow it," the salesman had mentioned in passing. Needless to say, speed was not something we worried about. It was a perfect backpacker's car, though. It got us where we wanted to go and back — and the price was right.

Our visit to the U.S. Military Academy at West Point the next day was for me a mixture of pride and nostalgia. Most of the upper classmen were gone from the Academy for the summer visiting active Army units in the field or at installations around the world or participating in tactical training programs of their own. The only cadets present were the plebes, the first year cadets who had only just arrived and were undergoing the first days of their academy experience. It is a most difficult time for them; unlike anything they had experienced before. If they survived — and most do, they would develop into the great soldiers and leaders the country has learned to rely on in times of national peril or emergency.

Illustrious members of the Academy alumni include names like Eisenhower, Patton, MacArthur, Bradley, and Schwarzkopf. They are among the most famous, but they were supported by a host of very capable subordinate commanders and staff officers, most of whom remain unknown to the public but who epitomized the devotion MacArthur called for in the cause of "Duty, Honor, and Country."

We had arrived fairly late and were still taking in the sights when we noticed the cadets assembling in front of gray buildings. A glance at my watch told me it was time for the retreat ceremony. The duty day was over. The leaders went through the formalities to insure that all were accounted for and that the formation was correct. Then, when everything was set the cadets in formation stood at parade rest. As the scenario was unfolding, I told Cathy what was happening. "First the bugler plays, To the Colors, and the cadets stand at parade rest." It happened, and I stood at parade rest.

"What's that?" Cathy whispered.

"Hush," I said softly, "that's To the Colors."

The early evening air carried the bugle notes across the plain. The sound reverberated among the barracks, then echoed faintly in the hills behind. It became quiet. "Now everyone will come to attention and present arms," I whispered.

The Commander of Troops called out, "Bring your units to attention and present arms," and one by one the company commanders called their units "to attention and presented arms". When the last company complied, the Commander of Troops and Staff stood at attention and presented arms.

"What's that for?" Cathy asked.

"That's to show respect for the flag. Now they'll fire the cannon and play retreat." No sooner had I said it than the cannoneer pulled the lanyard, firing the cannon and setting in motion the bugler who played retreat. The Military Policemen began to lower the flag as the bugler played. I also stood at attention — complete with long hair, unkempt beard, stained shorts and scruffy hiking boots. Some things just never leave you.

"Wow, they did it. They fired the cannon, and you knew they were going to do it. How did you know it?" Cathy was like a kid at a parade.

Coming here to the Academy had been well worth the effort — for both of us.

The approach to the Bear Mountain Bridge over the Hudson River at 124 feet is the lowest point on the entire AT. I thought with some trepidation about the coming climbs to get back to the 6,000-foot level of some of the mountains in New Hampshire. But right then the walk across the bridge was a small treat. A slight breeze helped dissipate the heat, and the view of the Hudson Valley was truly inspiring. After reaching the east side of the bridge, the Trail followed the road for a short distance before ascending rather steeply up the ridge known as Anthony's Nose, then up Canada Hill.

The views of the Hudson Valley from the ridge were less than ideal because of the haze, but it was beautiful, nonetheless, with contrasting colors along the river and the hills with delicate differences in the blue and green hues that characterized the early summer scenery. West Point sits amid a very picturesque landscape of escarpments behind the river with mountains rising in the background — both to the north and south. Because of these mountains, only the tallest buildings could be seen from where we stood.

The well-maintained Trail made walking the ridge line easy, and we made good time reaching the Graymoor Monastery around 4:00 p. m. The monastery, founded in 1909 by a converted Episcopal clergyman, sits on a dome-like hill and dominates the surrounding countryside. It evokes memories of some of the medieval castle ruins one sees in Europe. The building itself, a massive, modern brick structure, however, appeared more like an asylum or correctional facility than a monastery. Its massive size was intimidating. We knew from the Philosopher's Guide that the monks were gracious hosts, and thoughts of a decent meal and good night's sleep urged us upward.

The road approach, a winding asphalt driveway, eventually ended in a narrow parking lot in front of the entrance where a number of late model cars were neatly parked in designated spaces as admonished by a prominently displayed sign. I had expected to see monks in traditional habits looking like St. Francis of Assisi or Friar Tuck from Robin Hood walking the grounds in meditation. Wrong again. We saw nobody, until entering the building and encountering a female receptionist who explained that Father Bosco was responsible for dealing with hikers.

From the name Bosco, I anticipated a heavy-set monk in a traditional monk's habit and sandals. The stereotype was demolished when a tall, very thin man approaching the end of middle age, wearing a short sleeve sport shirt and slacks, offered his hand. "I'm Father Bosco." After a short orientation covering the Monastery rules and meal times, we received a mimeographed information sheet to assist us in remembering what we had just been told and were led to our rooms in an older part of the building that no longer housed monks.

The rooms were austere monastic cells with a hard board bed (no inner spring mattresses here), but the cells did have a thin cotton mattress on the bed (not uncomfortable), a small sink with running water, a desk, a chair, and a narrow wall closet with a partition containing drawers. A bare bulb with a conical shade suspended from the center of the ceiling provided the only light. There was no air conditioning, and we were informed pointedly — smoking was forbidden.

The dining hall was huge, larger than many dining facilities in the Army. Diners sat at large circular tables with generous amounts of space between tables as well as diners. The tables took up about a third of the total floor space with 20 or 30 feet of unused space between the tables, the side walls and the kitchen entrance. Additionally behind the circular tables was an area half as large again with rows of long rectangular tables complete with benches, all unused. Obviously the facility had been designed for many more people than were now in residence.

Included among the diners at an adjacent table were four

people, three women and a man, along with Father Bosco. One woman was obviously older than the others were, a second seemed to be quite young. She had arrived limping very noticeably behind a seeing-eye dog that was pulling more than guiding. The third woman was closer in age to the older-looking woman. The man appeared to be middle aged. He looked like a thru-hiker in some respects with an unkempt beard and sloppy clothes, but he lacked the gaunt body of a thru-hiker, and he was wearing jeans.

Other than the guests, the diners in general, all men, were mostly in their 60s, some older and a couple much older. At one table, however, was a group of young men who were out of place. I guessed them to be workers or seminarians. The food was very good; the main course, a seafood Newburgh on rice, was excellent. I helped myself twice from the bowls placed in front of us. Not only that, the salad bar was brimming with fresh vegetables; I had three helpings from it, the last accompanied by some self inflicted embarrassment for appearing "gluttonous."

After a few minutes, Father Bosco came to our table and sat down. "Want to spend a little time with everybody," he said by way of introduction.

"How many monks live here?" Cathy asked.

"Forty right now," he replied. "We're getting smaller all the time. The number of people coming into the priesthood is getting smaller all the time."

"Why's that?" I asked.

"Moral decline." Father Bosco shook his head slowly and thoughtfully. "Look at the movies now. Listen to the music now. It's morally corrupt." A moment of silence followed. He looked like he was thinking, and I suspected he wanted to say more. Suddenly he looked me directly in the eyes. "What do you do? You look too old to be hiking the Trail."

"Oh, I'm hiking the Trail, all right. I'm a retired Army officer. I'm just hiking the Trail to sort of transition into being a civilian again. Of course, that's not quite correct. Officially I'm still an officer in the Army. It's just that I'm in retired status. Effectively, though, I'm a civilian."

Just then a very old man escorted, supported by a nurse, wobbled toward the dining room door. Father Bosco pointed to him. "He's a retired Army chaplain. He was in the second war.

Used to say mass from the back of a truck. He's senile now. We had another one, but he's dead. Died about a year ago."

"Are they monks?" I asked and pointed to the table with the younger men.

"They're undergoing rehabilitation," he replied. "They're alcoholics or drug addicts, derelicts of some sort. We pick 'em up from the city mostly, bring 'em up here and clean 'em up. We work 'em and try to rehabilitate 'em. Some make it. Most don't."

"The reason I asked is because I don't see any religious clothing."

"We don't wear the habit all the time. I only wear it on weekends. Most don't wear it except on special occasions or Sunday. It's a lot less strict now than it used to be. Before we had to be up at 5:30 a. m. and had to spend so much time in prayer and meditation, it was pretty regimented. We don't do that now. I mean, we don't get up at 5:30 anymore. We can stay in bed until breakfast, if we want to."

The word meditation immediately caught my attention. "How do you meditate?" I asked quickly. Here was a man who had spent his life doing the very thing I wanted to learn to do: to meditate, and to communicate with God. Maybe I could learn the secret . . .

The change in subject startled him and a slightly puzzled expression came over his face. He then bowed his head slightly and, looking at the table, said that they would take a "passage from the Bible" and use it as a starting point or a guide as they sought to understand the deeper meaning of the text. He talked in terms of "obtaining a more intense knowledge." He then reached into his pocket and handed us each a card on which was printed two prayers.

"God called me to the priesthood at an early age," he said. "I remember going to mass as a boy to hear the priest and thinking what a wonderful thing it was to be called by God like he was — to serve the Lord. It came to me while I was in church that I wanted to be a priest. I wanted to be like that priest. I started my training when I was thirteen." He stopped to reflect. as if he might be thinking back across the years, and he probably was. "I have a book for meditation. I'll bring it to breakfast. You'll eat breakfast, won't you?"

I nodded my head. "Wouldn't miss it for anything."

The majority of monks had left as had the other people, including the group with the dog. Father Bosco rose saying he was going to vespers, and we all departed the facility at the same time.

After a good night's sleep, we were already eating breakfast when the priest arrived. The other hikers had departed before breakfast. In fact, they had awakened me at about 5:00 a. m. when they had departed.

Since they were gone, Father Bosco gave us his undivided attention. He seemed to have a purpose as he came over. "You must have done a lot of shooting while you were in the Army. Like marksmanship shooting. How do you hold a rifle to shoot when you're standing up? I tried to hold it steady, but it waves all over on me. Is there some trick?"

"I haven't fired a rifle in years." I laughed. "In marksmanship, they refer to the standing position as the off-hand position. It's the most unstable position; you have only muscle support. We tried to get as much support as possible by wrapping the rifle sling around the arm in a certain way and holding the supporting elbow as close as possible to the body. I always found it tough to shoot well from the off-hand position. In the other marksmanship positions, we could get bone-to-bone support that really makes it much easier to hold your sight alignment. But getting into some of those positions can be a challenge."

"I used to have a .22 caliber rifle that I hunted rabbits and squirrels with. Sometimes I'd go to the dump and shoot rats. I've been thinking about getting another rifle. I got rid of the .22 rifle after Kennedy was assassinated."

"How do you feel killing those animals?" Cathy asked. "Didn't you feel guilty killing those little suckers?"

"Animals are put on earth for man's use. That doesn't mean we should kill them needlessly — just for the sake of killing, but to hunt for sport or food is not sinful." End of conversation with Cathy. He turned to me again.

I was struck by the fact that he almost never spoke to Cathy. He politely acknowledged her presence when she occasionally entered the conversation; otherwise, he spoke only to me, almost as if Cathy might not be present. I expected Cathy to show irritation, but if she was irritated, she hid it well.

"Is the Army boot camp like the Marines where they're always yellin' at guys or somebody?" he asked.

"In the Army they call it basic training, and it's probably not as demanding as the Marine version," I explained. "The concept is to put recruits through psychologically, physically, as well as emotionally demanding experiences which will help them endure the rigors of military life and the stress of combat."

"You serve in Viet Nam?"

"Two tours. Once as an advisor to a Vietnamese District Commander and once with a US unit."

"That must have been bad. I mean, everything I read about it, about not knowin' who the enemy was. Did the troops do a lot of stuff like My Lai? I couldn't see killin' a lot of innocent people."

"I didn't see or hear of anything like My Lai, while I was there. As far as I could see, our troops acted with remarkable restraint under extremely trying conditions."

"Did we have women in the Army in Viet Nam? I mean — other than nurses. I know we had nurses."

"We had some women, but women constituted a far smaller percentage of our forces than they do now."

"How are they as soldiers? I mean, how do they do their jobs? You can't treat 'em like men; It must be tough to discipline them, if they goof up."

"Women are in almost every MOS in the Army, except those requiring direct combat, such as the Infantry."

"What's that?"

"What's what?" I was baffled.

"The MOS or whatever you said."

"Oh, that. That's an acronym for Military Occupational Specialty. It's the code for your job and skill level."

"They any good?"

"They're soldiers, just like male soldiers, only in some ways a little different. You have to treat them equally. I could say that by and large female soldiers are as good as their male counterparts, and sometimes a good deal better and sometimes a good deal worse."

I wasn't sure he was hearing what he expected; he kept looking at me in a perplexed way. "The female officers who've worked for me have, with a couple of exceptions, been very good. One of them, a lieutenant, was an Academy grad, and she was one of the best lieutenants I've seen during my time in the Army."

That seemed to startle him. The dining room was starting to empty. It was getting late, and we had to be on our way. Still, Father Bosco remained seated, thinking over what I had said. I could understand with his monastic background the difficulty he had understanding and relating to women. Although we never talked about it, I think Cathy recognized the problem, and that was the reason she didn't get out of sorts when he spoke only to me. Clearly he seemed uncomfortable dealing with women.

Finally he rose from the table, and looking at me with a piercing intensity, handed me a small reddish-brown colored book about two inches square and about a quarter inch thick. "It's for meditating. I hope you find it useful. There's also a prayer with it."

We walked slowly out of the room together, then shook hands. I watched as he moved slightly stooped down the hall — then, Cathy and I went to get our packs.

On the way down the hill from the Monastery back to the Trail, we passed a van parked on a level area where a beautifully maintained lawn and shrubbery overlooked by a shrine. A man and a women — I recognized them from the group the previous night — were striking their tents. They were obviously occupied, and we continued on without disturbing them. Later in the morning we met them again at a road junction where the Trail crossed.

"You hikin' the Trail too?" Cathy asked.

"When we can, which is not too often. The Trail is just so tough," answered the woman.

"We're actually the support crew for Granma Soule," responded the man. "Granma is hiking the Trail, and we're supporting her by carrying her pack and stuff, and meeting her at Trail crossings."

"I was hiking the Trail — until I had to have my toe amputated," the woman cut in.

"That was in Pennsylvania — in Harrisburg. She can't hike again until the first of August," said the man.

"Well, I'm not supposed to," the woman responded, swinging her leg. "We'll see about that,"

"Which one is Granma Soule?" I asked.

The woman was clearly the spokesperson for the van crew.

"The little older woman. Her real name is Verna. The other woman is Dina. There're four of them who've hiked the Trail together before. They're known as "The Hiking Grandmas." The two that aren't here have hiked the whole Trail. Dina has completed most of it. Needs to do Massachusetts and Vermont to complete it. Granma has hiked several sections, but this year decided to do it end to end, and we're supporting her. Dina is only hiking for another week. Then she has to go back home."

I was really curious as to the reason for the amputation of her toe. But I didn't want to appear pushy.

Cathy didn't share my inhibitions."Why'd you have your toe amputated?"

"Injured it. Hit it against a rock in Pennsylvania. I'm a diabetic, and that's what caused the damage."

The man joined in. "She didn't want to stop. It's good we did, though. The doctor said she could've lost her foot or worse, if we hadn't got there when we did. What're your names?"

"I'm Cathy Morris and he's Jan Curran, the Old Soldier," said the ever friendly Cathy.

"We're Sue Lockwood and Gordon Smith. We're brother and sister," said Sue.

"It must get awfully crowded in the van with four packs and camping gear," Cathy observed.

"And that's only part of it. There's a lot of dialysis supplies and stuff we carry for Sue plus the dogs and their food. Sue's blind, and we have a seeing-eye dog for her.

We found them to be interesting people and wanted to talk longer, but the Trail awaited, and I told Cathy we needed to get on. Cathy held back for a moment, then said, "Hope we see one another again down the Trail."

The Trail through this stretch of New York led across open woodland, then followed a series of little used historic unpaved roads — Old West Point Road, Old Albany Post Road, Chapman Road and Canopus Hill Road. These roads were often used by soldiers from both sides during the Revolutionary War, and I found it mildly exhilarating to know I was walking on the same roads used by them over 200 years before. Toward the end of the day we hiked along an old narrow gauge railroad bed that connected Sunk Mine with Cold Spring Turnpike. The train carried ore from the mine during the mid-1800s.

Along the way we met John Newman, a.k.a. "Oliver Twist," from Callowhee, North Carolina, who was day-hiking portions of the Trail. He invited us to stay with him and his school teacher wife at their campsite in Fahnstock State Park about a mile down Highway 301 from the Trail crossing. He said he would give us a lift back to the Trail in the morning, and we accepted without hesitation.

Granma Soule, Sue and Gordon had also come to the park, and they and the Newmans were gathered in front of the Newmans' tent when we arrived. A lively conversation ensued during which it was agreed that the Trail was just plain tough, almost to the point of being too difficult. Granma related how she had to remove her pack when coming out of Lehigh Gap, fasten a rope to it and pull it up after her. "Just couldn't make it with these short little legs of mine," she said.

Granma, a thin, hickory-sapling-tough 5 feet 2 inches tall was 62 years old, but except for some sagging skin beneath her eyes, she looked much younger. He legs, particularly her calves, were highly muscled, reminding me of the comic strip character from Lil Abner called Mammy Yokum. Mammy was one tough lady, always punching someone to the moon. Her legs were like Granma's.

After a short time, Gordon asked Sue if they shouldn't "do a bag?" I suspected he was referring to Sue's dialysis treatment, and I was right. Sue acknowledged him but made no movement to comply. Gordon waited a few minutes, then went to the van and returned with some medical equipment, which Sue immediately used. I couldn't see exactly what was going on, but I guessed she was sampling blood sugar. At any rate, they then went to the van, and I could see them both wearing surgical masks inside.

The conversation then turned to various Trail experiences. Granma said while she was hiking in the Smokies she came upon a naked couple sitting along side the Trail. "What'd you do?" chimed in someone.

"Asked 'em if the Trail went through there," Granma replied matter of factly, "What was I going to say?"

Everyone laughed at Granma's predicament.

The talk then turned to the thru-hikers ahead of us. Someone asked if anyone had seen entries in any of the Trail Registers by Slim Jim or Daddy Long Legs. Another asked the same about the Blaze Brothers and the Brits. Then, the conversation slowed at that point, and Cathy and I excused ourselves and headed for the tent for some much needed sleep.

Gordon gave us a lift to the Trail the next morning, offering to take our packs along with Granma's and Dina's and meeting us at the point where the Trail crossed Highway 51 at day's end. We immediately accepted. As we were leaving the van, Gordon mentioned that the packs would bring a good price in town.

"You don't think he'd do that?" Cathy asked with some concern.

"Naw, just his way of joking. Besides, he knows I'd kill him if he did."

The day was hot and humid, and walking almost unencumbered was a real treat. We had borrowed a light, nylon day-pack from Gordon and filled it with our lunches and water and other necessities like toilet paper, and we took turns carrying to share the minimal weight.

The forest was mostly deciduous with some scrub growth and a few stands of hemlock. Several patches of wildflowers, including spotted wintergreen and hog peanut among others, brightened the pathway. At Highway 52, we stopped, picked up our packs and talked again with Sue and Gordon. Now that they knew us, they seemed to open up more. They were very unusual people.

Sue had been a school teacher in Michigan before the full onset of her illness. Neither worked in the conventional sense of having a job and lived from Social Security and Sue's pension. But Gordon "worked" by caring for Sue, doing errands, driving the van, helping with the dialysis and doing all those things for Sue that we who are not handicapped take for granted. In effect, Gordon's mission in life was to care for his sister.

They were devoted to one another and to Granma Soule and her mission, had helped in planning the hike, and had been with Granma since March when she started from Springer Mountain.

On occasion, when the Trail permitted, and sometimes when it didn't, Sue would hitch up Mack, the black Labrador retriever cum seeing-eye dog, and, with Gordon in tow, head for the Trail. Those periods were the highlight of her day; she was most happy then. It seemed the one time when she could escape the tyranny of her illness. Gordon kept track of her mileage and up to that time estimated Sue had walked about 700 miles of the Trail, pretty damn remarkable, considering her situation.

We learned that Dina was leaving the next day. She felt she was not in hiking shape and was holding Granma back. But now a new member of the Hiking Granma's group was coming to Pawling, New York, to join Granma on the Trail. I wondered how Granma felt about breaking in a new tenderfoot. As I had learned from the Blaze Brothers and The AT Believer example, one of the cardinal rules of hiking is "everyone hikes his own hike" and it can be extremely trying to be tied to someone who is too fast or too slow. It knocks you off your rhythm and has been the cause of a good number of partnership breakups on the Trail.

We were hit by a thunderstorm during the last hour of the day and were soaked when we arrived at the Morgan Stewart shelter, where we spent the night.

The next day we did running battle with mosquitoes and deer flies. Mosquitoes are pikers compared to deer flies. The deer flies bit right through the material in my shirt — and they hurt.

The following day was also uncomfortable. Although it was not raining, the woods were heavy with moisture as was the soil. That made rocks slippery. Thankfully there were no dangerous drop-offs. The air was sticky humid with absolutely no hint of a breeze, and we soon became soaked with perspiration. But by the time we reached Pawling, the sun had come out, and although it was hot, it helped dry out the countryside, and the air became less humid.

We decided to slack pack to Kent, Connecticut. We rented a car in Pawling and drove to Kent, where we booked a motel room for two nights. In the morning, we left our packs in the room, then returned to Pawling, dropped off the car and walked in comfort unencumbered back to Kent.

It was one of the most beautiful sections of the Trail we had hiked, since coming back on at Turner Gap. The hike across Ten Mile Creek over the Ned Anderson Bridge and along the Housatonic River was refreshing, and the views from Schaghticoke Mountain of the valley to the south were particularly scenic. Farther on, we encountered several groves of bright, almost silver cedars and also occasional heavy, damp hemlock groves. We startled a scarlet tanager that departed in a reddish streak from a low hanging branch, and we stopped to watch a couple of red wing black birds cavorting in a field near the river. It was almost a perfect day. We reached Conn. Route 341 about 5:00 p. m. and headed for Kent and the motel about a half mile to the east.

CHAPTER 8

By profession I am a soldier and take pride in that. But I am prouder — infinitely prouder — to be a father. A soldier destroys in order to build; the father only builds, never destroys. The one has the potentiality of death. The other embodies creation and life. And while the hordes of death are mighty, the battalions of life are mightier still. It is my hope that my son, when I am gone, will remember me not from the battle but in the home repeating with him our simple daily prayer.

— Douglas MacArthur

Kent, CT to Tyringham, MA

We encountered the Granma Soule entourage again at dinner that evening at a small Italian restaurant across the street from the motel. We were already seated when the parade through the dining area began. It was led by a waitress followed by Sue, limping behind a harness straining Mack, followed by Gordon, then Granma, and lastly Marge; Granma's new hiking companion brought up the rear. The place was packed nearly to capacity, and everyone stopped eating to watch the rain-bedraggled company march in to the beat of Sue's cast banging the floor. We exchanged greetings. Since they were seated close to us, we conversed between mouthfuls. I learned they were tent-camped in the rain.

That evening in bed I began thinking about Sue and how difficult her illness had made her life. I wondered how she approached life, and what sense of purpose she could discern in light of her disease and pain. I sensed Sue was still denying her limitations, still fighting a battle she couldn't win. She had not reached accord with reality. But eventually she must. Because it was not something she could will to change; it was she who had to adapt. And that was difficult to accept. Still and all, I admired her tenacity in trying to go on, as if nothing had changed in her life.

It seemed that the sense of purpose in our lives is not fixed in concrete, but that it changes as we mature. It develops according to the stages of our lives. When faced with momentous changes in our lives, so our sense of purpose changes. For us to be truly happy, we must recognize that fact and allow ourselves to be guided and counseled from our inner strength. We need to allow our inner state of consciousness to provide the direction in which we develop and how we are to react to situations beyond our ability to control. Essentially what is required is as simple as believing in the Lord's Prayer: "Thy will be done on Earth as it is in Heaven." It is the recognition that whatever our gifts or our afflictions, they are not only ours, they come from the Creator for a purpose, and it is up to us, with His help, to find what that may be.

Gordon and Sue dropped us off at the Trail in the morning, offering also to take our packs. We accepted the offer with pleasure. The day was clear, bright and cool, just made for pleasant hiking. Initially we crossed a cow pasture where a herd of cows and a young calf were grazing.

One of the cows, a heifer, apparently thought we were a threat or were violating her territory or just wanted to play, and charged. Although she was young, she also weighed several hundred pounds; even at a slow speed this could cause major hurt to brittle 53-year-olds. The object in such a case is to convince the animal that it could also be detrimental to its health or longevity. Using my hiking stick like a matador, but with nowhere near the grace or confidence, I managed to deflect her charges. After a third half-hearted charge, she turned and went back to the herd. I suspect that she just tired of playing and decided to look elsewhere for amusement. We didn't wait to find out. A huge oak tree had fallen directly across Macedonia Brook; it formed a bridge, which the Trail followed, and we hastened across and out of the herd's range.

The climbs up Pond Mountain and Caleb's Peak were a

breeze without packs. The highlight of the day was the St. John's Ledges and the spectacular overlook of the Housatonic Valley. We stopped for a breather and to admire the scenery.

Mike Bisceglia, a newspaper photographer for a paper in southern Connecticut, was there when we arrived. He asked if we knew Granma Soule and if she was behind us, and if so, how far back. We didn't know where Granma was, but we knew she had started before us and had certainly passed the Ledges some time before we arrived. We so informed Mike. Mike told us that Granma had become a celebrity of sorts, and he was there to get pictures for a story about her in his newspaper.

The hike down from St. John's Ledges to the Housatonic Valley followed an elaborate staircase of massive stone steps constructed by trail crews from the Appalachian Mountain Club, (AMC) of New Hampshire. The steps covered a 500-foot vertical drop and represented a major engineering effort. Despite the obvious advantages of the steps, the drop-offs between rocks was quite long and the stairway still quite steep and hikers; particularly those with short legs, were faced with the difficult challenge of stepping down three or four feet between rocks. For me they were difficult; for Cathy they were almost an obstacle. For Mike, who followed us down, they were a snap. He bounded down the mountain ahead of us, shooting frame after frame; once he shinnied out to the edge of a rock outcropping some 30 feet above the ground to get us going by. Straddling it like he would a horse, he shot more pictures, then with the briefest of departure ceremonies, he bounded back up towards St. John's Ledges.

The Trail then followed a well-worn old dirt road for six miles beside the Housatonic River. We passed fields of thickly waving golden Alexander and cool red pine plantations along picturesque stretches of the river, sometimes flowing in deep pools, sometimes foaming down rapids, or just shallow rocky river bottoms where occasional fish waggled in the flow.

Later in the day, we climbed out of the valley and met Gordon and Sue hiking along with Mack and Muggsy. Muggsy a nondescript little mutt with limitless energy and an independent streak was totally focused on Gordon. He was hooked to a leash, ostensibly to allow Gordon to control him. But in reality, it seemed that it was the device Muggsy used to pull Gordon along to where Muggsy wanted to go. It was all Gordon could do to hold the dog. Its other characteristic was its phenomenal leaping ability. His leaps were like rocket launches that propelled him into the air for journeys several times his own height.

The Trail from the ridge to Cornwell Bridge was a small treat. It crossed a deep ravine with a rambunctious mountain stream, and the hills and ridge sides were covered with extensive stands of hemlocks, pines, and spruce. The terrain was spectacularly rugged with gigantic boulders strewn along the chasm floor and up the hillsides. Countless skeletons of recent and not so recent dead falls laced the forest floor. Although the country was wild, the Trail was decently sited so that we could walk and still enjoy the beauty unfolding before us. It also made it easier for Sue who had been able to walk about two miles from the road.

The following day we started at about 6:30 a. m. and climbed Coltsfoot Mountain, passing Bonnie Brook along the way. The brook passed through a gap in a stone wall that at one time had been a dam. It was a picturesque little stream, containing several cascades with pools at their bases. We also visited several beautiful hemlock and pine groves interspersed with generous stands of white birches which reminded me of the poem, Birches, by Robert Frost.

The description contained in the Trail Guide, referring to the area we were about to walk, was quite eloquent: "Road passes through a lovely valley with handsome farms bordered by carefully tilled fields rimmed by majestic pine forests."

Majestic pine forests containing some of the largest pines I had ever seen rimmed the lush and beautiful farmsteads. I pointed them out to Cathy announcing authoritatively, "Those are gigantic pines."

"What kind of pines are they?" she asked.

"I think they're white pines. Look at the needles. If they have five to a bundle, they're white pines," I replied.

"That's not what you just called them."

"Well, I meant only that they were big trees as in gigantic."

"Maybe we'll see a grandfather tree," Cathy said excitedly.

"What kind of tree?"

"A grandfather tree. It's a tree from which all other trees in the forest come. Indians revered them and gave them gift offerings to insure that their spirits remained kindly disposed toward the Indians," Cathy explained.

"How do you know that?"

Cathy laughed. "I read it in a book."

"What're you gonna leave for an offering? A penny or something?"

"Jeez! Don't be colonelish! The Indians used to leave tobacco offerings. I'll break up a cigarette and leave some of the tobacco."

"At least, they'll be good for something!" I had been on her case for falling off the nicotine wagon.

"Never mind, you ain't been doin' so good with the beer."

She had a point there, and I shut up.

A short time later we came to a huge tree six or seven feet in diameter that towered over the surrounding trees. "There's a grandfather tree!" Cathy exclaimed. She went over and dropped some tobacco shreds at its base.

"Sure you can afford that?" I teased.

She ignored me. "Now we're gonna be safe and no harm will come to us, while we're on the Trail and under protection of the grandfather tree."

"Does that include up to Maine?"

"No, that only includes the immediate territory belonging to the grandfather tree."

"So what happens when we leave the grandfather tree's territory?"

"We have to find another grandfather tree."

"How will we know that we've left friendly territory?"

"Look! What's that?" she replied, pointing to a stand of flowers beside the road. Evidently she had no answer for me on the business of protection!

I did not sleep very well that night. We ended up camped in an area where camping was not authorized, and I was afraid a Ranger or someone would come by and throw us out. Not only that, but a raccoon or raccoons spent half the night rummaging through the garbage cans and just about wore out the can next to the picnic table where our tent was pitched.

We started off the next day with Verna and Marge. Verna led off climbing up the first ridge without apparent effort, leaving the rest of us struggling, Marge more so than Cathy or I.

Granma just took off jackrabbit style and soon was out of sight.

Granma was now 40 pounds lighter than when she had started on the Trail. She was now, she had told me, the same weight she was when she had gotten married. For a 62-year-old, she was in outstanding physical condition. Upon reflection I thought, Hell, she's in outstanding condition for any age.

The Trail wove through an area of beaver dams, crossing one particularly substantial one with the forest and a small brook to one side and a pond with a strange mixture of reflected sunlight and mists that shrouded the most distant tree skeletons on the other side.

We passed the Pine Knoll lean-to, now reduced to a jumbled pile of wood. A group of three people, three generations of backpackers, grandfather, son and grandson had tent-camped there and was preparing breakfast. The smell of bacon frying and campfire wood burning permeated the forest air mingling with the fragrance of firs and pines. Another future backpacker and hiker was being introduced to the Trail in the right way, I decided.

Dean Ravine was a special beauty with wild white water cascading down a precipice and tumbling into a rocky gorge some 50 feet below. The Trail followed along the rim, then dropped down to the floor of the ravine and followed the stream along a dappled course where sunlight colored the water in shallow pools golden.

In the afternoon, we hiked through Falls Village past a rock wall that formed a never used canal built in 1851. Falls Village was an industrial site from the past, manufacturing cannons during the Civil War and train wheels. It is now a quaint New England landmark.

The climb up Prospect Falls was very steep with large rock steps like St John's Ledges. However, here some log ladders had been constructed to aid climbers over particularly steep cliff and ledge faces. On the ridge top, the Trail followed a quiet path through mostly open forest. A large rock formation, known as "Giant's Thumb," stuck up from the ground like a "sore ____ " unless one were more inclined to take a phallic view of things. It definitely was a strange formation, since there were no other rocks in the vicinity. The Trail Guide indicated its origin was unknown.

Camping Zone 4 was an abandoned logging road cut into the hillside a couple hundred yards uphill from the parking area. The ground was rocky and the earth hard with little room to erect a tent, but after 17.8 miles, erect it we did. Granma and Marge arrived a few minutes later and set up their tents. Gordon and Sue remained in the parking area where they planned to set up their tents, despite the "no camping" signs posted all over.

It was at that time that Marge announced she was leaving the Trail the next day. As with Dina, Marge was unable to maintain Granma's pace, and felt she was holding Granma back. Not only that, she wanted to stay in motels and eat in restaurants whenever possible but being tied to the van crew made that difficult.

The climb up Lionhead, the first in a succession of ridges, was steep, but the view to the east of the just-risen sun was a fitting reward for the effort. We met a young man admiring the sunrise who informed us he had climbed to the ledge in the dark, so that he might photograph the sunrise. The sun was already well above the horizon by the time we arrived, but the views of the mists over Connecticut were impressive nonetheless. We next climbed Bear Mountain and then Race Mountain, which although not steep, seemed to take forever to climb.

All in all, the day was a hiker's dream: beautiful weather and a pathway rich with natural beauty. All the mountain tops had offered impressive views over the Connecticut and Massachusetts countryside, and the Trail had taken us through a number of hauntingly dark and beautiful pine and hemlock groves. We also passed stands of bright and airy birches as well as visiting occasional streams, alternately darkly flowing or flashing silver and golden in the sunlight.

After a short excursion through Sage's Ravine with a number of small pools and small falls, we started up Everett Mountain, the largest in the chain. A series of short ascents and descents, the kind that really take the measure of a hiker, led us to Jug End where the Trail dropped precipitously back down to the valley floor.

It was about 4:00 p. m. when we arrived at our pickup point; Granma and the crew were waiting.

The following day was interesting and rewarding. Early on

by a fenced field, we passed a marker indicating we were on the site of the last battle of Shay's Rebellion in 1787. We had several very good views of the mountains over which we had hiked the previous day. Lionhead, Race and Everett's Mountains were all clearly recognizable as was Jug End. They looked so far away it didn't seem possible that we had been there the day before. Then, after a series of ascents and descents into several small gorges, the Trail headed north and by early afternoon we had arrived at the campgrounds at Buell Lake where we spent the night.

As soon as we had set up our tents, we went swimming. The dirt and grime that had accumulated over the past couple of days quickly dissolved, and the cool water both exhilarated and soothed our bodies. And after swimming, we invited everyone to a wiener roast. We all stuffed ourselves with hot dogs and potato chips and sundry other junk foods which Cathy and I bought when Gordon took us into Great Barrington, Massachusetts, earlier in the day.

I awoke at 5:00 a. m. the next morning to the sound of Granma breaking camp. She left after taking a picture of Muggsy peeking out from beneath the flap of Gordon's bivy tent, and we got on the Trail about half an hour later. The path took us past a particularly pretty beaver pond where mist ascended on the warming dawn air and dead trees rose from their reflections on the water like the sinister beings inhabiting the imaginations of horror movie writers. The Trail then followed a series of roads down the mountain and presently we were in the picturesque New England village of Tyringham, nestled in a Berkshire Mountains valley.

CHAPTER 9

The courage of life is often a less dramatic spectacle than the courage of a final moment; but it is no less than a magnificent mixture of triumph and tragedy. A man does what he must — in spite of personal consequences, in spite of obstacles and dangers and pressure — and that is the basis of all human morality.
— *John F. Kennedy*

Tyringham, MA to North Adams, MA

After passing the small cluster of buildings that comprised the village proper, we encountered Sue; she was waiting for us with Mack rigged in harness. She had initially intended to hike with Granma but had missed her. So she had waited — until we came along. We followed the road up the hill past beautifully landscaped homes and estates with deep lawns and long winding driveways. Then, at the top of the rise, we came to a very large yellow farm house where the Trail turned right onto a dirt road that led farther uphill.

Just as we arrived at the house, a large, mean-looking, brown chow came racing down across the lawn toward Mack. There ensued a couple of tense moments when it looked like a dogfight might develop. Sue tried to position herself between the chow and Mack, but the chow simply went around her and came at Mack from a different angle. Everyone started yelling for the owner. Eventually a middle-aged gentleman hurried down from the house and grabbed the chow by the collar. Sue then took Mack to the van, which Gordon had parked at the road junction.

A conversation followed in which I learned that the farm-stead consisted of 400 acres; the place had been in the family for over 100 years. The owner told us he was a member of the "Massachusetts Club," as he put it, and that he often had done Trail maintenance along that section — but no longer. He was incensed that the National Park Service in conjunction with the ATC had condemned 40 acres of his land for a relocation; this would take the Trail off the road and "put it up on the ridges." He told us we would be one of the last hikers to enjoy the walk through the picturesque little village. He "didn't see any sense" in moving the Trail, since it "just made it harder to maintain." He said he had fought the condemnation for as long as his money had held out, then gave it up. He was a bitter man.

The Trail to Goose Pond and Upper Goose Pond led through a thickly canopied but open mature forest. Upper Goose Pond, which lies under the protection of the National Park Service, was dead still, its surface mirror smooth, and at the far end, a jumble of rocks formed the shoreline where a dark forest of pines and spruce stretched up the hill.

A small bouquet of black-eyed susans on a fence post along with a note addressed to "Old Soldier and AT Medic" greeted us at the place where the Trail crossed the Massachusetts Turn-pike. The note was from Sue and informed us that the van was parked on MA Highway 20, about a quarter mile to the left of the Trail crossing. It took us 15 minutes to cover the one-half mile from the Turnpike to Route 20. Upon arriving, we went immediately to the van and then up the hill from the crossing to the Gaslight Motel.

The motel sat among a stand of mature pines beside a beau-tiful little lake where mostly white wooden cottages dotted the shore and a flock Canada geese drifted contentedly just off the near the banks. Cathy and I sat out front after dinner, enjoying the warm evening air, watching the geese, and the setting sun. We were not long there before a tall, thin man emerged from a room several doors down from us and crossed the parking lot toward the geese. About half way across the lot, he stopped, picked up two fist-sized rocks, then tip-toed, hunch-shouldered, the remainder of the way to the edge of the pond. It was obvious to even the geese that this guy was answering a cave man's urge for a goose dinner.

The geese paddled out toward the center of the lake, keeping themselves well beyond throwing range. After the geese moved out of range, he returned to his room and waited a few minutes for the geese to come back toward the shore. He then repeated his sneak tactic, hunching his shoulders and tip toeing, albeit in plain sight, across the parking lot. He tried that approach three times, looking sillier each time. Every time he appeared, the wise geese moved slowly out to sea. Finally convinced that the sneak attack tactic wasn't going to work, he put the rocks out of sight in his pockets and remained by the shoreline, whistling as if he were just another tourist enjoying the scenery, and waited for the geese to return to the shore. The geese stayed out of range. He persisted in this tactic, until the deluge from a ferocious thunderstorm drenched the area, including the goose hunter who scurried back to his room soaking wet.

The following morning we began hiking in an invigoratingly cool breeze under skies that promised sun the entire day. We climbed Becket Mountain and signed the register after an entry by Granma in which she said she had seen two bear cubs. About two hours later, while approaching the October Mountain lean-to, we heard voices. Initially we thought a group of hikers was ahead of us. Then, as we approached nearer to the shelter, we saw a man in the clearing talking to someone in the shelter. He saw us as we broke out of the forest and called to us, saying he was just about to leave (It was about 10:00 a. m.) and that we could have the place to ourselves. I looked quickly to see who was in the shelter. It was empty.

The man, except for his delusions, was alone. He turned away from us and commenced babbling incoherently — alternately to himself and the shelter. Then, abruptly he stopped babbling and looked at us again, saying that he was leaving and that the shelter was ours, that he'd be gone in a "couple of hours." As we continued across in front of the shelter, I noticed a motorcycle parked near the edge of the clearing. After another 100 yards, we reached a dirt road; once across, we met Granma.

Granma's face was white. She told us that the man at the shelter had asked her if she were hiking alone. She told him no — that she was with two other people and went on her way, hoping we would hurry up and get there. A comment in the Trail Guide indicated that because the shelter was so close to a road, it was often used by non-hikers.

We spent the night at a motel on the outskirts of Pittsfield, Massachusetts. Gordon waited until after the arrangements had been made to tell the manager that a seeing-eye dog accompanied Sue. The gentleman was very adamant about not allowing dogs of any kind on the motel premises. Gordon told him point blank he had no choice and cited the Massachusetts law pertaining to working dogs. Still — the man was not convinced and proceeded to tell us horror stories to justify his refusal.

The first objection was that once a dog goes into a motel room, any other dogs that follow try to establish territorial custody by urinating. He related how a friend had brought a dog into one of his rooms, and as soon as it got inside, "It lifted its leg all over the bedspread." Then, he pointed out that his maid was allergic to animals and that she got asthma attacks and would quit work. Finally he told us about an experience he had after renting a room to a wedding party. It seems the following morning when the maid went to clean the room she was confronted by a growling dog. But that was not all. The room also contained a caged monkey, sitting on the bed and two guinea hens running around the place. The funereal expression on the manager's face was a sufficient deterrent to defer laughter — until later. Then, came the crowning argument, before capitulation. His wife would "raise holy hell."

His concern about his wife's reaction gave me an entree to ask about local restaurants. The nearest was a Vietnamese restaurant, about a mile and a half farther on, there was an Italian place. The decision was not difficult.

I greeted the Oriental man behind the maitre'd's stand in my best Vietnamese. He answered quickly, and I understood about two words. Seeing that I had just outrun my supply of Vietnamese, he switched to English. We had a lively conversation about Viet Nam, and he showed me pictures of the countryside, including a large wall poster of the Cham Temple just outside of the city of Phan Rang. I had been stationed there in 1965 and knew the place well. I often passed that same temple while on my way to the US airbase down the road. It was such an impressive structure that I stopped one time to walk inside, but it had been long abandoned, and there was nothing to see inside.

The host had served 15 years as a Vietnamese Special Forces Officer. He mentioned the names of a number of American Special Forces people, none of whom I recognized. He also knew Phan Rang well, since the Special Forces had a camp outside of Cam Ranh Bay, just to the north, and he often went there as well as to Nha Trang, just north of that, where the American Special Forces were headquartered.

He was businessman enough to recognize the possibility of an economic gain and indoctrinated us in Vietnamese cooking, suggesting that we try several dishes. I asked if he had any "nuoc mam," a pungent fish sauce I had often eaten in Viet Nam. Of course! Did I think any self-respecting Vietnamese establishment would not have the stuff?

Even as he explained the menu, he exhibited energy. I had noticed it immediately upon entering the place. It was an air of constant motion, of energy. But it was all directed energy and motion, and it swept up those with whom he was speaking and carried them along for the ride.

We talked about Saigon and Cholon, the Chinese section of the city, and of Francois', the superb French restaurant diagonally across from the Rex Hotel on the Street of Flowers. The Street of Flowers took its name from the huge number of open air flower pavilions that stretched down the promenade toward the Saigon River. The flowers, dazzling in color, exotic in variety, and brimming with the freshness and the richness of the Vietnamese countryside, brought an air of vivacity to streets and building facades weary from decades of conflict and neglect. The longer we talked, the more animated our host became.

When we left he gave us a copy of a newspaper feature about him written by Vinod Chhabra in the Sunday Times Union from Albany, New York. The article chronicled his success as a restaurateur as well as that part of his life after the fall of Saigon to the Communists. It described how he was treated in captivity by the Communists, how he escaped, how he survived as a "boat person," how he came to America under the patronage of Arlo Guthrie, and how he had created a new life for himself.

It was a truly heroic story about a heroic man in the most elemental sense of the term. It told of a man who had looked death in the face and did not flinch; who refused to give an inch to his captors, who, despite physical humiliation beyond belief, would not surrender his soul. He had survived. He had held his head high through it all, and none could bow it.

Kim Van Huynh has scars to be sure, scars enough for ten men. But they will never achieve dominance over him. This was a man who had all the reasons in the world to be negative, to think the world owed him for his pain, to sit on his tail, collect welfare, and pine away for a culture and a country lost. But he refused to be defeated; he saw the possibilities and recognized that in order to see them he had to be positive.

As soon we started walking the next morning, Granma took the lead, and with her short legs pumping with machine-like precision, was soon out of sight. Granma had only one speed, not a race speed, but a brisk pace that remained constant whether she was going uphill or down, or on a level stretch. It never changed. It was not hard to stay with or even pass her on level ground or going downhill; as for climbs, she left us like we were turtles.

It was still ideal hiking weather, slightly overcast and cool. We soon reached Gore Pond, which reminded me of Upper Goose Pond in that it appeared to sit in the midst of a wilderness undisturbed by the Twentieth Century. That idyll was soon dispelled by the sound of a motorcycle, and we came to an area where the cyclist had torn up the Trail, chewing large gouges from the path and spewing dirt and rocks as he cut around switchbacks.

It was Saturday and a mail drop was waiting for me in Cheshire, Massachusetts. The drop contained an assortment of food, but most important, were the Trail Guides and maps for Vermont, New Hampshire, and Maine. I was concerned that if I arrived after noon, the place would be closed, and I would have to lay over for the weekend. Consequently I stepped up the pace to a level Cathy couldn't maintain, and she dropped off, saying she would meet me later in Cheshire.

In my haste I passed Granma; she was sitting on a rock admiring the view in the bright sunlight. Her expression indicated more than surprise but something less than shock as I cruised by. Not only that, I also surprised Gordon and Sue; they were parked along the road into Cheshire, waiting for Granma. In fact, I surprised myself by keeping up the pace.

I reached the Post Office at 11:40 a. m. to learn that they had expanded their operating hours for the summer to 3:00 p. m. on Saturdays. However, I was sure that if I had arrived at 12:01, the place would have been closed and the Postmaster, the only one with a key, would have left for Boston for the weekend. I believed in Murphy's Law.

St. Mary's of the Assumption offered a large community room/gymnasium in the rear of the church for use by hikers. There were no showers and no sleeping accommodations other than the floor, but it did have toilets and sinks with running water, and best of all, it had a roof. I was in the process of claiming my piece of the floor for the night when an elderly lady clad in baggy, denim bib-overalls entered the hall. Seventy-year-old Edna Williams from Melrose, Florida, was just coming in from the Trail to the north. She had hiked just about the whole Trail in bits and pieces and was determined to complete the last sections this summer. She was talkative and delightfully articulate in describing her experiences and ambitions. I learned that she had twice broken a leg while hiking, and the previous summer had been carried out of Mahoosuc Notch after breaking a hip. Her Trail name, "Seventy-Years-Young," was an apt description of her outlook on the Trail and life in general.

Two south bounders, Brett Hensley, (The Fireman) from Dow, Georgia, and Troy Buenneke (Shaggy) from Moscow, Idaho, arrived soon after Edna. They said the Trail in Maine was really difficult, very steep and rocky with lots of exposed tree roots to contend with. I was surprised when they told me the White Mountains had not been too difficult. I suspected that they were most impressed with the difficulty of the mountains after just coming on the Trail as I had been impressed by the climbs in Georgia right after coming on the Trail.

Troy, 6 feet 7 inches tall, said he had had difficulty negotiating the Trail in places with low hanging branches. I nodded in sympathy, recalling my exasperation on more than one occasion when low hanging laurel or rhododendron branches had caught my pack and knocked me off balance or held me back. And I was only 5 feet 10 inches tall. Troy indicated he was going to spend some time in Cheshire; he had slipped on a log puncheon and injured his right shin, and he wanted to "get it right" before moving on again.

Cathy had become pensive. Tomorrow was to be her last day on the Trail. She had to return to Miami and the work-filled days that awaited her; she was not a happy camper. Her usual upbeat, "Hang in there, Old Soldier, You can do it," encouragement was gone. I had become accustomed to her positive approach toward the difficulties of the Trail and enthusiasm for hiking, and I knew I would miss her encouraging comments that seemed to ease the path.

We started off the next day with a great breakfast of bacon and eggs at a small diner across the road from the church. The weather was ideal, sunny and cool. We climbed for about six miles, including a jaunt over Saddleball Ridge with nice views, then past a beautiful old water supply pond just before reaching the summit of Mt. Greylock. At Bascom Lodge we met Granma who was leaving to get back on the Trail, and Gordon and Sue who joined us for a delicious lunch of hamburgers and iced tea.

Before I left, I wrote my name and hometown in the guest register. The view from the summit was spectacular and several people had written glowing praises. Others had written that they had seen a red shouldered hawk or red tailed hawk or a deer or a bear, each describing the encounter with enthusiasm. I had seen only a couple of chipmunks and didn't consider them sufficiently regal for comment in the register.

The Trail down from Greylock was long and, in places, fairly steep; we had to proceed with caution. Thankfully it was dry. Then, it ascended steeply up Williams Mountain where we enjoyed first class views of Williamstown and the campus of Williams College. From there, we headed directly down toward North Adams.

About half way down, Cathy stopped and sat on a long rock beside the Trail and told me to go on. I could tell she wanted to be alone to collect her thoughts and emotions. I proceeded without comment. After going a few hundred yards, I stopped and waited. Not more than ten minutes elapsed before she appeared on the path above me, moving slowly, as if trying to delay the inevitable.

Shortly afterward, we ran into Brett Hensley. Brett was climbing up from the north to complete the section between North Adams and Cheshire. Troy did not accompany him; Troy's shin was still hurting; he had remained at the church as he had indicated he would. We also encountered a hiker who called himself, "Bushmaster." He had hiked the entire Trail the preceding year, and I remembered reading some of his entries in Trail registers in the south the previous summer. This year he was taking a more leisurely approach to hiking.

When we reached the point where the Trail followed the streets through North Adams, Gordon, Sue, and Granma met us. They were waiting to hike the last part of the Trail with Cathy before she departed. Gordon and Sue had grown quite friendly with Cathy as had Granma, and I thought they would miss her. And, in fact, they did, often mentioning her later in our hikes and asking if I had heard anything from her; or they would remark that Cathy would have said or done so and so.

Cathy accompanied me back to the Trail in the morning, carrying my pack to allow me to save my energy for the Trail. We sat by the roadside and waited for Gordon and Granma to arrive. The sun was just starting to rise as everyone hugged Cathy goodbye for the last time. It was an emotional departure.

We started off with Granma in the lead as usual. The climb out of North Adams followed the streets initially, then passed over two foot bridges and along a spillway which released water from a circular dam to cross under a power line by a creek. Granma left me as soon as I took my first 30-minute break there.

My mind started automatically assessing my situation without Cathy. I felt strangely pensive and lonely knowing that Cathy would not be there to talk with or to provided the little insights we shared on the Trail. She would not be there to break the occasional monotony of the hike or support my morale when the conditions became miserable. There is much truth in the adage, "misery loves company." I started to wonder what it would be like without her and wondered why I had not considered that before. I also empathized with her having to go back to work.

I acknowledged that I felt really alone for the first time on the Trail this year; realized that I was, in fact, really alone for the first time — since coming on the Trail in June. I didn't like the feeling. Sure, there was Granma and Sue and Gordon, but they would not, indeed, could not provide the camaraderie and

intellectual stimulation Cathy brought to the hike. My step was
not so lively, and my confidence was a notch lower when I started
off again.

CHAPTER 10

Reshaping life! People who can say that have never under-stood anything about life — they have never felt its breath, its heart beat, however much they may have seen or done. They look on it as a lump of raw material that needs to be processed by them, to be ennobled by their touch. But life is never a mate-rial, a substance to be molded . . . life is constantly renewing and remaking itself.

— Boris Pasternak

North Adams, MA to Griffith Lake, VT

Four miles after starting from North Adams I came to the Vermont-Massachusetts border and the start of the Vermont Long Trail which the AT also uses for its initial northward thrust into the Green Mountains. The Trail skirted several beaver ponds and crossed the dam holding another pond. It was spongy walk-ing, but I stopped anyway to look over the construction and to watch water flowing from the base of the tangle of saplings be-neath my feet. I have always been impressed by beaver dams, how efficiently they serve their purpose, and almost always take the time to inspect their dams, as if I were an engineer. I have never regretted spending the time.

The hiking was relatively easy, and I made good time, stop-ping only twice. Once for water at Congdon Cabin, a primitive but functional hiker's cabin complete with caretaker and then after crossing the stream outlet for Sucker Pond, to contem-plate the foundations of a 19th Century hotel set on a knoll there. Otherwise, most of the day was made up of crossing swampy areas by way of corduroy log paths or puncheons. I was surprised to find I had covered 18 miles for the day — when I arrived at VT. Route 9 where Granma and her van crew were waiting.

The foundations of the hotel had tweaked my curiosity. I wondered why anyone would have built a hotel there, and after having built it, abandoned it. It seemed there was a lesson hidden somewhere in my reflections. It was a microcosmic example that reiterated the transitory nature of life. Nothing in life is permanent except change. For me, the ruins reinforced that.

We repeatedly form attachments and experience detachments in life. Lovers grow into oneness, whether in puppy loves or first loves, or lasting loves. Then come the separations. We age, we change, we grow and leave our former loves. Mostly it is by circumstances of choice, either our own or our partners, and then — ultimately we become separated by death. Children grow, mature, and leave. Friends move to distant places, either physically or spiritually, or we move. There is a constant flow to life, a surging and an ebbing in all relationships, and in fortunes.

Most of us wish we could outmaneuver life and in some way — suspend time — so that it doesn't interfere with our magical moments. But that is impossible. And we also can't shorten the duration of or make disappear the times when we are in pain. Pain is often part of the process of change, and we must complete the process before we can overcome the pain. We have to understand that life is a kaleidoscope of experiences and each attachment or loss is followed by other attachments and losses. The secret to our success is to recognize the rewards each of those experiences brings. It is in recognizing that loss and death and pain are parts of life as well as the joys and abundance of favorable times that peace comes, and that by accepting and fully living the full cycle of seasons, we become full participants in the process of creation.

I went right to sleep as soon as I crawled into my sleeping bag. I didn't realize how exhausted I had become — trying to hold to Granma's schedule and not taking a break every eight days as recommended by Laidlaw. I figured slack-packing obviated the need for that. I was wrong. I awoke at about 1:30 a. m. to go to the bathroom and discovered I had a full blown case of atrial fibrillation.

I took an Inderal tablet and three digitalis as suggested by the doctor — then tried to go back to sleep, hoping everything would clear up by morning. The fibrillation was severe enough to keep me tossing and turning as I tried to find a position that would not accentuate the irregularity. I found that lying on my left side increased my discomfort as did lying on my back. I felt best when I was on my right side and raised my head and shoulders. Of course, there was a drastic increase in my anxiety level. I tried not to panic; I tried to stay calm and look at the situation from a detached and unemotional standpoint. But this was beyond me.

I thought about my reflections earlier in the day at the old hotel foundations and determined that it was easier to be dispassionate from a distance than it was while undergoing one of those "moments of pain." When things started to get personal I tended to get emotional. After all, I thought, It's my damn heart, and if it goes, I'm gone.

As the duration of the attack continued, it became clear I was in for a miserable night. It also became clear that the plans Granma and I had made to meet at the Kid Gore or Caughnawaga shelter the next night were going to have to be revised. I wondered on and off about the wisdom of continuing on the Trail. At the darkest moments, it seemed like the adventure had come to a premature end. I had really given the Trail a good shot, and I could come off and hold my head up and say I'd walked from Georgia to Vermont, but my heart couldn't take the stress. I "had" to come off.

I supposed that if I were in Georgia or North Carolina and this had happened, I might very well have said, "To hell with it!" But here I was in Vermont with somewhere around 500 miles to go. I'd already invested 1500 miles of sweat and pain as well as joy in the Trail. In fact, I had already invested a considerable piece of my self-respect in the journey. The words seemed somewhat hollow as I framed them in my mind. What is this compulsion? I asked myself. Why do I go through this agony? What's so damn important about finishing this thing?

I thrashed the question over and over during the night. The Trail was no longer a "fun hike." I'd seen enough trees and vistas, waterfalls and flowers, and breathed more than enough of the sweet mountain air. It was now an endurance contest with endless climbs, rock scrambles, root hopping, and tripping, slipping and slogging in rain. I also thought about the mundane. It was a colossal pain just to attend to the logistics required to stay on the Trail, to resupply, send mail, do laundry, and perform the myriad tasks thru-hikers contend with on their quest. Then, I remembered the first attack of atrial fibrillation I had suffered at Plum Orchard Gap in Georgia. I hadn't quit then. Why was this any different?

Now I posed an even deeper question. Why exactly was I on the Trail? And why did always something within cry out for a second opinion every time I considered quitting? Somehow I could not accept quitting the Trail as a reasonable outcome. Common sense told me it was ridiculous for a fifty-three-year-old man with a finicky heart to continue pushing the limits, continue battling the climbs, the weather and everything else that made the Trail so tough. I wasn't 21 anymore. Sure, the Slim Jims and the Blaze Brothers and the others could hang in there; the resilience of youth gave them an edge in their battle with the Trail. I didn't have that weapon in my arsenal. I needed something else to give me an even chance.

I'd peeled back all the layers of the onion only to find another layer, no answers, only layers. It seemed I had become part of the Trail. I had set out to master the Trail, to conquer it and hang it up in the trophy room of my memory as something I could personally point to and say, "I won!" Now the tables had turned . . . The Trail had become the master and would not let me go — at least not let me go with my self respect intact.

It became clear that I had no alternative but to reach deep down and find some hidden reservoir of determination. That had to be my weapon. It was all I had. Determination to succeed. I had called on it before. I would call on it once more.

In the end, I decided I had only one really viable alternative: to come off the Trail, until I had recuperated enough to get back on. That would take one day at the most, and I could ride in the van. That meant I would skip a 30-mile stretch, but I could come back and finish it at a later date.

I was tented next to Granma and heard her packing her gear for the day. I looked at my watch. It was 5:15 a. m. Jeez, woman, cut it some slack, I thought. "Granma," I whispered as I unzipped my tent.

"Yes?"

"You're going to have to go on alone today. My heart's fibrillating," I replied evenly to give the impression of being in control.

"Oh, that's too bad. You feeling all right?"

"Well, not really, but I'm in no danger. This'll clear up later — I'm sure."

"Is there anything we can do? Take you to a doctor?"

"No, this thing will convert by itself. It's just going to take some time."

"Well, I hope everything turns out okay for you," she concluded and went back to striking her tent. Eventually she finished packing and went to Sue's tent. "Sue," she called, "Soldier's not going with me today. His heart's giving him problems."

"I heard," Sue responded.

After about half an hour, I heard the van take off. I could imagine feeling worse, but I didn't know how. I went through the motions of stuffing food down my throat and packing. Every action required more effort than I could afford to expend. I had to stop frequently to rest.

After breakfast, I took a short walk. When I returned Gordon was taking Sue's blood pressure. I asked him to take mine, which he did, and pronounced that it was 112 over 78, but that my heartbeat was "highly irregular." No kidding, I thought. Shortly after 7:30 a. m. the conversion occurred, and my heart marched to its normal rhythm; except for feeling drained, I felt fine. The episode had lasted slightly longer than the usual five and a half hours.

Gordon and I packed up the van later in the morning and off we went. The interlude gave me the opportunity to get to know Gordon and Sue better. We talked first about Granma. They were concerned about the pace she was setting. She was steadily losing weight, they said, and they were afraid she was reducing her defenses against disease and might fall ill. They also expressed disapproval of Granma's speed; they thought she was missing a lot along the Trail.

I slept for a while afterwards and awoke much refreshed. I was able to review at my leisure the Trail Guide and maps for New Hampshire and the White Mountains; and what I read and saw was intimidating. I hoped I would be able to stay with the van and slack-pack the Whites. Gordon told me Granma planned to reach the Maine state line in another 15 days. After that, it was about 280 miles of basic wilderness as I saw it. It would be a challenge.

The climb up Bromley Mountain the next day was the kind of experience that one imagines when thinking about the Trail. Although it was a fairly long trek, it was not difficult. I took my time and made sure to take hourly breaks. The moments were special like when nearing the summit over a grassy ski trail, the sun, peeking across the mountain top, illuminated the forest edge and bathed the grassy run in the most intense green I have ever seen. And the summit afforded spectacular views in all directions. Despite a shivering chill, I climbed the wooden observation tower and spent several minutes admiring the panorama before scurrying back down to escape the wind. I wondered if the chill was a portent of things to come. It was late July, and the briskness of the temperature surprised me.

An irritating anxiety characterized the initial part of the hike which I countered by meditating, making a very conscious effort to attain and maintain a positive attitude. I came to the conclusion that it was much easier to hike with a partner than to hike alone. It is a pleasure to share the observations and experiences of the Trail with someone else. And from a logistical standpoint. Having a partner is a major advantage. However, in a way, it is better to hike alone. The sense of the hike is much more intense. I was able to achieve a deeper concentration and for longer periods — when I was alone. I surmised that each has its unique advantages and disadvantages, that depending on one's changing moods and motivations, contributed to the fabric of the hike. It was apparent that I missed Cathy and her exhortations when I was getting low or there was a tough climb coming. "You can do it, Old Soldier!!" she'd say. "You can do it!"

The Trail on Bromley's summit was poorly marked, but eventually I found a marking on the side of the ski tow pylon and was soon an my way to North Bromley and Peru Peak. I particularly enjoyed the long stretches through evergreen forests where the pure northwoods' aroma of spruce permeated the crisp mountain air. The climbs to Styles Peak and Peru Peak were steep. Peru Peak was covered by forest and offered no views, but on Styles Peak, the panorama of the green mountains was a rare treat.

"Hugh, The White Rabbit," from England, was on Styles Peak when I met him. I learned he had hiked with Brett Hensley for a while before dropping off the Trail to spend some time in New Hampshire with his English girlfriend. They had stayed at the home of an acquaintance in Hanover, and later when the acquaintance and his family went on a short trip Hugh and his girlfriend were invited to take over the house for three days. We didn't talk for long. His visit with his girlfriend had put him far behind schedule, and he was trying to make up for time lost.

At the Peru Peak shelter, I met Carleton Matthews, a.k.a. "The Jersey Kid." Carleton was the first and only African-American thru-hiker I had met on the Trail. He informed me Granma was about ten minutes ahead of me. While taking my break there, I read some of the recent entries in the shelter journal, Granma's among them. She always drew a sketch with Mount Springer at one end and Katahdin at the other, and in between, she sketched herself on some form of transportation — one time it was a tank, another a bird, then a plane, and a motorcycle. This time she was on a horse.

Trail registers are interesting reading with humorous comments as well as deeply philosophical reflections, and full of messages left by hikers for friends following. It was a way to keep up with the progress of one's fellow hikers. Occasionally some very talented artist would leave a sample of his work. Mostly the entries were sensible and interesting reading, but sometimes some troglodyte would trash it with pornography that demeaned the otherwise uplifting character of the document. I almost always wrote something in the shelter journals. In this, my contribution reflected my feelings about the Trail marking on Mount Bromley.

I met Carleton later on at the Lost Pond shelter where he was resting and airing his feet. He had a blister and was out of Band-Aids; I gave him my last one, and after expressing condolences over his misfortune, left him tending his wounded foot.

The climb up Baker Mountain followed some granite ledges created during the collision of tectonic plates millions of years ago. I stopped periodically to view Otter Creek, the valley below, and Pico and Killington Peaks. Dorset Mountain, just across the valley, seemed so close one could almost reach out and touch it. Actually the mountain was miles away. Not noticeable from the outside was a massive marble quarry that I was told ran for about two miles inside the mountain. The ceiling was reputed to be about 30 feet high and supported every 50 feet or so by marble pillars formed by removing the marble around them. A German firm supposedly owned the quarry.

The Trail Guide called the mountain, Dorset Mountain, but the owner of the campground where we stayed called it — Danby Mountain. He said that the name depended on which side of the mountain you were from. If you were from Danby, it was called Danby Mountain, and if you were from Dorset, it was called Dorset Mountain. It was all perfectly logical if you were a Vermonter, I thought. He also mentioned that nearby was a large talc mine; I heard the huge trailered dump trucks and saw billowing clouds of dust or talc as the they rumbled by the campground in the early morning.

The suspension bridge over Big Branch swayed and bounced precariously as I crossed, but the view of the stream was reward enough for the unsettling conditions. It was a quiet stream with almost no white water, a rarity in Vermont. But small trees and bushes whose branches hung out over the shaded bank lined it. Some even trailed their branches in the water like day dreamers might.

Griffith Lake reminded me of the picturesque oil paintings of wilderness lakes from the Romantic Period one finds in art galleries. In several small coves, rocks lined the water's edge, until it narrowed and populations of yellow water lilies gathered in small settlements to enjoy the sunlight. It seemed almost obligatory to have a fly rod to lure a strike from the lunker trout that surely must have been lying in wait to ambush a tasty fly.

CHAPTER 11

Life's a pretty precious and wonderful thing. You don't sit down and let it lap around you...you have to plunge into it; you have to dive through it! And you can't save it, you can't store it up; you can't hoard it in a vault. You've got to taste it; you've got to use it. The more you use, the more you have . . . That's the miracle of it.

— *Kyle S. Chrichton*

Griffith Lake, VT to West Hartford, VT

We set up camp that evening in a nearby campground next to Otter creek. It rained most of the night. When I awoke the grass was soaked, and the air was heavy with moisture. While striking my tent, I startled a great blue heron along the creek bed. It took off sailing noiselessly through the overhanging mists — until it was enveloped by the grayness. Although over in a matter of seconds, the scene was timeless in quality. For me mists have a haunting quality that suspends the passage of time. I thought the vision would last and was surprised when it ended.

I started hiking about 7:30 a.m. I soon climbed above the low hanging clouds and into a sunlit mountain morning. From above, the valleys, filled with mist, created the illusion of lakes reflecting sunlight with mountains and ridges rising from their shorelines.

I quickly passed a number of young people whom I initially took to be day-hikers but who were in reality members of an archeological team doing a survey of an Indian quartz mine. They informed me that the Indians used quartz to make many tools and this area was a "stone tool manufacturing site."

A little farther up the Trail, I found a piece of quartz embedded in a layer of soil covering a large rock. I noticed the tip was shaped much like a knife; it appeared to have been worked, and I picked it up. It was a stone knife with the blade beveled on one side and a small notch carved on the left side of the "handle." My thumb fit perfectly into the notch when I held it in my hand.

Rays of sunlight shining through the dark green of over-hanging trees and the deep blue of the cloudless sky together with eerie wisps of mist swirling gently in the morning air made Little Rock Pond a scene one remembers for life. The Trail passed through a magnificent forest of large spruce trees, the air pure with their aroma and the forest floor soft from years and layers of shed spruce needles. A scattering of young spruce trees, thrusting their tips in search of sunlight, reminded me of Cathy and her grandfather tree. But even among the mature trees, there were no candidates for the honor. After passing the spruce forest the Trail led to an area of white rocks with stark over-hangs and jagged outcroppings that filled my mind's eye with visions of early creation. I slipped down the mountain side with caution.

Clarendon Gorge is one of the many great natural beauties of Vermont. The Trail crosses it on a suspension footbridge about 50 feet above swift flowing water. There the stream is channeled into a more quiet version of what one sees farther up the gorge where primordial boulders and sharp rock cliff edges create unimaginable turbulence. The water, raging to froth, gushes down the gorge, as if in a panic to escape the torture.

A group of people doing television filming had taken over the bridge and were using it as a prop for a scene. They were wearing brown shirt uniforms with red armbands containing a peculiar black diagonal symbol on a white background. They obviously intended it to be reminiscent of the Swastika of the Nazi brown shirts before the Second World War. One young man standing in the center of the bridge cradled a toy submachine gun in his arms. As I passed, I asked him what was going on; he replied only that he felt like a fool. The circumstances were a disappointment for me, since it prevented me from stopping on the bridge to admire the spectacular natural beauty unfolding down the gorge.

We started off at 6:00 a. m. the following morning with Granma in the lead as usual which meant that I would soon be alone. And I was. The Clarendon shelter journal contained another of Granma's sketches. This time she had roller skates on her feet. Today was the 29th of July, my birthday, and marked the end of the 53rd year of my life. I was now working on year 54. God, I'm getting old, I thought. I hadn't felt old when I sat down, but when I reflected on my age, how far I had come, and how far I had to go, I suddenly felt old. For some nonsensical reason, I entered the words of the birthday jingle to me in the register. I was a little more somber after getting back on the Trail. "And miles to go before I sleep," the refrain from Robert Frosts poem, "Stopping By Woods On A Snowy Eve," kept reverberating in my mind as I climbed Beacon Hill.

I spent the day in the woods — always climbing, it seemed. I saw nothing but trees and more trees, and roots and rocks. That was pretty much it, until I reached Killington Peak where a short side trail led to the summit; the summit was supposed to offer "great views." I decided to pass. I was very tired.

The climb up Killington had been long and tough over some very difficult trail packed with large roots and rocks, and steep little ledges. Toward noon my legs got rubbery, and I felt slightly weak and dizzy. I stopped at Consultation Point for lunch. This did much to restore my strength and energy. At Pico Camp, I sat in the clearing in warm sunlight and admired the scenery, including a splendid view back toward Killington.

Gordon and Sue were waiting for me at Sherburne Pass in front of the inn located there. They told me that Granma had stopped earlier, gotten a bite to eat, then continued to the campground a couple of miles farther on. They also told me that "G-Man" was at the inn, trying to work for a meal. G-Man was Tom Gertsma from Berkeley Heights, New Jersey.

I had seen G-Man's back earlier in the day when he had left Clarendon shelter just as I was arriving. About an hour later, I met him coming up the Trail behind me. I wondered how I had passed him. He said he had missed a turn in the Trail, and I knew exactly where he had gone astray. I had also missed the turn. However, since I lost the blazes right away, I immediately backtracked and found the turn. I remembered hearing someone shouting earlier, and he said it had been him screaming in frustration.

The Trail from Sherburne Pass to Gifford Woods State Park was testy. It climbed the face of a massive almost vertical rock slab on a long thick vine that ran diagonally across the entire length. There was a rock scramble, and then the Trail degenerated into a climb up a loose dirt and rock path that took the remaining starch out of me. A makeshift sign told me I had reached the point where the AT split off from the Long Trail. The AT headed east toward New Hampshire, while the Long Trail continued north toward Canada. At that point the Trail leveled out following the ridge for a while before heading down to the campground.

It had been a tough day, and I was not in a great mood when I arrived. Even Granma was not her usual chipper self. She told me the climb up Killington had gotten to her also, and she was tired. I calmed down after a few minutes of bitching about the Trail; that seemed to relieve some frustration.

After a hearty helping of my chicken and noodle casserole concoction, the world seemed more civilized. As soon as I had eaten, Sue went to the van. When she returned she was carrying a small birthday cake with two brightly flaming candles and started singing, Happy Birthday. Everyone joined in. I was stunned. How did they know? I thought. It must have been Cathy. Sue sat the cake in front of me.

"You got to blow out all the candles," said Sue. "And make a wish."

Gordon handed me a balloon on which was written "Happy 53rd" which I promptly broke. It had come from Granma's state line celebration balloon stash. Whenever Granma crossed a state line Sue would give her a blown up balloon, which Granma then broke to celebrate the crossing.

"You don't look a day over 50," Gordon laughed.

"You have to cut the cake. This isn't all fun," Sue teased.

Granma said nothing, just smiled, but obviously enjoyed the event.

"How did you all know?"

"A little bird," Gordon piped up.

"It was the birthday fairy," Sue said.

"Really, How did you find out?"

"We saw your entry in the Clarendon shelter journal," Sue confessed.

"It's absolutely beautiful," I said as I cut the cake. And it was not an overstatement. Sue had cut a small map of Vermont from a post card and attached to it two small white paper ovals which read "Happy Birthday -53-" on one and had the AT symbol on the other. Two thin sticks stuck into the icing supported the little map — it looked like a flag flying over the cake.

I cut several large pieces that disappeared in a nanosecond. And as sated as I was after dinner, I still managed to devour three pieces. We were all sitting around afterwards, reviewing the day's events when Carleton came by on his way to where he was to camp with G-Man. I offered him some cake. Initially he refused, then changed his mind after some cajoling, and I cut him an extra large piece that he almost inhaled.

As we were eating, two woodpeckers (I think they were red breasted woodpeckers) joined us on a large bush next to the table where we were sitting and started feasting on the clusters of berries that covered the bush. "I guess everyone's celebrating my birthday," I observed. It was a delightful and thoughtful climax to a very tough, 17.8 mile day. It wasn't long before Granma and I headed for out respective tents.

The Trail out of the campground the next morning, except for a short stretch along Kent Pond, was a road walk for the first two miles. Then, after crossing Quimby Brook, it followed a series of wooded roads, crossed or followed a series of creeks, and several tough little climbs before reaching Vermont Route 12 — some 14 miles farther on. Granma had arrived about 30 minutes before me. We all then loaded into the van and went to Silver Lake State Campground. Granma and I opted to spend the night in a shelter. Gordon and Sue chose to tent camp. It was a fortuitous decision, because the rain came early in the evening and stayed late.

Later, after the rain stopped, I heard Gordon calling softly to Sue. Evidently he had heard Sue moaning in her sleep, a signal that her blood sugar was low. He called several times, each call becoming increasingly louder, and in the process woke both Granma and me. Eventually Sue responded, and he told her to drink a Coke. After some time had passed, he called again, asking if she had drunk her Coke. Sue responded that she had, and it became quiet again. Then he called again, telling her to drink her Coke. Finally he went to her tent to force her to drink.

Sue was sitting in the middle of her tent, holding the Coke can over her head. But she wouldn't drink it. Gordon threatened, cajoled, then pleaded in turn with her to drink. He kept at her with remarkable persistence. So persistent was he that in a fit of frustration Sue screamed, "Gordon," her voice rising shrilly at the end of his name, but she drank. Sue snapped out of her stupor and reacted with remarkable clarity — just as if nothing had happened. Gordon told me later that if Sue had not drunk the Coke, he would have been forced to take her to the hospital.

The next day began with a climb up a side hill field with beautiful views to the south and west. The higher ridge lines were decorated with layers of cottony clouds and deeper in the valleys, the mist played hide and seek with the lower reaches of the ridges. A profusion of bugle shaped yellow flowers entertained my climb. The Trail again followed several wooded roads, making hiking easier. A second climb led to the top of a no-name mountain with an open summit (in the south it would have called a bald) full of wildflowers, particularly lavender bergamot, viper bugloss and black-eyed susans, and the omnipresent yarrow. It was a feast of color spattered across fields of green, sometimes golden and sometimes rust colored grass, all gently swaying in shifts with the breeze. Suddenly the Trail seemed a little less rigorous.

I retained my good mood, despite having to face down a dog which I thought might be dangerous. The cause of my concern was scuttlebutt I had heard along the Trail about a vicious dog that had been snacking on hikers. This was not the bad dog, however. The vicious one lived in a house farther along the Trail; I passed later in the morning. Thankfully the dog was inside at the time.

G-Man had not been so fortunate. The dog had attacked him. He said he had asked to the owner who was standing outside the house to call off the dog, but the man ignored his plea and went inside the house. He showed me where the dog had bitten him. G-Man was not the only hiker to have problems with the dog. Several thru-hikers recounted in shelter registers experiences with the dog, and stories were circulating within the thru-hiker community telling of people being bitten, and warning notes had been posted at nearby shelters.

The Bunker Hill Burying Ground, a small lonesome hillside cemetery with that name on its gate was a burying ground in every sense of the term. Surrounded by an austere stone wall and protected by the canopy of a lone, large shade tree, it seemed a fitting resting place for the farmers and tradespeople that scratched a livelihood from a barren, rock-strewn land. I was irresistibly drawn inside. No massive granite or marble monuments offended the simplicity of its beauty. It was very old with some graves identified only by field stones set in the ground where the lawn sagged. Other graves contained regular headstones, but were so old that the writing was illegible. A few had legible inscriptions. The most prominent was well marked with a black slate stone that read:

Mr. John Gibson Jr.
Departed Dec 29 1815
35 yrs 10 mos in
The Triumph of Faith
Stop Traveler as you pass by,
As you are now, so once was I.
As I am now, you soon must be,
Prepare for death and follow me.

I passed several small farms, then a large one that seemed like an estate in comparison with a number of horses and a lone farmer haying a huge field. The Trail then headed down the mountain on a tractor path that passed within about 10 feet of a small wooden house. A man with wrinkled skin and a baseball cap with a shock of pure white hair peering out from beneath it was sitting on the porch when I came by. He offered me a glass of water from the tap in his house, saying it came directly from a spring. It was, he assured me, "the sweetest water there is," in a Vermont accent that could only belong to an original. He mentioned that he often invited hikers to take a break from the ardors of the Trail and by innuendo included me. But I had spent so much time admiring the scenery and the wildflowers and visiting the cemetery that I politely declined. I was more than a little behind Granma.

I then passed through a deciduous forest where a number

of what I first thought were electrical cables or phone lines were strung between trees and along the Trail. Closer inspection showed them to be plastic tubing, and I realized they were attached only to maple trees. Then I came to an area where they were in profusion; I realized they were conduits for collecting maple sap for syrup. It didn't fit the image I had formed at the University of Vermont many years ago of horse drawn sleds with wooden vats and little buckets hanging from tree taps.

Later in the afternoon, the Trail followed an improved dirt road past a large farm where hay was being gathered. The walking was easy, and I lapsed into reverie. My mind wandered back to the Bunker Hill Burying Ground. The starkness and simplicity of the scene and the other worldly air which seemed to surround the place conjured up thoughts about life and death — normally reserved for poets. In fact, as I was walking among the graves, I sensed the same emotions I remembered from reading Alexander Pope's poem "Elegy in a Country Church Yard." It seemed more an experience than a poem at the time, and that was how it affected me.

In such moments one tends to philosophize about life and death and ponder the great questions which all of us silently ask and which the braver among us ask out loud. My own experience had become an effort to understand life. There would surely be time enough for dealing with death later. But life was where I was now, and despite John Gibson's admonition several lifetimes ago, the first order of the living is to understand this marvelous gift, if for other reason than to more fully appreciate that gift.

It was becoming apparent that the experience of the Trail paralleled the experience of life. As on the Trail, life consisted of mountains and valleys. Sometimes we look at life from the mountain top, and it is beautiful and gentle and kind. And the next day we slide down to the bottom where our view is one of discouragement and despair. Then we climb the mountain again, and we forget the preceding day and drink in the joys of that day from our exalted perch. And so it goes through life. We are constantly moving through valleys and over mountain tops.

And every mountain is followed by a valley, and every valley is followed by a mountain.

The secret seemed to lay in spending more time on the mountain tops than in the valleys. But how to do that was something mankind has been wrestling with since Eve gave Adam that fateful apple. One must get down to the basic fact that life is not fair — it just is — and we can't do anything about it. If we can accept that, then we can move forward. And feeling sorry for ourselves in that "life is not fair to us" is no solution. Since we cannot escape pain, we must learn to accept it. We progress when we recognize that the solution to dealing with pain is to choose a positive response to our hurt.

If one believes in God, then one accepts there is a reason for everything in life — including the pain. And if one can unload the burden of negative self indulgence and look only toward the positive impact created from learning our divinely intended lesson, we can make the climb to the next mountain top unencumbered by doubt and anxiety. It's called faith. With faith, we can breathe sunlight from the mountain tops. Without it, we spend our days groping through dark valleys.

Shortly after passing the haying operation, I looked back and could see another hiker in the distance bearing down on me. He caught up to me at the point where the road I was following and the Trail turned onto the paved road leading to West Hartford. "Smokin' Joe," a 53-year-old, had started at Springer and was headed for Katahdin. (I never did learn his real name, and none of the other hikers I met knew him by anything other than Smokin' Joe.) We walked together down to West Hartford. I was to meet Joe on many other occasions during my hike through New Hampshire.

We stayed the night at Quechee Gorge State Campground, just down the road from a beautiful, Clarendon-like gorge, deep with rushing water and filled with boulders and ledges. After showering and putting on clean clothes, I went to a nearby restaurant for dinner. Granma had preceded me and was sitting in a booth. Gordon and Sue had elected to eat at the campground. I spied Granma and walked past the group of people waiting to be seated to join her.

"Did you hear that business with Sue last night?" Granma asked as soon as I sat down. "Seems she's gettin' worse."

"Yeah, it woke me up. Did she do that before?"

"No. That's the first I heard it. I never heard her like that before. I was gettin' scared. I was glad Gordon got her to drink that Coke."

I realized that this was the first time in a long time that I had been able to talk with Granma alone. She was basically a shy, retiring person who was more comfortable staying in the background during group discussions. That is not to say that she wasn't on top of everything. She had a mission and was adamant about protecting her ability to conclude it. She opened up a bit to me, saying she missed her family and that there were times on the Trail when she had sat and cried, because she was alone and felt overwhelmed by loneliness. She said that had occurred while she was hiking in the south and that she had passed that stage now.

She had spoken with her husband, and he was coming to meet her in Monson, Maine, and that her grandson was going to join her there and hike with her from Monson to Katahdin. She described how she had started him hiking when he was very young. He was so small, she said, "all you could see was two tiny legs stickin' down from the pack." Now he was a "strappin' 20-year-old."

Granma was a very positive person with a tremendous amount of grit and staying power. I admired her personal courage in the face of the many adversities she had faced on the Trail. She had taken everything the Trail had thrown at her from being stranded in the Nantahalas and the Smokies during snowstorms to dealing with the Trail alone when Sue was hospitalized with her toe amputation. At age 62, she had forged on in conditions that would have daunted many 20-year-olds. She had overcome inhospitable weather and inhospitable trail conditions — never losing sight of Katahdin or her personal place in the scheme of things on the Trail. She had started off as a "pudgy 140-pound little old lady," and by the time I had met her she had been transformed into lean, mean, seasoned hiking machine with an inspiring desire to succeed.

Whenever I thought of Granma, I thought of the song by Frank Sinatra, with the refrain, "I did it my way." This small, thin, retiring, elderly grandmother had become a hard-nosed individualist who was more than the equal of any man I had met on the Trail. She possessed a fire that could never be extinguished. The fire had been lit now, and she was forever changed by it. Her personal history, although a part of her makeup, would cease to exercise a dominance in her life. The Trail would take on that role. She may have sat at times in the midst of the wilderness in the dark of the night and cried from loneliness and from separation from her family, her husband, her children and grandchildren, and her home. And she might do that again. But she had fought her personal demons and had defeated them and would always defeat them whatever the place, whatever the time. In those battles no quarter is given, or if it is, it must be refused. Victory in such circumstances must be complete and absolute.

Granma was a winner!

CHAPTER 12

*Adversity is like the period of the former and latter rain —
cold, comfortless, unfriendly to man and to animal; yet from that
season have their birth the flower and the fruit, the date, the
rose, and the pomegranate.*

— *Sir Walter Scott*

West Hartford, VT to Warren, NH

It was now the first of August. I started the day walking
with Granma to the first climb. For a small woman, she had an
enormous stride. She was only five feet two inches tall but her
stride was a longer stride than mine. Not only that, she covered
a lot of territory in a relatively short time. She left me, as usual,
at the first climb, but I caught up to her on the ridge top, which
surprised her. We walked together for a while, until I took my
hourly break, and she went alone.

The van crew, along with Granma, were waiting for me when
I arrived at the point where the Trail crossed Hopson Road.
Gordon had secured our mail from the Norwich, Vermont, Post
Office, and we took a break to read the letters and sort out the
goodies. Cathy had sent a number of small presents for my birth-
day, including a diminutive bottle of Grand Mariner and candy.
Each of the others got a T-shirt with an appropriate inscription.
Granma's read "Gallopin' Granma," Gordon's, "Good Hearted
Gordon," and Sue's "Scrappy Sue."

After the break, we walked through town and crossed the

Connecticut River. Here Granma celebrated her balloon breaking ritual. We were now in New Hampshire — twelve states down,
two to go!

We marched the main street in Hanover in single file, Sue
in the lead with Mack pulling and wheezing. At one point, a
young Irish setter tried to get too friendly with Mack, and he
sent it yelping and cowering into the middle of the street, holding up traffic and causing a general commotion. The owner was
finally able to coax the terrified animal back to the sidewalk,
and Mack swaggered on like Leslie Nelson in the movie, Naked
Gun, oblivious to the confusion reigning around him.

The College Episcopal Student Center (The Edgerton House)
often allowed hikers to spend the night; we headed there. Gordon accompanied me when I went in to make arrangements, the
first time he had done that. We were directed to the church
where we found Chaplain Patricia Henking and a couple of help-
ers applying a coat of paint to some white wooden furniture.
(The Chaplain had applied as much paint to herself as she had
to the wood.) She told us that the student center was currently
available for hikers, but that she planned to stop that practice
in the coming year. She also informed us there were no showers
and no cooking facilities, and to just go over and make ourselves at home; she would come along later to check us in.

We thanked her and left without commitment. "No showers," I said to Gordon as we departed the front door. "That's the
pits!" Suddenly I hit on the bright idea of going to one of the
fraternity houses on campus. I had read in a shelter register an
entry by Happy Feet, saying they were planning to stay at the
local chapter of Bill Foot's college fraternity. I suggested that
the idea had merit and asked them to let me try to do the same
— to find accommodations in one of the frat houses. They agreed,
but the negative energy was palpable.

I walked into the first likely looking building where a group
of young men were sitting around enjoying the last days of summer. It was a friendly group who showed a mild interest in me.
I mentioned that I was with a group hiking the Trail and indicated we needed a place to stay overnight. Everyone looked at
everyone else, until one fellow with a beer in hand said he belonged to the Tabbard House, a former chapter of Sigma Chi
but now unaffiliated, and that they let hikers stay there. I got

directions and headed off again.

Curtis, a member of the executive board of the Tabbard house after hearing my story, gave me approval for us to stay the night. As I was leaving to get the others, Smokin' Joe came from one of the rooms. He greeted me like a long lost relative and took me in tow like he was the owner, showing me the shower rooms and laundry, and the room where he had spent the night. He said the kids were really "great," and he was having a really good time. I was pleased with myself, thinking I had just hit the jackpot in the way of accommodations. As soon as I could, I broke loose from Smokin' Joe and hurried back to get the others.

We pulled the van up in front of the fraternity, a large, attractive, red-brick house with gleaming white trim and splendid landscaping. It seemed to be an effort for Granma and her crew to even go into the place. It was obvious the total college scene, let alone the fraternity, was alien to them and a bit intimidating; I tried to tried to reassure and encourage them. Once inside I attempted to sell them on the place without appearing "pushy." It was a super soft sell, and I think I had them just about convinced when Smokin' Joe came by talking about the great party they had the previous evening which lasted until 2:00 a.m. Sue suggested tactfully that they would wait if I wanted to take a shower, which is exactly what I did.

By the time we returned to The Edgerton House, G-Man, The Jersey Kid, and two south bounders had arrived there. Granma and I went about selecting and preparing our "sleeping quarters," conversing intermittently with the other hikers about what most interests hikers, the Trail, our experiences along it, and what to expect and what should concern us ahead. The south bounders played down the difficulty of the mountains in New Hampshire — but not the mountains in Maine.

G-Man talked about the dog that bit him, and I mentioned reading an entry at the Happy Hill Cabin register by a hiker complaining about the dog's owner, and how the owner allowed the dog to attack him. I wondered aloud if the ATC was aware of the situation. As we talked, more hikers arrived. As the day wore on, the place filled up — not with students, only hikers. I could see why the Chaplain wanted to put a stop to it.

Later, after getting settled, I went into town and bought a

light-weight down sleeping bag rated to below freezing. My other bag was not warm enough to keep me comfortable during the cooler nights I was now experiencing. It was also getting cold on the ridge crests during the day, particularly when it was windy. My thin poplin shirt was next to useless; I also purchased a green woolen sweater.

The next day began with a road walk through town. On the outskirts, the Trail skirted a ball field before entering the forest. We walked in heavy mist, and my feet immediately became wet from water clinging to the grass. For once, I had started ahead of Granma; she had decided to wear her gaiters, and it took Gordon some time to find them amid the jumble of gear in the back of the van. Not only was he carrying Granma's and my gear, he had now included G-Man's and The Jersey Kid's packs — adding to the confusion.

I took it easy as I normally did when starting off the day, and Granma soon caught up to me. We walked together over a fairly easy path, until we hit a short but steep rocky incline, and Granma pulled ahead. The Trail ascended gently at the beginning of its climb to Velvet rocks, until it reached a saddle and appeared as if it would continue over the other side. Wrong again! On either side of the saddle were steep inclines, and the Trail took a right angle turn, then ascended almost vertically for about 400 feet to the top of the ridge line.

Just before climbing Moose Mountain I switched to the Harris Trail, a former route for the AT; I followed it for four and a half miles until reaching Goose Pond Road. It was a provident detour. I finally saw a white tail deer. I was fast becoming convinced that the deer population in northern New England had come to extinction, and the sight, although rare, was a welcome treat. I also came upon a huge bear track and the largest birch tree I had ever seen. The tree must have been four feet in diameter. On the way up to Holt's Ledge, the Trail crossed over a beaver dam, and the quiet pond it created exuded a timelessness found only in wilderness. It was a period conducive to meditation. I tried to put the experience in a spiritual perspective, but my mind was not receptive.

A portion of the summit of Holt's Ledge had been fenced, and the Trail rerouted to provide a protected area for breeding and nesting of Peregrine falcons. An exquisite view of the valley to the south rewarded those who made the arduous climb.

Granma and I walked together down to the Lyme-Dorchester Road and our pickup point. We talked about the Trail and the degree of difficulty we were now experiencing. We both agreed that the Trail had become more demanding over the years, and we suspected it would become even more so as future planned relocations from roads and villages became reality. We conjectured, as the population aged, there might develop pressure to make the Trail more accessible. I wondered, if in future centuries, it might evolve as had many of the hiking Trails in Europe with inns and bed and breakfast places offering accommodations to hikers.

That, I thought, would destroy the wilderness aspect of the trail. But much had already been destroyed, and I was not sure that the ATC could, in the long run with population growth expanding, succeed in keeping development from encroaching and destroying even more of the wilderness experience. I was sure we were talking about issues the ATC had spent hours and hours debating and would spend more hours debating with many disagreements and probably some emotional cataclysms along the way. But we agreed the ATC was doing an outstanding job of protecting the Trail in its present configuration and would likely do so in the future.

The Dartmouth Ski Center with its dark-green, wooden buildings and large, level gravel parking lot appeared to offer a pleasant place to spend the night. We could get away from traffic noise at the Lyme-Dorchester road, and level places at the bottom of the ski runs looked like they might accommodate a tent or two.

The fist size gravel of the parking lot was less than ideal for tent sites, but the base of the newly cleared ski run with its hay patches looked inviting, and we chose to stay there. I started my supper, then erected my tent. I had no sooner started eating when it began to rain. It rained the entire night and was still coming down heavily when I awoke in the morning. Leaving the comfort of the tent for a downpour was really difficult, but I heard Granma stirring. I figured I'd better get with it.

When I got out of my sleeping bag I was greeted by the shock of cold water and discovered it had become wet in places. Investigation showed the whole bottom of the bag to be wet as well as the floor of the tent. The tent had obviously sprung a leak — an unpleasant surprise.

I packed a now thoroughly soggy sleeping bag and a soggy tent into a soggy pack, forced down a soggy breakfast, and prepared for a soggy day. Gordon and Sue had spent the night in the van and were not much interested in leaving it; Granma and I broke camp alone.

The climb up Smart Mountain was, considering my mood, easier than I had expected. And it seemed all was not lost; the rain stopped about mid-morning, and Trail conditions were reasonable. I reached the Cube Mountain Shelter about 2:00 p.m. and headed for the summit. About half way up, I ran out of gas. My heart began palpitating. I slowed my pace and took frequent breaks to reduce the exertion. Upon reaching the summit of Cube Mountain, I expected to just cross over it and start down the other side. But the Trail wandered all over the summit before deciding to head down hill, and I felt like it took forever to get started down.

That I was not in one of my more positive moods did not help my disposition when I started to encounter the rock scrambles. Trying to control my descent over the wet and slippery rocks could best be described as difficult. And that was an understatement. But, in some places, Trail crews had imbedded a series of 6" by 6" wooden beam sections into the rock ledges to form stairways; these were very helpful under the conditions. Although the wetness and steepness presented hazardous conditions, the hike was not without rewards. The path followed a cascading mountain stream; a series of small water falls and pools amid some unusual rock formations brightened the day, and I forgot my irritation.

The Mount Cube House, a picturesque old brick structure, was, according to the "Philosopher's Guide," the home of former New Hampshire State Governor, M. Thomson. A large, white, hay-filled barn and several smaller white buildings with farm equipment and machinery attested to the fact that this was a working farm. Across the road from the house, another small, white building, backed by a lush cornfield, served as a gift shop with a limited snack menu. The gift shop sold crafts as well as homemade preserves. But they were much less interesting to ravenous hikers than the apple pies, the scent of which brought to mind memories of gourmet hallucinations, the kind hikers suffer from during periods of prolonged fresh food deprivation.

Granma had arrived just before closing time and succumbed to the temptations. The kitchen was closed by the time I appeared, but I must have been a pitiful spectacle; the owner reopened the place and served me a large wedge of the tastiest apple pie I have ever eaten, and it was topped with two very generous scoops of vanilla ice cream. Granma, who had already finished one pie, was tempted into a second helping.

The "Philosopher's Guide" also indicated that the owner of Mount Cube House allowed hikers to stay overnight in the barn, and all of us looked forward to the prospect of bedding down in a loft full of soft hay. The woman, whom I assumed to be Mrs. Thomson, personally showed us to the barn. She opened the door to a fusillade of barks from three dogs chained to timbers beside the entrance. The dogs barked the entire time we were being shown around the premises. They were not vicious and made no attempt to strain at their chains or in any way to come after us. In fact, they looked pathetic, somewhat sad or lonely, and certainly bored, with barking their lives away. In truth, they were two dumb old mongrels and one dumb young mongrel happy to please. They were probably a real pain to keep track of, and that no doubt was the reason they were chained. They were certainly a good alarm system. Any movement anywhere around them was sure to set them off. But other than that, they were affable in the way of old derelicts.

Granma and I selected our respective places in the hay loft and set about laying out our sleeping gear. We also spread out our tents as well as the contents of our packs to allow everything to dry. My initial vision of sleeping in soft hay with no need of an air mattress disappeared in a collision with reality. This was not loose hay but stacked hay bales, and trying to find a suitable soft spot, even with an air mattress, proved to be a challenge.

We were all bone weary. Shortly after dinner, Granma and I headed to the barn, while Gordon and Sue began putting up their tents. As we approached the barn, the dogs went into a chorus that lasted for at least ten minutes. Every time one of us moved or whenever someone went by on the road or whenever a dog, however distant, barked, the trio launched into a barking frenzy. Initially earsplitting, the barking gradually subsided until one or two of the dogs would woof once at intervals like it was an afterthought. The intervals between the woofs increased until at last all was quiet. Then the next eruption would occur, and the cycle was repeated. I found myself awaiting the next eruption.

G-Man and The Jersey Kid arrived at about 9:00 p.m. and departed about half an hour later, after trying to handle the bales and going through a couple of episodes with the dogs. I rolled around attempting to find a spot where my legs or arms would not slide down between bales or where a sharp end of hay was not sticking into me. I could hear Granma breathing easily in her sleep.

After about the tenth eruption from the trio, I called it quits in the barn. Trying not to waken Granma, I collected my gear and dragged myself and my equipment across the road. It became a race between me and the mosquitoes — to see whether I could get the tent up in time or whether the mosquitoes would drain me before I could get into it.

I started the day a half an hour late without Granma and without enthusiasm, basically just counting off the miles. When starting the climb up what I thought was Ore Hill my heart started to palpitate, and I experienced several episodes of light headedness. Now it dawned on me; I had forgotten to take my medicine. I did it then and slowed my pace, resting frequently. During the course of the climb, I realized that I was not on Ore Hill but on the ridge line to the west of it.

I was basically exhausted physically and mentally, not a happy camper, and I decided to call it a day when I reached New Hampshire Route 25C. I hitched into Warren, New Hampshire, where I headed straight for the town center. But first I stopped at the local bank to replenish my cash supply. Some outstanding water colors decorating the walls contained the name Judi Kline, the same name as the teller who waited on me. I asked if she were the artist. Judi said they were her paintings. I learned she had started to paint by herself initially, then had taken lessons. She said her maiden name was Currier — as in Currier & Ives — and was a direct descendent of Currier.

On the way back to the Trail, I got a ride from a very heavy man in an old Oldsmobile with its trunk open. He was going somewhere to pick up an old stove. "Seen any animals?" he asked.

"Not really. A deer yesterday."

"Don't surprise me none. They all been killed."

"How's that?" I asked.

"Everyone around here has a dog. They let the dogs run and hunt with 'em, and kill anything that moves," he replied in a tone of confidence that suggested expertise. "They're ruinin' the environment, that's what they're doin'. Won't be any deer left pretty soon — or anything else for that matter."

I explained that I had seen a plenty of deer in Pennsylvania and Virginia, and that those states had great conservation programs; perhaps New Hampshire could benefit from something similar.

"People don't care any more. All they care about is their selves. Everyone's livin' above their means. All they want is money. Use to — you could buy a house for ten, twelve thousand dollars. People bought those houses and sold 'em for thirty thousand and then they was sold again for sixty thousand."

"Seems like some one made a lot of money."

"Didn't make no money. Only caused inflation. Dollar's hardly worth anything any more. People on fixed incomes can't make it." He was on a roll. "How can anyone expect to make it when inflation's runnin' at ten or twelve percent?"

I was tempted to tell him that inflation rates had been considerably below that level for some time but reconsidered. My host was very much in the "send" and not the least interested in the "receive" mode, so I nodded my head. He continued rambling on from subject to subject for the next three or four miles — until dropping me off at the AT.

"Hey, man, I been stung five times today! You got that? Five times, man!" Carleton punctuated his excitement by waving his arms wildly. "That's two times in three days. I been stung eleven times. Any of you been stung? Nooo! Only me. These bees goin' after me cause I'm black? They got prejudiced bees up here?"

"They weren't bees," G-Man said calmly. "They were yellow jackets."

"A bee sting is a bee sting. Don't make no difference when

you're gettin' stung, if it's bees or yellow jackets after you. Look how my arm is swoll up."

"What happened?" asked Granma.

"Dunno for sure," Carlton said. "All I remember is I lay down by my hikin' stick, and next thing I know I'm being chased by bees. I ran off, but some of 'em got under my shirt and started stingin'."

Carlton was wearing a cut off type T-shirt, very much in vogue with young athletes. The shirt fits over the shoulders and arms but is cut off well above the navel. It looks macho on guys with well developed torsos and flat bellies. Carleton, slender with highly developed shoulder and arm muscles, was the type who could wear one. The shirt, not tucked into the trousers, allowed air to circulate around the body for cooling, but also, in this case, gave the yellow jackets an avenue of attack.

"You need to get a shirt you can stick in your pants," I suggested.

"I gotta stay cool. I don't like all them clothes like you're wearin' when I'm hiking." He grimaced, as if even the thought caused discomfort. Then he became immersed in reflection. "Maybe there's a message here," he mused aloud. "Maybe it's time to come off the Trail." A very serious look embraced his countenance. "I wonder if I'm allergic to bee stings? My arm is still swollen from those stings three days ago. Should it still be swollen after three days?"

If they knew, no one offered an answer. I was about to say his arm didn't look swollen to me, Carleton beat me to the punch.

"Nah, I ain't gonna wimp out. I'm gonna hang tough," he allowed.

Gordon and Sue arrived during the latter part of the conversation, which caused everyone to think about where to spend the night. "Where we going to camp tonight?" G-Man asked, looking at Carleton.

"I don't know. Anywhere there's no bees."

"How about Beaver Brook shelter?" G-Man suggested.

"How far's that?" asked Carleton.

"On the other side of Moosilauke — about nine miles."

"You crazy or somethin'? Nine miles. And me with bee stings."

They were still in the process of trying to reach an agreement when we left in the van. I didn't know why they were devoting so much time to the discussion. They seldom spent the night together, since they had differing hiking philosophies. G-Man was willing to carry a lot of extra gear for comfort and bear the weight. Carleton was interested in speed; he carried less weight and had fewer comfort items. G-Man and I had discussed their differing ideas earlier on Smart Mountain, and he had told me their tents were illustrative of their differences. G-Man carried a six or eight pound hexagonal tent in which he could sit upright and feel relatively comfortable. Carlton, on the other hand, carried a tubular, bivy type shelter, which allowed him only to lie down.

Once again, everybody had to hike their own hike!

CHAPTER 13

The idea of God stands for a possible attempt at an impossible conception. We know nothing of the nature of God.
— *Edgar Allen Poe*

Warren, NH to Franconia Notch, NH

The hike the next day was punctuated with several meditative periods and even a few minutes of prayer. Evidently the solitude was productive. I engaged in some extended spiritual searching, trying to ascertain my relationship to God — to determine the function of God in my life — or better said, the function my life had in God's plan. It was a period spent primarily with questions, since that was the level of my awareness and development. My knowledge was so limited that I could only ask questions. And each question I asked led to another question which led in turn to another. How does one get to know God? Even more essential: What is God? What does God mean to me personally? There were no flashes of light or insight, no answers. But ideas were fermenting.

Before sleeping, I reminisced about the day and periods of meditation. The quotation, "I can of mine own self do nothing . . . The Father within me, He doeth the works," repeated itself. I remembered Father Bosco saying he took a piece of Scripture and used it as a focal point, trying to learn fully the significance of what was said. When I reflected on that phrase it seemed a burst of understanding came. What was this power within me? It certainly had nothing to do with my physical or mental self. It was spiritual self, a spiritual consciousness. It was a level of consciousness unreachable by human effort or the human mind. It was the sense of doing nothing and allowing the Father to take over.

The more I thought about it, the more convinced I became that I had been trying too hard to contact God. I couldn't contact God. I could only make myself receptive to His revelation by removing the egotistical "I" from my consciousness, by cleansing it of mortal concerns to make a place for the Father to reveal Himself. That seemed to be the key I had been searching for. It was all so simple; why had I not come to it before? The answer? It was obvious; I had not reached the point where I was ready. Was I now at that point?

I started up Mount Moosilauke and almost immediately met a young man struggling with a very heavy pack. He was, he informed me, preparing to establish a base camp for a group of students studying the effects of acid rain. Two of the students, men, from Dartmouth College and a third, a woman from Yale, were all working under the guidance of a Dartmouth professor. They were busy marking plots on the mountain where they would conduct long term studies of the effects of acid rain on the forest by taking bore and ring samples of selected trees over time.

The woman from Yale told me that acid rain was the popular term for a photo/chemical reaction caused by fossil fuel emissions combining with ozone and sunlight to form acids that were subsequently deposited on earth.

I mentioned that the West Germans were very concerned about their acid rain problems and had ascertained that most of their forests had in some way been affected. I had read that some studies showed that up to half of some forests were damaged. She was familiar with the German studies and responded that they were skewed; their statistics included the destruction of all the trees in the forest and in any forest a large percentage of trees die off from the process of natural selection. Therefore, these could not be taken into account.

The climb up Moosilauke was fairly tough and long as I had anticipated; and it took most of the morning to reach the summit. The views were spectacular. I could see the White Mountains all the way to Mount Washington. They were like nothing else I had seen. I had imagined the Whites to be upgraded versions of the Green Mountains, but these were magnificent — a completely different mountain chain rising up before me. They were in a class by themselves.

A number of people were already on the summit, lying in the grass, eating lunch, or admiring the scenery. A small fold in the terrain in front of a rock formation with a view of the Whites provided enough shelter to hunker down out of the wind and eat lunch. I could not imagine a more beautiful place to dine. The Trail down was very steep and difficult, much more so than the climb from the other side had been. It followed a stream down the mountain much the way the Trail did on Cube Mountain. But this stream flowed over several awesome cataracts, some of them dropping fifty feet or more. The scenery was so breathtaking, I didn't even think of complaining about the difficulty.

I stopped at the Beaver Brook shelter and learned from the Trail Register that the Blaze Brothers, The AT Believer and Screamin' Night Hog had all passed the Happy Feet. The Happy Feet were only nine days ahead; this amazed me, considering my slow pace. Carleton had passed me and was talking with Granma when I arrived. I had done only 8.9 miles for the day, but they were really tough miles and I was glad to see the van.

Gordon took us to the Wildwood Campground where we spent the night. I slept well and felt refreshed when I awoke. But for some reason, I was in a hyper mood. I couldn't explain it, but I was extremely anxious and uptight. That was not a good sign.

Granma and I had decided to take two days to do the stretch between Kinsman Notch and Franconia Notch. The distance was not all that great, but the terrain was rugged. As a result, we both carried our packs, but only with sleeping bags, stoves, food and comfort items. The rest we stashed in the back of the van. Light as it was, it was heavy enough to let me know I had a load on my back.

The initial ascent out of Kinsman Notch went pretty well, but after about 30 minutes, I began to experience arrhythmia. My body was telling me I was pushing it too hard. I needed to slack off. Granma had zoomed out of sight as soon as we had started to climb. So — here I was again alone, my heart palpitating after walking for only about half a mile. I had climbed only a very small portion of what promised to be a very tough Trail. But I felt it would be unwise to push on. That meant I would have to come off the Trail; and if I did that, I would probably also have to leave the van.

I considered my options. They were the same as I had considered during previous deliberations. If I came off and stayed with the van that would mean skipping another section. I was not happy with that option. I sat for about 30 minutes — assessing my situation. Then, I decided, to Hell with it; I'm going to continue. I arose from the rock where I was sitting and started walking, climbing and resting as my heart rate shot up. I went only a short ways, and the palpitations recurred. I simply could not ignore them. I could not continue in my present condition. I had to take a day off to rest.

I was less than elated as I turned around and headed back down toward Kinsman Notch. I hoped that Granma wouldn't be worried when I failed to show up at the shelter as we had planned. Then I realized that was not likely to happen. She would probably finish the whole stretch in one day. I realized that I had seen the last of Granma and was not even able to say goodbye.

When I arrived at the Notch I headed down Highway 112 for North Woodstock, sticking out my thumb at every passing vehicle. No one stopped. But it was just as well; it gave me the opportunity to do some soul searching as I walked. I had learned the same lesson all over again, I thought. You can only hike your own hike, not someone else's. I thought that life was like that. I could remember a poem in German hanging on the wall in my German girlfriend, Anna's house. Translated it read:

"No one knows
"The path that lies
"Before you.
"No one has gone
"The way that you will go.
"It is your path
"Unalterable.
"You may take counsel,
"But you must decide.
"Listen to the voice
"Of your inner Teacher.
"God has not left you alone.

"He speaks to you in your thoughts.

"Trust Him and yourself."

We are all on a path that no one has ever trod before. It is our own uniquely personal journey. We can ask all the advice we want, but ultimately we must make the decisions and take responsibility for them — and for the direction we take. We must determine what is important in our lives and do it our way. I had also hit on another recently neglected human attribute: responsibility. We must assume responsibility for our decisions and actions. And we are not allowed to substitute evasion of responsibility in searching for comfort as an acceptable alternative to the discomfort of challenge or honesty, and doing what we know in our hearts to be right.

I stopped at the Lost River Campground for some ice cream. After about 20 minutes, I got back on the road again. And as luck would have it, Gordon and Sue came by on the way to Lafayette Campground. That was really provident; in North Woodstock, I would have had to hitch a ride to the Lafayette Campground to inform the crew that I had decided to slow down and hike by myself at my pace. I was slightly surprised that Gordon and Sue seemed not surprised to see me. I told them what had transpired, how I needed to come off the Trail to rest and sort things out. Then I asked them to take me to a motel in North Woodstock.

I had my pick of motels. The town was full of them. After checking prices and amenities, I chose the Mount Coolidge Motel. Gordon dropped me off, agreeing he would return the following day, and we'd take it from there.

I borrowed Gordon's maps of the White Mountains; I had lost mine. Where, I was not sure. Perhaps it was in Hanover at The Edgerton House; and I was highly annoyed with myself for losing them. I promised Gordon I'd return them the next day. I planned to copy the maps before returning them and set out after lunch to do just that. That North Woodstock had not yet entered the 20th Century in business equipment soon became apparent. Most places had no copier, or if they did have one, it was too small or was not working. Eventually I gave up on that effort and set about writing down in sequence every terrain feature I would meet — reference points during the upcoming journey.

I studied the maps at length, planning in detail how to handle the White Mountains. There were no shelters per se in the White Mountains. Instead the Appalachian Mountain Club (AMC) managed a hut system that offered visitors not only a roof and four walls but also bunks with mattresses, pillows and blankets, even hot breakfasts and suppers. That was the way to go! I thought, pumping the air vigorously with my fist.

I formulated my plan accordingly. Because I would be carrying unaccustomed weight, I would hike slowly. Initially I planned to go from the Lafayette Campground up to the Greenleaf Hut the first day. Then it would be: Galehead Hut, Zealand Hut and the Crawford House. From the Crawford House, it was on to the Mispah Hut, Lake of the Clouds Hut, Madison Hut and the AMC headquarters at Pinkham Notch.

The AMC had an excellent reservation system; and it was recommended, even mandatory at this time of the year with the press of tourists, to make reservations to stay at the huts. And the fact that one was thru-hiking the Trail entitled one to absolutely no preference, either in regard to reservations or cost. The over nights, including meals, were quite expensive, over $50 per night, but as far as I was concerned, it worth every penny. But for some of the thru-hikers, especially those with low budgets, the price was pretty steep.

I was able to reserve space at Greenleaf, Galehead and Zealand Huts and the Crawford House Hostel; everything else was booked. At Lake of the Clouds Hut reservations were restricted to less than 48 hours in advance; that was also not an option. I would deal with that later. The plan should work out well; I would not be hiking more than eight miles in any one day which would give me the opportunity to become accustomed again to carrying the full weight of my pack.

I calculated that, with no unforeseen problems, I would reach Gorham, New Hampshire, by the 18th of August and would probably be in Monson, Maine, by the first week in September. I figured my progress on the basis of an eight-mile day with several days off for rest and recuperation.

I called Cathy and asked if she wanted to join me in Maine for my final assault up Katahdin. She was excited by the prospect but also expressed some reservations, saying it would be difficult to work around some of the problems entailing the job at her end. She had already used a significant portion of her vacation time and would have to do some bargaining to find additional days. She suggested meeting me in Stratton, Maine, and accompanying me from there. This was good news. I was secretly excited that I was in the planning range for Maine. That meant I was nearing the end.

I began meditating again. But this time it was more soul searching than meditating. I needed to relax and go with what my body would give me. I was relearning that lesson for the umpteenth time. I couldn't do it any other way. I had gotten outside of myself, out of control, concerned with trying to control things that were beyond my ability to control. Increasingly focused on Trail locations, the weather, the climbs, and my heart performance, I was becoming frustrated by my inadequacy in dealing with these factors.

I lay on the motel bed looking at the ceiling and vowed to get it together. I would succeed. I would ignore that which was impossible to control and be patient in my efforts to deal with that which was susceptible to my influence. The first thing I could influence was the amount of rest I needed, and I focused on that right then. I was still tired and needed to rest another day. It was working. It seemed a weight had been lifted. Resting another day was provident; the weather forecast called for rain. I was putting things into perspective. I only had 383 miles to go. I could hear Cathy saying, "You can do it, Old Soldier! You can do it!!"

Ray Pawelka, the motel owner, gave me a ride back to the Trail in a style that could only be described as grandiose. Although to a casual observer, it must have been a humorous sight, me clad in scruffy clothes, ragged shirt, patched britches, shaggy beard and disreputable hat with my hiking stick poking through the sun roof of a gleaming new, golden, S Class Mercedes Benz. New Hampshire had not been spared the commercialization of some of its most priceless natural beauty, and the ride up to Franconia Notch again proved there is no defense against bad taste in the pursuit of money. We passed carnival type rides and huge water slides along with a small gauge railroad; and even at this early hour, the press of tourists had begun. The gift shops I had visited the previous day seemed to have in common with gift shops in tourist places all over the world — a full inventory of tasteless plastic souvenirs for sale.

The carnival-like atmosphere seemed more appropriate for Coney Island or Busch Gardens and was, for me, totally out of character with the magnificent landscape in which it was set. I thought back to state fairs or carnivals I had visited, and it seemed like some had come to North Woodstock. But when they departed, they had left bits and pieces behind that had taken root and become a permanent part of the place. I was glad to be leaving. A car in front of us had a bumper sticker that read: "Welcome to New Hampshire. Now go home!" I could understand the message.

Ray dropped me off at a small roadside turn off, just opposite the "Old Man" viewing site and Profile Lake. I thanked him profusely for his generosity and promised to periodically let him know how I was doing, and he then drove off. I initially started walking in the wrong direction. Some people in the parking lot told me that Lafayette Campground was about two miles back in the direction I had just come. Ray had overshot the mark a bit. I reached the campground about 45 minutes later and ran right into the "Bridal Path," the name of the trail leading to Greenleaf Hut. I was finally on my way through the Whites.

CHAPTER 14

Why should we be in such desperate haste to succeed, and in such desperate enterprises? If a man does not keep pace with his companions, perhaps it is because he hears a different drummer.

— *Henry David Thoreau*

Franconia Notch, NH to Crawford Notch, NH

The climb to Greenleaf Hut was only two-and-a-half miles, but there were some very steep sections. I climbed with determination, if not speed, and made surprisingly good time. I thought it might be difficult getting used to a full pack again, but it seemed I had not lost any conditioning in that regard. I moved well and was surprised that I felt as good as I did — even with the weight. The rest had definitely helped and so did my concentration on thinking positively about the Trail and the hike. I did have a few palpitations initially, but they disappeared as soon as I got into the rhythm of the climb. More surprising than the ease of the climb was the number of fellow hikers on the trail, probably 50 or more just on that stretch. All were in high spirits, if not in great shape.

Initially the trail stayed in the woods and I was not particularly impressed, but after passing a section called "Agony" the scenery was spectacular. The trail had passed above tree line and the views were unlike anything I had seen before on the Trail. The course of the Trail along the ridge spine could be determined by watching the hikers moving like multicolored ants across the gray rocks or silhouetted against the skyline.

The hut, a large wood and stone building, sat on an Alpine meadow right at tree line. Behind it a collection of small evergreens provided a measure of protection from the wind coming up the valley. The front was open toward Mount Lafayette and overlooked magnificent Eagle Lake, a glacial pond hearkening back in time to when the country was in the grip of the ice age. The trail led from the shelter, contoured the lake a short ways, then headed straight to the summit of the mountain which towered over the landscape. It dominated the panorama with its massiveness and intimidated this viewer with the awesomeness of its stark, barren rock fields, boulder formations, and its raw beauty.

After checking in with one of the young people running the place, I returned to the front steps to admire the scenery. It was irresistible to the point of breathtaking, this mass of raw rock. It was so high, so overpowering as to be held almost in reverence. As I looked up, the thought crossed my mind that in the morning I would become a part of that mountain. I would be part of it, not like the essence of its rock, but I would be enfolded by its immensity. My life would be entwined with the beauty, the mystery, the exhilaration that comes with the first steps into the unknown. It looked so far to the top; then as my eyes dropped down to the lake below it seemed not so far from that perspective. But I could barely see the people on the summit, and those ascending and descending looked to be make believe; and that made it even more awesome. They were moving to be sure, but their pace was so exaggeratedly slow that the impression was surrealistic.

Then two Peregrine falcons initiated a display of aerial acrobatics above the lake with the mountain as a backdrop. They soared and dove and soared again, crested to an apogee, then folded their wings and dove with impossible speed straight down. I expected to hear the screaming sound that accompanies such maneuvers by aircraft, but there was only an infinitely more impressive silence. I lost sight of them as they dipped below a low ridge directly to the left of the hut. I then picked them up again as they pulled out of their dives and flew horizontally across the lake at eye level, to swoop up to an apogee and repeat the process.

I was reminded of the swallows I had watched at the Rainbow Springs Campground in North Carolina doing the same type of acrobatics. They were beautiful but had neither the range, speed nor power these birds exhibited. It seemed like they were putting on a matinee show. I watched for a few minutes — entranced — then looked around for someone with whom to share my reactions. About ten people were milling around in front of the hut, but no one was watching the display. I was amazed. I felt like yelling, "Hey, people, look up there! Look around you. Why the Hell are you up here?"

Thirty people, six children included, were guests for the night, and by mid-afternoon most had already arrived. Several who had finished checking in were sitting around relaxing in the sunshine and admiring the beauty. One of them, a man named Jack, an environmentalist/naturalist of sorts, impressed me; he sat as motionless as the chunk of granite under him. He stared up at the mountain like he was trying to drink in the scene or engrave the vision in his memory. Perhaps he was meditating.

I learned he was planning to hike basically as I was — through the Whites, going to Galehead the next day and eventually over to Carter Notch Hut. Another young man stood out; he was wearing battle dress camouflage pants with Army issue jungle boots, normal load carrying web harness and an Army issue rucksack, from which dangled two canteens and a throwing knife.

I hadn't seen any wildlife on the trail. But the hut had attracted some. First I saw the falcons and later a red squirrel. The squirrel came right up to the hut, obviously looking for a hand-out; since it was a no-no to feed the animals, perhaps he hoped for a morsel inadvertently dropped on the grounds.

Just before supper, I wandered to the rear of the hut where two huge snowshoe hares munched quietly on the grass and sniffed the ferns. They ignored the gathering crowd until one photographer came to within about two feet and one of the hares moved off.

Supper was served family style at three large tables. The menu consisted of soup served from steaming tureens, bowls of fresh lettuce and tomato salad and a main entree of roast beef, baked potatoes and green beans. A pumpkin/raisin pan cake dessert topped off the meal. Although the food was plain, it was delicious, more than ample, and, best of all, I didn't have to haul it up on my back.

Heavy item support for the hut was supplied by helicopter in mid-summer; the 'copter delivered staples and canned goods and took out trash and waste from the toilets. Water was piped from the lake into a large water tank to the rear of the hut and heated by solar energy generated by panels outside the hut. The hut caretakers carried the daily resupply of fresh food and supplies up in rucksacks or A-frame back packs. The "Croo," as they were called, were five young people, probably college students, who did an outstanding job of catering to and supporting the daily flood of tired, hungry people. They handled themselves with great tact, responding positively and politely toward all their guests.

The walls of the hut were covered with a number of information bulletins, notes and pictures. One of the more interesting was a historical explanation of the origin of the glacier pond in front of the hut, accompanied by a mock eulogy to its eventual demise. The crystalline character of the waters had changed over the years through the natural process of silting and now was becoming overrun with vegetation, which in turn was speeding the process of silting. At some time in the distant future, the lake would become a marsh, then probably disappear altogether.

Also posted was a list of people who had worked as "croo" in the hut with the records of weights they had carried on resupply runs up the mountain and the amount of time it had taken to make their climbs. The overall champion was Tom Dean who carried a record 178 pounds up the mountain in a time of two hours and 28 minutes. On reflection, I realized that he was carrying the equivalent of my body weight up the mountain and it had taken him less time to do that than it took me to carry less than a quarter of that weight. He also owned the speed record, carrying 56 pounds up the same distance in 49 minutes.

Sleeping accommodations were provided by triple-decked, wooden bunks built into place. Normal mattresses were supplied along with pillows and a blanket. Guests were separated by gender and the toilet was located in the far right rear of the men's quarters which meant that everyone had to pass by where I was sleeping. It really didn't matter much to me; I went to sleep almost immediately after getting in bed and I didn't hear a thing until morning.

Breakfast was as much an event as a meal, although the food was definitely the main focus of interest. Buckwheat pancakes, oatmeal, juice, coffee and tea started us on the day. Before leaving, the "croo" put on a humorous little skit, the purpose of which was to remind everyone to make their bunks and fold their blankets.

The trail initially dropped down from the hut to the shore of Eagle Lake, which at that point was below tree line. Then began a steady and sometimes steep ascent up to the summit. After passing above tree line, the trail was marked by blazes painted on rocks or by rock cairns every hundred feet or so. The day was gorgeous with sunshine, blue sky and only occasional clouds. But the wind was brisk and the temperature chilly enough that despite the exertion, I put on my wind breaker.

The immensity of the mountain and the splendor of the scenery were exhilarating. I stopped often to admire the views, thinking I could remain there forever, and subsequently had to push myself to continue. I tried to anticipate where the trail would go as I looked up toward the various rock formations. What seemed to be perfectly logical routes from one perspective became impossible formations up close and the trail would change direction and take a route not imaginable from below. The farther up I climbed from the hut, the smaller it became, until it was almost invisible from the summit. Some wispy clouds drifted by on the summit and some passed below me.

At 5,243 feet the summit was 1.1 miles from the hut. I had made the climb in 45 minutes and had experienced no palpitations along the way. The view from the summit was an event that one remembers for life and becomes the standard by which all subsequent views are judged. There were peaks in every direction and drop-offs from the peaks to the valleys were long, steep and deep. The clarity of the panorama was astounding without haze of any kind. I recognized Mount Moosilauke in the distance and in the other direction, Mount Washington and closer yet, Mount Garfield. I could see the whole world it seemed.

The Trail followed the spine of the mountain crest, weaving its way through rock formations and outcroppings, each formation bringing a fresh image and perspective, and in between each, miniature alpine meadows of a few feet in diameter brightened the path.

The Garfield Ridge trail was one of the toughest sections of the White Mountains. The drop-off into the saddle between Lafayette and Garfield was precipitous and very rough. The Trail then followed a series of changes in elevation that were both longish and steep where the protected cols (passes) between the high points were heavily vegetated and swampy. The final climb to the summit of Mount Garfield was short but steep. The Trail passed below the crest but a short side trail led to the rocky summit and I went there. Again the views were absolutely spectacular.

The climb down from Mount Garfield was very steep and several sheer ledges made the descent more exciting than usual. I was glad it was dry. It would have been treacherous in wet weather. The sky began to cloud over in the afternoon, and as the wind picked up, it became chilly. But down in the cols, protected from the wind and with heavy underbrush and boulders, the tough hiking made it very warm. Consequently I was constantly putting on my sweater and wind breaker at the higher elevations, then removing them in the cols. The total distance from Greenleaf hut to Galehead hut was only seven miles, but it was the toughest seven miles I had done on the Trail and it took me until 4:30 p. m. to reach Galehead.

Again, the number of people on the Trail surprised me. I had expected some hikers but not the number I was seeing. I would have liked a little more solitude to enjoy the beauty. Despite the company, I was able to do some meditating and praying. I'm sure it was the beauty of the surroundings, but I felt a little closer to God.

Galehead hut was very similar in construction to the Greenleaf hut and the hut Croo similarly helpful and pleasant. The Trail register contained entries by Granma, G-Man and the Jersey Kid, but I didn't see any from the Blaze Brothers, the AT Believer, Screamin' Night Hog or the Happy Feet.

One wall contained a time-yellowed newspaper article about Emily Kluge, a native German who immigrated to The United States and had trained as a nurse in Brooklyn, New York. Emily began climbing the White Mountains in 1914. Her equipment consisted of half a sleeping bag, a huge cape and a wide skirt. She carried a small back pack and wore breeches under her skirt. She secured the hem of her skirt to her waist belt and carried her things in the pouch the skirt formed. She became a legend of the White Mountains, stopping at huts to rest or eat, always helping with the chores or dishes, or sewing patches or darning socks — whatever she could do to help.

One spring she wrote to the people at Pinkham Notch that she would be unable to come to the mountains; some of the elderly patients she cared for "just would not die." Although she could only contribute $15 at a time, she became a life member of the AMC. She returned to Germany and sent many cards and letters to the AMC, never once mentioning the World War I, which started a short time later. A picture of her dressed in her hiking skirt adorned the wall next to the article.

Galehead was also home to "Doodah," a large minx bob-tailed cat. Doodah was clearly in charge at Galehead. He strolled about the hut in the way of a manor lord surveying his estate, sometimes allowing guests to pamper him, sometimes withdrawing in displeasure. He also abided no competitors. At one time the hut had a real problem with mice, that is, until Doodah arrived. There is no longer a mouse problem. He also had been known to dispatch small snowshoe hares. I thought the cartoon cat "Garfield" had to have been modeled on Doodah. No other animal I seen had as much a mind of its own as Doodah or exhibited that certain air of detached self-assurance that those blessed with natural superiority so clearly carry.

The next morning, after a breakfast of oatmeal, bacon and eggs, the Croo put on their skit using the theme of Snow White who would respond only to the prince who could properly fold the blanket.

The weather clouded over at the outset of the hike, threatening to rain and then deteriorated after that. The climb up South Twin Mountain was steep, but the footing fine, and I made good time. I was about half way to the top of the mountain when I was passed by a young boy barely into his teens. I encountered him again a short while later and stopped to talk. He was hiking with two other family members but had left them behind and now had decided to stop to allow them to catch up. I went on and didn't see him again, until the next morning at Zealand Hut. Farther on, I met George Schmidt, a retired Air Force pilot. He was also headed for Zealand hut and we walked together a short ways. George was 69 years old and a lot slower than I was. I moved ahead.

I reached the Trail junction just below the summit of South Twin Mountain shortly before George and the rain, which had been light up to that point, now came down hard. Clouds engulfed the summit, and the wind blew the mist and rain in horizontal sheets. The Trail then took a right angle turn and headed for Mount Guyot. Unfortunately with visibility reduced to about 50 feet, there were no views.

The Twinway, as the Trail was called at that point, was not well maintained, and it was sometimes a struggle to push through the wet bushes and tree branches, which responded to my intrusion by donating their accumulated moisture to my clothing. Sometimes the vegetation obscured the path to the extent I thought I was bush-whacking. At one point, the Trail crossed a boulder field, which required rock hopping. Vegetation had overgrown the path and I couldn't see where to hop next. Consequently I missed some intended hopping spots and slipped between the rocks. Thankfully, other than some major aggravation and a couple of barked shins, I came through the ordeal unscathed.

It took what seemed like a long time to climb Mount Guyot and at times I feared I had lost the Trail. I felt sorry for George. The wind and rain had lowered the temperature close to the freezing point, making for some very cold and uncomfortable conditions and causing me to think this was no place for 53-year-old, let alone a 69-year-old. I had seen his legs behind me as I descended from South Twin, so I knew he had been right behind me. But he was now nowhere to be seen.

Actually the climb up Mount Guyot was fairly short — but steep — and once I broke above the tree line, the wind became vicious. The Trail also became increasingly difficult to follow because the visibility was so poor I couldn't see the blazes ahead; it became a matter of guessing the right direction to take. Eventually, I reached the point where the Twin Mountain Trail became the Bondcliff Trail and the AT separated at that point, leading to the left over the Summit of Mount Guyot (4560 feet) and descended its northeast ridge. It was somewhat confusing to follow, and I had to pay close attention to be sure I was making the right turns.

It was very cold on the mountain making my hands so numb I had trouble holding my hiking stick. I changed hands frequently, warming one hand in my pocket, while carrying the stick in the other. On the way down, I stopped to eat lunch and discovered my hands had become so cold I couldn't peel back the top of the sardine can. My fingers simply did not have sufficient strength to turn the key and peel the metal back. I tried several times to get my fingers to work, all to no avail; then in an act of colossal stupidity, I held the key in my teeth while I tried to turn the can. A sharp snap and the shrill rush of cold air against the exposed tooth nerve informed me that I had broken my tooth.

I felt around my mouth with my tongue, located the broken end and spit it into my hand. In my mouth it felt like a boulder, but in my hand it looked as small as a $20 diamond. I tried to inspect it. But it was so small and my glasses were so wet and fogged up, I gave up and dropped it in my food stack, intending to give it a closer look when I got to the hut. But when the time arrived, I couldn't find the damn thing.

In the meantime, the rush of adrenaline to my angry response served to warm up my hands sufficiently so that I was able to open the can. I ate the fish without taste, concentrating instead on feeling the rough edges of my newly broken tooth and trying to cover it with my tongue to protect it from the cold air.

After lunch, the main objective in life was to get down off the mountain and into a warm hut. At 2:15 p. m., after negotiating a couple of very steep drop-offs and bitching silently about the weather and my funny feeling tooth, I arrived at Zealand hut. It seemed like the state of New Hampshire had congregated inside the hut; finding a place to sit was as tough as opening the sardine can had been.

I wondered how the hut was going to accommodate all those people for the night, then realized that most were day-hikers who would soon be headed back to their cars at Crawford Notch, a couple of easy miles down the hill.

As time wore on, the crowd began to thin. Then I realized that George Schmidt had not shown up. He had been right on my heels on the way down South Twin Mountain; he should have arrived minutes after I did. Two hours after my arrival, I became sufficiently concerned that I mentioned it to some people.

At 4:30 p. m. still no George, and my concern turned into worry. Then at 4:40 p. m. I heard someone outside say, "You must be George. There's someone in there that's going to be mighty glad to see you."

Then I heard George saying, "Not nearly as glad as I am to be here."

The sense of relief was palpable. The Trail conditions were downright dangerous for anyone in such weather, and for someone pushing 70 years old, the peril was magnified. He was even colder and wetter than I had been and set out immediately trying to restore his body heat and dry his clothes.

The hut had a very functional clothes/equipment drying apparatus. Three eight-to-ten foot wooden clothes racks were suspended from the ceiling by thin nylon ropes. The ropes ran through pulleys that allowed them to be raised or lowered as necessary and were then tied off to pegs in the wall. George and I added our jackets, shirts and trousers to one of the already burdened racks and then hauled it back to the ceiling out of the way. It was not wise to stand beneath the racks.

The Zealand Notch area had been heavily logged around the turn of the century. In 1903, a forest fire left the place looking like a wasteland. In the intervening years, the area was reforested by hardwood trees. But now spruce trees had reintroduced themselves and it was hoped that the place would gradually return to a spruce forest.

A brook about a hundred yards off to the side of the hut developed into Zealand Falls, a series of picturesque cascades and a small water fall. In the evening, before it turned dark, the rain ceased, the clouds started to break up and the sun shone weakly through the trees across the falls.

I sat and watched the water course its way down to Whitewall Brook that in turn would lead to the north fork of the east branch of the Pemigewasset River. Such are the humble beginnings of all great rivers, I thought.

Later, after it became dark and the wind had picked up, I left the coziness and warmth of the hut to stand for a short time in the clearing in front of the hut. The moonlight cast the shadows of trees across the silver clearing and made the blackness of forest more intense. The sky seemed like black velvet, punctuated by countless tiny points of light twinkling across the light years. The wind was just enough to impart a chill and I was not sure if the chill came from the wind or from exhilaration of it all.

I awoke in the morning to the softly pleasant air of "Country Road" being sung by the Croo accompanied by guitar. What a pleasant way to wake up! The boy I had met the previous day on the climb up South Twin Mountain now occupied the bunk below mine, which had been vacant when I went to bed. I dimly remembered hearing someone come in during the night but had gone right back to sleep.

I learned the family had arrived at 10:00 p. m. by flashlight. They had missed the turn in the Trail near the summit of Mount Guyot and continued straight ahead. They had walked the Bondcliff Trail in its entirety and had to retrace their steps to find out where they had missed the turn on the AT.

Considering the conditions, it was pretty dangerous. They had been on the trail for 15 hours in absolutely miserable conditions of wind and rain, and I imagined they must have been very grateful to have reached the hut. They had come perilously close to disaster. The boy was so exhausted by the ordeal that he didn't even stir, while the rest of us were getting ready to take on the day.

I arranged with the Croo to include in their daily radio contact with the base camp at Pinkham Notch, a request for me to use the shuttle to go from the AT to the Crawford Notch hostel. It was arranged, and I was on my way. The Guide book indicated the Trail passed Thoreau Falls and Ethan Pond, and I looked forward to seeing them both. I was disappointed. The falls were nothing special and the pond could not be seen from the Trail.

After that, the most interesting part of the walk was the passage along the west face of White Wall Mountain. The Trail followed an abandoned railroad bed through a massive rock slide that had probably occurred during glacial times. The rocks were not your garden variety boulders of the type that comprised "devil's racecourse." These were massive boulders — the size of railroad boxcars lying in a vertical jumble that stretched from the valley floor up the side of the mountain for several hundred feet. Some rocks were perched precariously over the Trail, and I felt slightly apprehensive walking beneath them. I had not seen anything quite so desolate as the boulder-strewn valley floor and had nothing to compare it with, until I came to Mahoosuc Notch in Maine.

After passing the rock slide, I encountered some grouse walking like tourists down the Trail ahead of me. Most flew off as I approached. However, two courageous birds, or perhaps foolhardy might be a better description, remained behind. One of them stayed on the Trail walking directly in front of me like we were both out on a stroll. The other bird hopped up to a head-high tree limb beside the path. I walked right up to the bird, expecting it to erupt into flight.

Eye to eye we stood, until it side stepped nervously away from me along the branch. It didn't so much as ruffle a wing. I decided to see just how tough this bird was and tapped it gently with my hiking stick. No response. I tapped a little harder and it hopped to the next higher limb. I blinked first by continuing down toward Crawford Station. The triumphant bird remained on his branch and the other one just ambled to the side of the Trail to let me pass.

Granma, The Jersey Kid and G-Man had all signed the register at the Crawford Station; I did likewise. Then it was down to the Willey House Station parking lot and a one mile road walk up to the Willey House.

The house was overrun with tourists who showed a mild curiosity when I arrived. But that soon evaporated after I plunked myself down on the front porch of the gift shop to eat an ice cream bar and await the AMC shuttle.

CHAPTER 15

It would surprise any of us if we realized how much store we unconsciously set by beauty and how little savor there would be left in life if it were withdrawn.

— *John Galsworthy*

Crawford Notch, NH to Pinkham Notch, NH

At the hostel I was able to call the AMC headquarters and reserve a bunk for successive nights at Mizpah hut, Lakes of the Clouds hut by Mount Washington and the Inn at Pinkham Notch. I could not get into Madison hut; the Croos had reserved it solely for their use for their annual season ending bash. I wouldn't have minded except the associated tent site was half a mile down the mountain and the hut was the only hut on the loop of the Presidential Range from Lake of the Clouds to Pinkham Notch. I would even have camped outside the hut, if I could have used the facilities. But hikers were not allowed to camp within a certain distance of huts throughout the Whites. It was a sensible rule that prevented what certainly would have been massive over-use with its attending mini-environmental tragedies around the huts.

The next morning I started out for the Mizpah hut using the Crawford path, the oldest continuously used mountain trail in America. It originated in 1819 when Abel Crawford and his son Ethan Allen cleared a path to the top of Mount Clinton and from there guided many groups to the summit of Mount Washington. In 1840 they improved the trail to a bridle path with Abel making the ascent at age 75 by horse. In 1875 it reverted to a footpath; since then, many thousands of people have traveled this path to the Presidential Range and Mount Washington.

I expected the climb to be difficult, but it was not nearly as bad as I had imagined. I reached Mizpah hut by 11:00 a. m. The early arrival called for a change in plans. A quick call to the very accommodating AMC booked me into Lake of the Clouds hut that evening. A comment by Granma in the hut register from the previous night indicated the weather had been miserable — windy and rainy.

The climb from Mizpah to the summit of Mount Pierce was quite long and fairly steep, but the weather was beautiful, full sunshine and blue skies with the only clouds visible being on the horizon. On the summit, I again encountered John Dodge, a spry 78-year-old I had met earlier during my climb to Mizpah. He was sitting on a large rock eating lunch and admiring the scenery, and the Trail up to Mount Eisenhower and Mount Washington. He told me he had been hiking the White Mountains since 1935, and I quickly calculated he had been wandering around the mountains for 52 years.

He pointed out a plume of black smoke rising from the horizon near Mount Washington and told me it was from the train that plied the cog railway. The tracks lay just over the ridge from the summit of Washington, and he said that as I got closer I would be able to see the railway and, if it was running, the train.

He invited me over to his rock to have lunch, saying I should be careful to step only on the rocks as he had done; the terrain was ecologically fragile at that elevation and was easily damaged by walking on it. He also introduced me to mountain cranberry, holding one out for me to see. "Makes a great jam, and a great sauce!"

I thought there could not have been a more beautiful place in the world. Ahead were the stark summits of the Presidential Range and the ridges between the peaks all above tree line. The rock formations were unusual and exotic to the degree that if you looked creatively, you could get them to resemble familiar shapes in your mind like kids do with cloud formations. The alpine flavor of the vegetation was special. All sorts of interesting little flowers, some of which bloom only in that part of the world, and small meadows of fragile grass clung to life between the rocks.

The landscape was extremely vulnerable to damage by foot traffic and several erosion scars were evident. To minimize the impact, stone steps and pathway borders had been constructed to keep hikers on the trail and to allow damaged sections to regenerate.

The tree line began at 4200 feet and everything above that was alpine tundra, punctuated by dwarfed spruce called krummholz. The weather was extremely changeable and unpredictable with fierce storms and extreme drops in temperature, both without warning. Signs along the trails carried warnings about sudden weather changes, as did several pamphlets available at huts and the AMC facilities in the valleys. Hikers were to stay off the mountains in bad weather, not to go up, if bad weather was forecast, and that, if caught in a sudden change of weather, to immediately head for lower ground and shelter. A number of people had lost their lives while hiking the Whites and Mount Washington in particular; they had not heeded the admonitions and were improperly clothed or prepared for the hypothermia which followed.

After visiting with Mr. Dodge for few minutes, I returned to the Trail, being careful to step only on rocks and to stay within the confines of the pathway. I had not gone far, and was as usual immersed in admiring the fantastic landscape, when I met Louis Lanier, a short, slightly-built thru-hiker from Atlanta, Georgia, who caught up to me from behind. Louis's Trail name was, "The Georgia Ridge Runner;" had started from Springer Mountain in April. He may have been slight of build, but the muscles in his legs were like spring steel and he bubbled with an enthusiasm that matched in intensity his bright blue eyes. We talked for only a minute, but before leaving, he informed me that Smokin' Joe was right behind him. Sure enough, Joe, his bandy legs pumping furiously, caught up to me shortly thereafter. We exchanged greetings, and he too passed by, hurrying along as usual. Louis was a fast hiker, but his speed was a natural speed, and he seemed comfortable. Joe, on the other hand, didn't seem to be enjoying the hike. He was rushing to keep up with Louis, I thought.

The pass between Mount Monroe and Mount Washington contained a beautiful alpine meadow and a small glacial pond that looked as pure and fresh and cold as it must have been for thousands of years. A small sign informed hikers to please not disturb the rare dwarf cinquefoils — a small hairy yellow flower supposedly found nowhere else in the world. I suspected I was getting close to the Lakes of the Clouds hut, since trails from the ridges were congregating in the saddle to form one big trail that headed down the mountain instead of up toward the summit of Mount Washington. The hut became visible a short time later.

An elderly lady in charge of the Croo, the first older person I had seen working in a hut, already had the Georgia Ridge Runner and Smokin' Joe under control. They were being allowed to work in the kitchen as payment for their room and board for the night. She was briefing them on their duties and it would not be an easy evening.

The two scruffy, dirty hikers had become beaming choirboys. Their previously uncivilized hair had been washed squeaky clean and combed into unaccustomed order and the fact they were wearing long white bib aprons added to the angelic impression. It was only when a closer look revealed the underlying garb that the comity of their appearance became apparent. Louis' skinny, hairy legs peaking from beneath the apron were comical, but Joe with long blue tights under red nylon hiking shorts and red baseball cap was outrageous.

Their first job was cutting and grating cheese. Joe's job was to cut the cheese into manageable chunks, which Louis then grated for the meal. I heard someone ask them if they were friends from the Trail. "I'm his probation officer," Louis said in mock seriousness. Joe only smiled and stuffed a piece of cheese in his mouth. A second impression emerged in which they looked like two schoolboys working off punishment for misbehaving. Every so often Joe would wink at someone and pop a piece of cheese in his mouth. He ate almost as much as he cut. I suspected the boss lady was on to his tricks, but she didn't let on if she did.

That evening I did a lot of thinking about how to continue the Trail through the Whites, reviewing my options from different perspectives. Always the sticking point was the inability to stay at Madison hut. That left basically two alternatives, neither of which was completely satisfactory. The first alternative was to camp at the Madison tent site which was more than half a mile down a steep mountain side and the second was to take the bad weather route across the pass between Mount Washington and Mount Franklin to Tuckerman Ravine, then down to Pinkham Notch. I wanted to walk the part of the Presidential Range which looped the great Gulf Wilderness, but I didn't want to walk more than half a mile down what the maps indicated was a steep mountain and then back up again — just to spend the night. I decided to take the Tuckerman Ravine route.

The day started with breakfast and a Croo skit take-off from "Star Wars," where the warrior had to accomplish three tasks, obviously the most important of which was to properly fold a blanket. I climbed to the summit of Mount Washington without pack, intending only to pick up a mail drop, return to the hut, retrieve my pack and head for Tuckerman Ravine. The climb was long and fairly steep, but the weather perfect — not a cloud in sight and only a slight breeze. I stopped often to rest and breathe in the scenery. Louis and Joe both carrying full packs passed me as did others I had met the previous evening along with a couple I had met at Zealand hut three days previous.

Just as I arrived at the summit, the cog train pulled into its "station;" the little black engine belched smoke that matched its color. It was a diminutive; real, coal-fired steam engine that looked like it came from my childhood book about "The Little Engine That Could." The engine was black with soot and oil and the engineer and his helper looked more like miners just emerging from a week in a coal mine, than train operators. Both the engine and its lone passenger car were slanted forward about fifteen degrees, so that they remained level on steep mountain slopes.

I mentioned to the engineer, in an off-hand way, my delight in seeing an honest-to-God coal-fired steam engine still operating during the jet age. He feigned surprise, saying somewhat sarcastically, that he thought he had been hauling around little black rocks. I guessed he'd had it up to his nose with inane comments from tourists and just couldn't resist the impulse.

Louis and Smokin' Joe also had mail drops at the summit. Louis left almost immediately after picking up his mail, but Joe remained for a while. He was resting next to the Post Office cubicle when I arrived. I said goodbye, and after taking several photographs of the panorama from the summit, started back down to Lakes of the Clouds hut. I knew I had seen the last of Louis but wasn't sure about Joe. He had a habit of popping up at the most surprising places.

The atmosphere was crystal clear and I could see forever. All the mountains of the Presidential Range spread out before me in both directions at my feet. I looked back across Mount Franklin and Mount Eisenhower, and the path I had followed to get here. I had felt so high then. But now they looked far below me. Nowhere else on the Trail were the mountains so rugged, so wild, so captivatingly beautiful.

The descent from the summit back to Lakes of the Clouds hut took an hour. By the time I had sorted out and packed all my gear along with the contents from my mail drop, it was close to noon. I started out on the Crossover Trail to Tuckerman Ravine, absorbed in the beauty of the landscape. Everywhere I looked the scenery was breathtaking, and as I crossed over the shoulder of the ridge, every look up at the giant gave me a different perspective. I was paying more attention to the scenery than the trail. Before crossing Bigelow Lawn, the flat area south of the cone of Mount Washington, I got off the Tuckerman Crossover and ended up instead on Davis Path, which followed the ridge to Boott Spur. I recognized my mistake when I reached the junction of the trail from Davis Path to Tuckerman Junction. At that point, I stopped for lunch and sat for about an hour drinking in the serenity and the grandeur.

The Trail at that point crossed a massive boulder field marked by stone cairns about every hundred yards. Expansive fields of jumbled rocks that resembled a moonscape spread out for about as far as I could see along the ridge and only the occasional patches of grass resembling swamp bogs provided assurance that I was still earthbound.

The cairns looked like miniature lighthouses in a sea of gray rock, and I half expected occasional light beams to sweep across the landscape. Farther on, because of the tricks distance plays with perspective, I imagined them to be a line of hikers marching up to Tuckerman Junction. I also observed a group of hikers climbing the trail from Tuckerman Junction up Mount Washington.

The place was literally crawling with hikers. I watched people hurrying to the Junction, and once arriving, milling around in confusion for several minutes, until they had oriented themselves as to which trail they wanted to follow, then going hurrying on as before. I enjoyed the mix of colors of the hikers' clothing, the reds and yellows mostly with occasional greens and blues standing out in sharp contrast to the massive gray of the mountain.

The wind picked up a little as I started again. I wondered if I would have to stop and mill around as the others had at Tuckerman Junction. I stopped thinking about it until I arrived at the Junction, then I became confused and understood what I had seen earlier. Several trails converged there and it took a few minutes to get my bearings before I determined the correct path to take.

Before I left, I talked with a boy who was totally perplexed by the maze of trails. He knew generally where he was, but not at which trail junction. I showed him on the map where he was and pointed to the trail he wanted to take, then started down to the ravine.

I chose to take the Alpine Garden Trail to Lion Head and take that trail down to rejoin the Tuckerman Ravine Trail. The descent was steep with a treacherous path of loose dirt and stones that required caution. My planned route worked perfectly and again, the scenery was spectacular, marred only by the scars of erosion caused by constant usage of the trails into the ravine.

A rock outcropping beside the trail with splendid views of Pinkham Notch and Tuckerman Ravine invited me to stop for moment to enjoy the scene. High above me to the rear, the summit of Mount Washington had accumulated a halo of clouds. In between drifts, I spied a man in what appeared to be an ultralight airplane or a hang glider waiting for the right moment to launch. I identified it as a hang glider. Since he flew directly over me before soaring out across the expanse of valley leading to Pinkham Notch. He flew initially toward the mountains across the valley, then in a wide sweeping arc flew down the length of the valley and eventually dropped below my elevation. He then circled the parking lot at the Wildcat Mountain ski lift and at that point dropped out of sight. His flight lasted about half an hour. What a thrill that must've been!

Shortly afterward, a helicopter took off from almost the same point and headed for the top of Wildcat Mountain. It made several more trips as I made my way down the ravine. I later learned it was ferrying cement up to where workers were constructing a pylon for a ski lift.

The trail down Lion Head was steep and rocky but less so than the initial dive off Tuckerman Ravine, and I could pay more attention to my surroundings. The scenery never ceased to impress me. Everywhere I looked was a special view or a special rock formation, or the sweep of another ridge extending to another summit or a precipice that dropped into some mysteriously deep chasm. Not only were the ridges and peaks jagged above the tree line, but their size was awesome; the infinitely intricate folds and corners into which they tucked before sweeping upward produced the indescribable grandeur that was so pleasing to the eye and made the Whites so unique.

After dropping down the nose of Lion Head, the trail turned down the long draw connecting Hermit Lake shelters and the Pinkham Notch camp. I passed a number of people, mostly families with children on an afternoon outing. The children were universally excited about being in the great outdoors and their exuberance could be heard long before they were seen.

I arrived at the camp at 4:30 p. m. A check with the reservations desk disclosed that my plans to stay at the Carter Notch hut would have to be altered; the hut was booked full. What lousy luck, I thought. I didn't have much choice but to try to talk the Croo into letting me stay there over night — even on the floor, if necessary. Then I thought I might be able to work in the kitchen as Louis and Joe had done. Perhaps they might even have a no-show or a cancellation. I decided to stay on the Trail and take a break at Gorham, New Hampshire, before launching across the Androscoggin River and heading for Maine.

I shared a room with three other men, two friends from Philadelphia and one lone hiker from Manchester, Massachusetts. All were planning on leaving the Whites the next day to return home. Unfortunately two rooms down the hall was a family with two rooms directly across the hall from one another. The children were totally out of control, yelling back and forth across the hall, playing out their sibling rivalries as if the fate of the world rested on the outcome. The parents appeared oblivious to their children's behavior. Although I heard occasional words of admonishment from them, there was no discernable reaction on the part of the children except to raise the decibel level in a show of defiance.

The rooms were divided by flimsy wooden partitions for walls and the sound reverberating down the hallway entered the rooms with little loss in volume. Finally the family left to watch a short film presentation put on by the AMC — and I fell asleep. But they returned at 10:30 with increased irritability and increased noise, which woke me. The parents' pleas had no effect. Finally I got up at 11:00 p. m. to go to the bathroom; and on returning, I yelled at them to shut up." I was successful only in that they were a little less loud than before. I was angry now and did not sleep at all well.

The next morning I awoke, tired and irritable. As soon as I shouldered my pack, I knew I was not going to hike that day. If I had been able to sleep properly the previous night, I could have continued. But with the steep climbs and the physical exertion added to the lack of sleep, I had reached my physical limit. I went to the reservations desk, and to my dismay, learned the camp was booked full. The way my luck was going, I'd probably have been booked next door to the out-of-control kids. I also checked again on getting into Carter Notch the following night and learned it was booked full for that night too.

The gentleman from Manchester gave me a ride into Gorham. I rented a room at the Town and Country Motel on the outskirts of town, just up the road from where the Trail crossed. It was early when I checked in; I headed into town to shop and wash my clothes. I was even able to order a prescription refill with enough medicine to take me through the rest of the hike. (The woman could not dispense medicine without a prescription, and since it would take a day to get that authorization, I was told to come back on Monday.)

Back at the motel, I reviewed the "Trail Data Book" and trail guides for Maine and planned in detail what I wanted to accomplish each day for the rest of the hike. The maps of Maine were representations of three dimensional terrain map models that had been given certain lighting effects, then photographed. The idea was good, but the technique needed improvement.

The problem was that excess light or shadow covered some

of the detail of the terrain representation, which made the maps difficult to read. Also, the fact that the maps were monochromatic further complicated reading. An additional feature, the exaggerated slope representation of the Trail profile added an element of intimidation to those not skilled in reading maps from contour lines alone. Even I had a problem.

When I first looked at the profiles, I thought, Holy cow, they got to be kidding! Then I read the statement: "Slopes are exaggerated for clarity." I breathed a sigh of relief, but then started wondering what the mountains really looked like. I was preparing for the worst based on conversations I had with hikers who had recently come through Maine.

According to the schedule I worked out, I figured to climb to the summit of Katahdin on September 25th. That was a little later than I wanted; I would be so far north and winter starts early at that latitude. But I hoped the weather Gods would prove kindly.

I talked to Cathy and arranged for her to send food drops to the Post Offices at Rangeley, Stratton, Caratunk and Monson. The idea was that the food would be ultra-light packs of freeze-dried food that would reduce my pack weight. She also told me she planned to come to Monson to do the last hundred-mile wilderness stretch with me. That was good news.

Now is the time to gather my guts together, I told myself, and finish this rascal. I planned to take three days to make the stretch from Pinkham Notch to Gorham and made a reservation for three days hence. I figured I'd make Carter Notch the first night, Imp shelter the second night and return to the motel in Gorham for the third.

CHAPTER 16

Happy the man who can endure the highest and lowest fortune. He who has endured such vicissitudes with equanimity has deprived misfortune of its power.

— Seneca

Pinkham Notch, NH to Full Goose Shelter

After crossing the road, the Trail out of Pinkham Notch wandered by Lost Pond, meandered lazily along its shoreline and lulled me into thinking the hike was going to be a piece of cake — until I crossed some feeder streams and suddenly turned left to begin one of the steepest climbs I had yet made on the Trail. It went up almost vertically for about 1,500 feet. The hiker was required to hold on with both hands while climbing up steeply constructed stone steps and wooden ladders. It took almost two hours to reach the ridge top, which was only one mile from the road.

Another two hours passed. I staggered and stumbled my way along Wildcat Ridge, climbing and dropping off testy rock ledges and jump-ups on a path that seemed to be comprised solely of roots and rocks. It was lined with bushes and small trees whose only purpose seemed to be to tug at my clothes and pack.

My ill humor increased proportionally to the difficulty and the duration of the exertion. However, as in all such circumstances, an event occurs that lightens the load and brings a smile to one's face. In this case a group of three grouse appeared miraculously on the Trail in front of me. These were the strangest behaving birds I had yet seen. They sauntered down the path way before me like they were out on a Sunday stroll and even when I approached to within a foot or two, they refused to pick up speed or to yield the right of way in any fashion. I walked at their saunter for about 20 yards and then seeing they were not about to voluntarily yield, took matters into my own hands and prodded one with my hiking stick to push it sideward. The bird then sidled grudgingly and barely off the path to let me pass. I repeated the process with the remaining grouse. When I had passed the last one I looked around and found that they had reassembled back on the path and were continuing as nonchalantly as before.

My name was not on the reservation list at Carter Notch hut and my query about working for the night's stay was met with evasiveness, and the comment that a number of thru-hikers had stayed recently and there was not a lot of work to do. I was informed that sometimes guests didn't show and I might get a slot from a cancellation; the resupply Croo would arrive shortly and they would have an updated reservations list.

About an hour later, the two-person resupply Croo arrived carrying huge pack-boards on which had been tied boxes containing supplies. The tall young man and shorter, heavier looking young woman had hiked up from the parking lot via the 19 Mile Brook Trail which was a lot easier than trying to handle the AT up Wildcat Ridge. I wandered inside behind them and waited conspicuously, while they sorted out the supplies and updated the reservations list. No one wanted to volunteer any information; I forced the issue. I was informed that all the bunks had been reserved, but I could wait, if I wanted, in case of no-shows. It was only 4:00 p. m. and I decided to wait.

A tall slender young woman with long straight black hair flowing over her shoulders came into the hut and registered for one of the bunks. One of the Croo asked if she belonged to the AMC. (AMC members got a four-dollar break on the fees.) "Not any more," she replied with a hint of regret in her voice. After the arrangements were made, the woman sat directly across the table from me and began a conversation with a little girl who was looking for anything to amuse herself.

"Were you a member of the AMC for a long time," I asked, trying to break the ice.

"Eight years," she shot back.

"Why did you leave?"

Her response was so emotional I didn't understand her.

"Sorry," I said. "What did you say?"

She repeated herself, still talking rapidly, as if it was so painful she wanted to get it out as quickly as possible.

I still didn't understand. "It's okay," I told her, "if you don't want to talk about it, but I was interested to hear you say you no longer belonged to the AMC," I was trying to reassure her.

"I resigned over his firing my best friend."

"Who's he?"

"Tom Dean, the executive director of the AMC."

"Isn't he the guy with all the records for carrying stuff up to the hut that I saw at Greenleaf?"

"You mean — Mega Hut Man?" She smiled. "I worked for the AMC and got too close to the organization. I was just too close — and that's not good."

"Did you work full time?"

"Yes, I was a full time paid employee."

"Seems to be a big operation," I observed. "How many folks work for the AMC?"

"We had 57 full-time employees, and during the summer peak season, we could have as many as 300 additional people signed up."

"They have any clique problems in the AMC? Most clubs have them."

"There's an 'in group'," she replied. "It's been taken over by the former hut workers. There's a lot more to the AMC than just the huts, but the hut people have taken control and they run the show. The huts get all the money and recognition and everything else gets what's left over."

"How did the club get started?"

"It started in 1876 as the 'White Mountain Club' which was basically a hiking club. But another club already had that name and so it changed to the "Appalachian Mountain Club." She continued on, explaining that the AMC became quite powerful politically and was instrumental in getting the U.S. Forest Service organized at the national level. A very special relationship developed between the Forest Service and the AMC. It was so close, that the AMC was hired under a contract with the Forest

Service to provide trail maintenance in selected areas. That lasted until the legal bureaucracy caught up with the organizations on the minimum wage issue. To observe the minimum wage law became too costly for the Club and a new arrangement was worked out whereby the club and The Forest Service shared trail maintenance responsibilities.

"What else does the AMC do?" I asked.

"All sorts of programs. Education, trail maintenance, canoeing, nature studies. All sorts of things," she replied. "What are you doing here?" she asked turning the tables.

"I'm hiking the Appalachian Trail. I'm here trying to see if I can spend the night. The place is booked solid and I'm hoping for a no-show or a cancellation."

"Oh! I feel guilty. I probably took your spot. I apologize," she replied dolefully.

"You shouldn't apologize." I laughed. "If I can't stay here, I can go down the Trail. It's really not a great problem," I almost choked on my words.

"I know," she said seriously. "But you have more of a right to the space than I do. You're a real hiker and the huts are really for people like you. I'm just here for the night. I could get a motel room or something much more easily than you. I feel terrible."

I agreed with her logic, but it conflicted with my sense of chivalry and I tried to ease her discomfort a little. "Please don't feel guilty. I can handle it; it's really no problem."

A young man who had been hanging around outside the hut came to the door and one of the Croo asked how many were in his party. He replied there were seven, but assured the Croo member they had all agreed to leave home at the same time and would be there shortly. I had determined that they would be the last to arrive. All the other people with reservations had shown up, so I decided to go on. I asked the Croo member if he could recommend any good tent sites. "Just go down the Trail 'til you find one," was the reply. I looked over at the woman and she looked down in obvious embarrassment.

I headed down 19-Mile Brook Trail. After about a mile, I came to a very nice area with level grass tent sites and put up for the night. After supper, I lay in my sleeping bag reflecting on the day's events and the Trail over Wildcat Ridge. It was, I considered, the toughest hiking I had done on any portion of the Trail so far, and if it was to be like that through Maine, I was in for a serious challenge.

An unconscious comparison of my condition with the condition of those who had hiked Wildcat Mountain at the hut indicated that I was in better physical shape than most, including younger men. Several of them appeared to be at the point of exhaustion. That knowledge buoyed my spirits and I slept a deep sleep, undisturbed by people coming and going or children quarreling.

The hike up to Carter Dome was not nearly as tough as the climb up Wildcat Ridge and I made good steady progress. The weather was again ideal and the views from Mount Hight compared with those of Wildcat Ridge the previous day.

It was shortly before noon when I reached the trail to the Imp campsite where I had planned to spend the night; I decided to push on. After a series of climbs and descents along the ridgeline and the Carter Mountains, I reached the Rattle River shelter where I again thought about spending the night. A check of the "Trail Guide" showed that it was only a mile and a half to the road into Gorham and the motel. I moved on. Fortunately the motel had a room; I took it and canceled the reservation I had made for the following night.

I called Cathy to tell her about my progress. She said I now was down to 300 miles. I hadn't thought about that; I was only focused on getting through the mountains in Maine. That was really good news. She also mentioned that I sounded much better, much more positive — now that I had banished the van from my life.

I checked out of the motel the next morning and headed into town. I intended to stop at the Post Office to drop off some mail and at the pharmacy to pick up my medication, then take the Mahoosuc Trail up to Mt. Hayes. (It's western terminus was only half a mile up the road from the pharmacy.)

At the Post Office I met another thru-hiker, Kevin Pendleton from Ohio; he went by the Trail name of "Buckeye." He was a tall, strong, free-spirited young man, who seemed to be having the time of his life, although he appeared a bit worse for the wear right then. His skimpy shorts, a ragged T-shirt, worn hiking boots with holes and a filthy pack attested to the physical challenges he had experienced. Not only that, but he smelled as bad as he looked.

Buckeye had emptied his parcel on the floor of the Post Office lobby and was sorting out the contents and shaking his head with each can he extracted. When he was finished he pushed away the empty box and brown wrapping paper. "Jeez, I told her not to send all this heavy stuff," he said, pointing to pile of cans. "She just doesn't listen. Now I got to carry all this stuff. I'll need a damn pack horse."

During our conversation, he mentioned that he had gotten lost while coming down from the Madison hut. The hut leader would not let him spend the night and a woman had sent him down the wrong trail to the tent sites. He ended up sleeping on the levelest piece of ground he could find in the dark and when morning came he continued down the mountain until coming to some railroad tracks which he followed into Gorham.

The trail crossed the Androscoggin River on a wooden footbridge, constructed directly beneath railroad bridge. It was interesting, since the footbridge hung from the lower railroad trusses. I had to remove my pack to get on and get off the bridge; the walkway passed between two steel support beams for the railroad bridge and the space was too restricted to get through with my pack on my back. I wondered what it would be like if a train came over the trestle while I was beneath it. Fortunately I was spared that experience.

After a short road walk, the Trail crossed a narrow branch of the river, passed between two small hydro-electric plants with dirty low windows before following the retaining dam and another short road walk, then headed for Mount Hayes. The weather had turned hot and the air humid — I sweated profusely as I climbed. I reached the summit by mid-afternoon accompanied by thunderclaps coming from somewhere to the west over the Whites. I decided to call it quits around 5:00 p.m. and set up camp in the Trident Col campsite.

I had not seen any hikers on the Trail until Izak Matlin, "Zakman," a south bounder, came by. We talked about our respective recent experiences with the Trail to give each other hints of what was to come. Zakman felt that the Mahoosuc Range was tough, but after that it got easier. That was really good news to me. A short time later we were joined by two other south bounders, Wayne Price, "Wandering River Guide" from Ocobee, Tennessee, and Jason Anthony, "Cloud Finder" from Cape Cod, Massachusetts. They had met Granma, Carleton and G-Man at Full Goose shelter and Smokin' Joe at Gentian Pond shelter, but when asked, said they hadn't seen any short wiry Georgians by the name of Louis Lanier.

I cooked up some of the freeze dried food Cathy had sent and supplemented it with more noodles to increase the carbo load. It wasn't bad, but I liked my homemade "casserole" better.

During our conversation, Zakman mentioned he had not been feeling well; he was having intestinal problems and suspected he may have contracted a case of giardia. I asked if he knew where he might have gotten the bug and he said he couldn't be sure, but that it might have been from the water at Full Goose shelter. Zakman must have really been feeling bad; he had already left for Gorham to see a doctor by the time I got up in the morning.

Page Pond was a beautiful, small, north woods lake with several patches of aquatic vegetation in which I could visualize moose feeding in the mist of the early summer morning.

I then passed Dream Lake and Moss Lake following some very jagged, rocky evergreen shoreline, then entered a magnificent old forest with some unusual rock formations. The air was fresh and crisp with the cleansing scent of spruce. The pathway was spongy underfoot, filled with roots and small rocks, and the forest floor was covered with large patches of green, almost frothy moss.

It was early afternoon when I reached Gentian Pond and the shelter. No one was around and I didn't expect to have company. I stripped and went for a swim. I expected a cold reception when entering the water but was pleasantly surprised. A beaver dam, partly responsible for the pond had trapped some still water and it was warm and luxurious. Farther out toward the center of the pond, though, it became much colder. I went back to the beaver dam.

After swimming I climbed back to the shelter to eat lunch and admire the view. The shelter built on the mountainside a very short distance from the pond, sits on the edge of a steep drop-off with a breathtaking view to the south and east over Austin Mill Brook and the Androscoggin River Valley. The day was sunny and very clear and the view almost limitless, the kind of day and view when the beauty suspends one's sense of time.

The shelter itself was a masterpiece as far as shelters go. It was made of logs; in front, the builders had constructed two narrow, two or three foot floor to roof walls on either side of the opening which helped greatly in protecting the occupants from the weather, but which also left sufficient space for those wishing to enjoy the views.

While I was eating, a young AMC trail worker came by to do some sign repair. He told me the stretch of Trail between Carlo Col shelter and Speck Pond shelter was "doable, but tough." I had been considering continuing on to Carlo Col shelter that afternoon and then going from Carlo Col to Speck Pond campsite. That would have bypassed Full Goose shelter, but it would have been a difficult nine-mile stretch. I wanted to keep moving, but suspected I needed to take it slow through here. As things turned out, it was a good decision.

I opted to stay put for the night, planning to head for Full Goose in the morning and then tackle Mahoosuc Notch and the climb up Mahoosuc Arm the following day. The trail worker left shortly, and I responded to the silence and the wind by going to sleep for an hour and a half. I would have slept longer, but some hikers stumbling down the Trail awakened me.

Bob Guba, Charlie Smith and Bill McClure introduced themselves on a more formal basis. They had passed me going up Wildcat Ridge and I had seen them at the Carter Notch overlook and later at the hut. Bill, was a postal worker from Acton, Massachusetts. Bob, also from Acton and Charlie from Waltham, Massachusetts, were electrical engineers working on integrated microwave circuits for Raytheon.

Bob and Bill were experienced hikers, but Charlie was on his first ever hike. What an introduction!! I thought. Charlie was feeling the strain. He had injured his knee and you could tell it was painful. But he was "hangin' in there" on sheer determination. I really felt sorry for him; they were coming to, without question, the toughest part of the whole AT through Mahoosuc Notch and Mahoosuc Arm. And after that, they were planning to hike another 30 some odd miles over very difficult terrain to Andover, Maine before heading back to civilization.

I never ceased to be amazed at the diverse talents and backgrounds of people I met on the Trail. It was like running into a cross section of America. I had met people from all professions and all walks of life — from college professors to blue collar workers to corporate executives, to clergy, to military men. There were grandmothers and grandfathers, wives and husbands, physicians and lawyers, bums and college kids, and businessmen and engineers. And that didn't count the foreigners I had met or those whose backgrounds I didn't know.

Later we were joined by Will McLaughlin from Wilmington Delaware, who was planning to hike to Katahdin, albeit at a very slow pace, as he described it. Buckeye also arrived and told me that Louis Lanier was a couple of days behind us. Louis had become ill and dropped off the Trail in Gorham to recuperate but was now back on and ready for the final push.

We all talked about our Trail experiences coming through the Whites and whatever else came to mind. Bob Guba and Bill McClure recounted passing three naked young women beside the Trail on Wocket Ledges about three miles back. The women were sunbathing and made no effort to cover up when the men came by. I guessed I had come through that area a little too early. Quite a bit of discussion ensued about Charlie dropping off the Trail and conjecture about where he could come off, if necessary. Charlie, a bachelor, must have been really hurting; he never mentioned anything about the scenery around Wocket Ledges.

Despite the number of people at the shelter, I slept very well, and after an early start easily crossed over several approach knobs before reaching the summit of Mount Success. It was a tough climb to the summit, but I made slow and steady progress. About halfway up, Buckeye, loping like a moose on his strong young legs, passed me with no discernible effort. The summit offered an array of marvelous views of a sea of mountains extending to the horizon in every direction. After Mount Success, the Trail crossed a series of smaller peaks before dropping into a small wooded canyon where a sign proclaimed the border between New Hampshire and Maine.

Bob, Charlie and Bill were taking a break there when I arrived and Bob took my picture beside the sign. Normally I would have been excited over entering the last state on my journey, but the Trail had been tough, and I was subdued. Also Mahoosuc Notch and Mahoosuc Arm were in the back of my mind. I wondered if Granma had gone through her traditional balloon breaking border celebration, and it was my guess she had. Whatever, I now was 279 miles from the top of Katahdin.

I arrived at Full Goose shelter at 5:00 p. m. after a fast one-mile walk with Bob Guba on my heels. I asked if he wanted to go by me and he said, "No," that he was comfortable with the pace I was setting. I had passed Charlie and Bill earlier. Bill had stopped to take a smoke break. Charlie had stopped to rest his knee and wait for Bill. It was almost an hour before Bill and Charlie appeared. In fact, they had fallen so far behind that Bob became concerned and had gone back to look for them. He had not gone very far before they appeared.

I had used all my water early in the day and could find none along the way. I even ate lunch without water. Needless to say, I was very thirsty when I arrived and headed straight for the spring. The AMC was conducting an intermediate level backpacking class and about 20 people were congregated around the spring when I arrived. Fortunately they all had tents; there would be space in the shelter.

After some of them cleared away, I drank three cups of water right off. During a conversation with the woman from the AMC leading the class I learned that some people had become sick from drinking water at the shelter. She said she herself had contracted giardia. It had been established that giardia could be transmitted through beaver, moose, dog and human feces. Evidently they had just discovered the link between dogs and the disease. That made me queasy right away realizing I had drunk water that was possibly contaminated. Then I thought about what Zakman had said about the water there. Needless to say, I was an "apprehensive camper" at that moment.

Buckeye was at the shelter when I arrived which surprised me; when he had passed me earlier he said he was planning to go to Grafton Notch. I fell asleep early and snored. To shut me up, Buckeye wakened me, and I had trouble going back to sleep. The result: I was less than refreshed when I arose in the morning.

CHAPTER 17

The world's battlefields have been in the heart chiefly; more heroism has been displayed in the household and the closet, than on the most memorable battlefields of history.
— Henry Ward Beecher

Full Goose Shelter to Andover, ME

The Trail from Full Goose climbed about 500 feet to Fulling Mill Mountain before dropping down to infamous Mahoosuc Notch. The initial stretch of Trail into the notch was deceiving; it followed a peacefully gurgling stream through a quiet spruce forest with a soft easy walking needle floor. Then it climbed slightly to cross a rock ledge and without warning plunged into a narrow, deep canyon filled with the most ferocious tangle of rocks I had ever seen. Rocks as big as houses and railroad cars lay in heaps in eternally grotesque postures like the casualties of some great battle between the gods. Along one side of the canyon, the gurgling stream was transformed into a tortured waterway crashing down a boulder-strewn course, as if trying to fight its way through its agony. And on the other side, the sheer rock walls rose hundreds of feet above the desolation. The silence was as awesome as the scene. Only the brook could be heard, and it soon disappeared, probably underground. Otherwise no sound penetrated the deathly stillness.

In what seemed a fitting caption to the scene was a dead moose lying in the stream. It had fallen from the ledges above the canyon, broken its legs and could not get out. It struggled in vain to extricate itself from the stream until a Ranger administered the final solution, leaving it as a temporary reminder of the permanence of danger to the unwary in nature.

The Trail went right down the middle of the canyon, little white blazes indicating the general route one was to follow — if possible. Many moss and fungus covered boulders were still wet from the morning dew and slippery enough that footing was hazardous at best. At one point the blazes and painted arrows indicated where the Trail went through a narrow, very short tunnel formed by two monoliths leaning against one another. The aperture was so narrow and small that I had to remove my pack, crawl through and haul my pack after me. At another place the drop off was so long that I had to lower my pack down by rope, then lay on my belly atop the rock to drop down to the floor.

I wondered how Granma with her short legs made it through there. And then I thought of Edna Williams and her broken hip, wondering how she could possibly have come through this gauntlet.

In many places the Trail footing followed narrow ledges below over-hanging boulders and if not careful in passing through, the top of one's pack might bump the overhanging boulder, causing a loss of balance and quick trip off the ledge. In some places that would have been an inconvenience but in others it could have made for disaster.

The entire canyon was only a mile long, but it took me a full two hours to make it through. Granted — I was being extra careful; still the going was as tough as I had expected. Charlie, Bill and Bob passed me but never got very far ahead. I'd see them ahead of me occasionally, stopped, trying to figure out how to approach the challenge of the moment. I would soon reach that point and learn first hand why they had stopped.

As I was negotiating one particularly dicey little ledge and boulder, I thought about Cathy and the experience going over the Knife Edge. That had been tough enough, but this was several times more demanding and I wondered how she would handle it. I had no doubt, though, that handle it she would.

About a quarter mile into the Notch on the north side, a sheer rock cliff rose about 100 feet above the canyon floor. Buckeye, minus his pack, was hanging onto the face of the rocks about 30 feet up, apparently stymied in his attempt to do a technical climb. He then started back down, and I watched as he tested hand and foot holds. Waiting until he had safely reached the ground, I told him that I thought that what he was doing was stupid.

"Suppose you fall and hurt yourself, man?" I asked smartly. "Who's gonna get you outta here?" He looked at me sheepishly. "Somebody's gonna have to haul your ass outta here and that's going to screw up someone's hike. If you want to do that crap, climb some goddamn cliff, wait 'til you get where it won't affect other people if you bust your butt."

Basically I was unloading on him; I was still angry with him for waking me the night before. Nevertheless, what I said had evidently sunk in; Bob Guba told me later that Buckeye had told him that I had "chewed his ass."

The canyon ended in an open pine forest with soft level ground and an open fire pit. I rested for about 20 minutes, trying to collect my wits and savoring my victory before challenging Mahoosuc Arm. After the interlude, the Trail became steep again, climbing over many boulders that could be described as a slightly milder version of a vertical Mahoosuc Notch. The main feature, however, was the really massive, steep stone slab that looked like a cliff that had been tilted slighted on its side. I thought the climb would never end.

Just when I reached the point where I could see some clear sky ahead and the Trail started to become reasonable, off it would go climbing again as steeply as before with even tougher little ledges thrown in like punishment for my expectations of more lenient conditions. Near the top I was overtaken by Craig Upshaw, "The Lone Angler" whose entries I had remembered from several Trail journals. He mentioned that a friend of his had told him about seeing my picture in one of the Boston newspapers; I think it may have been the "Globe." (It was the photo that Stephen Helber had taken at Bear's Den Rocks in Virginia.)

Craig Upshaw and Buckeye were deep in conversation when I arrived at the Speck Pond shelter. Bob, Bill and Charlie were likewise occupied discussing whether to stay in the shelter or to tent camp on one of the platforms. The forecast was for clear weather that made it easy for me to decide where to spend the night. I was tired when I had started in the morning and was now exhausted. I didn't need anyone disturbing my sleep as could quite possibly happen in the shelter.

The tent platforms were constructed much like the deck of a house in the woods, not as high and without the railings, but the floor was the same. Nails around the perimeter of the platforms provided anchors to which tent ropes could be tied, eliminating the need for tent pegs. While I was cooking supper, Sam Thornstrom, the AMC caretaker, came by to collect the three-dollar camping fee.

"You thru-hiking?" he asked.

"Yeah, I'm thru-hiking. How'd you guess?" I laughed.

"You can always tell a thru-hiker. There's something about them. I can't describe it, but there's something that says 'I'm a thru-hiker'."

"How'd you get this job? Pretty cushy I'd say."

"I've worked for the AMC for the past three summers. Last year I worked the Naumann tent sites." I must have looked at him strangely, because he stopped. "You know, the tent sites by Mizpah hut?"

I nodded my head.

"I like it here. I'm my own boss and do what I want so long as I keep up with the things I'm required to do. The composting isn't a lot of fun, but it's not that bad either."

"How does the composting work?" I asked.

"You mix sewage with tree bark and let it dry out," he replied. "We use pine bark. It absorbs the moisture from the sewage and bacterial action works on the waste; in the process generates very high heat — up to 60 and 80 degrees Celsius. We use the same bark over and over, until we can't use it any more. Once the process is complete in one bin, I just use it to replace the bin in the toilet — and the process starts over again."

Interesting, I thought, as he moved on. I turned my attention to Speck Pond, an idyllic little lake nestled in the embrace of spruce covered hills with water as cold as crystal is clear. After eating, I sat on the shore, breathing in the solitude and the silence it suggested, until three young men entered the water whooping and shrieking as the cold waters enveloped their warm bodies.

On the way back to my tent, I met another thru-hiker who had just arrived. Ken Patrick, the "Homeless Hiker" from Roanoke, Virginia, was a Methodist minister who had received a four-month sabbatical from his Bishop to hike the Trail. I wondered why the Bishop would just give him time off to wander the Trail. It seemed there had to be some purpose behind the sabbatical and there was. His Trail name was the first clue. And to confirm it, Ken told me he was hiking to raise money for the homeless, that for every mile he walked, he received pledges of donations.

He said he had been told at the ATC Headquarters in Harpers Ferry that 750 people had registered to do a thru-hike beginning at Springer Mountain. The smart money was betting on about 80 to finish the whole thing. I doubted that so many would finish and told him that my guess was 50. He also questioned the 80 figure, but less skeptically than I.

The climb up Old Speck Mountain the next morning was an adventure in itself. Clouds covered the mountain and a very strong wind blew in gusts that probably reached 50 miles per hour. Below the tree line, the forest offered some protection, but above the tree line — out on the open ridge — the wind blew with such velocity that gusts repeatedly knocked me off balance. At certain places between the rocks, I was able to grip some of the taller branches of krummholz for support, which helped maintain my balance. Because of the mist and a slight rain, I initially wore the pack cover over my pack. As I neared the summit, the wind blew with such force that it tore the cover completely off my pack sending it sailing over my head. Fortunately, it wrapped itself around my hiking stick and I was able to retrieve it before it became untangled and blew off the mountain.

Just below the summit, the Trail cleared the cloud line and climbed into a sun-filled blue sky. The view back across the valley was spectacular; the cloud layer just below me filled all the folds in the ridges and stretched across to another peak. It looked almost like one could step off and walk straight over to the next ridge. Occasionally a piece of cloud torn from the layer below would sweep by, the wind playing with it, twirling or spinning it, holding it momentarily motionless, then sweeping it shrieking up the ridge again.

Before I had left the tree line, I encountered a flock of ruffed grouse that sauntered down the Trail ahead of me. Not one flew off. They all stayed on the Trail, until I came too close, then just ducked into the nearest bushes. One stayed on the Trail for about 50 yards, maintaining a comfortable distance between us, until we neared the tree line; then it too slipped into a thick stand of spruce.

I wondered if the wind had anything to do with their reluctance to fly. But then I remembered some other grouse in New Hampshire who seemed to forget they had wings. I decided that the grouse in the north were very unlike their relatives to the south who flew off in great bursts whenever anyone came within a certain range.

The climb up Bald Pate began fairly easily, then as so often was the case, turned off into a reasonably graded old logging road and headed straight up a dry creek bed that had it been filled with water would have been a water fall. An almost vertical climb over several hundred feet put me on the summit of West Bald Pate. After that, the Trail dropped down about a 100 feet into a small col, then began a more gradual ascent to East Bald Pate.

The Trail out of the col crossed a couple of nasty little ledges, but once it cleared them, followed a magnificent stone slab for several hundred yards up to the summit of East Bald Pate. The Trail was marked by the usual white blazes painted on rocks initially, and then by stone cairns, a la Tuckerman Crossover.

On first view, the trail up the massive slab was intimidating, but a closer reading showed that the Trail had been angled across the rock layers, rather than going straight up — and that was reassuring. The higher I climbed the better the scenery and the warming sun at three in the afternoon was delightful. The summit was fully 500 yards across; from there it dropped rather precipitously to little Bald Pate and then seemed to go straight down.

I arrived at the Frye Notch shelter at about 5:00 p. m., expecting to find other hikers in residence and was surprised to see it empty. By now, I had become conditioned to expect company in the shelters and was delighted at the prospect of having the place to myself for the night. My delight was short lived. Bob, Bill and Charlie arrived about 30 minutes later.

I had done 10.3 miles for the day, quite an improvement over the five miles I had traveled the previous day. Of course, the Trail was also much easier. It was difficult to accept and even more difficult to explain that it had taken me seven hours to do the five miles the day before.

The next day began with a climb over the nose of Surplus Mountain, after which I meandered down its east arm before finally dropping down to Dunn Notch and a gorge with a waterfall whose beauty could only be divinely inspired. The scenery was truly breathtaking. The path crossed the stream right above the ledge where the water began a free fall of what seemed like a 100 feet into a spectacular rock-framed gorge. The view created one of those rare moments when we become so entranced with the beauty that it becomes its own significance to the exclusion of all other facets of consciousness.

After crossing the stream, the Trail led steeply up to the crest of the ridge, then angled down the side of it and contoured above the precipices that formed the gorge. So wild, so primordial, so mesmerizing was the scene that — for me — time ceased to exist. The roar of water and the infinitely varied projections of rock and the turbulence created captured my undivided attention. I don't know if I stayed ten minutes or 30 minutes or an hour or longer. I knew only that it took a conscious effort to continue.

The Trail crossed B-Hill Road about eight miles northwest of the village of Andover where I thought I had a mail drop. I reached the junction sometime after ten and headed down the road, hoping to get a hitch into town before the Post Office closed. It was a Saturday and I was concerned about having to spend the weekend hanging around waiting for it to open on Monday.

I walked for an hour and a half, during which time I was passed by a total of five cars, before a young man with long hair and a massive beard, driving a dark green Chevy pickup loaded me in the back. I had just before crossed the town line as indicated by a road side sign and expected a short hitch. I learned that what the towns in Maine lacked in population, they more than made up for in territory. It was at least another five miles to the outskirts of the town proper.

A large, beautiful white church with a massive square tower and the town square with a gazebo where teenagers gathered seemed like an island of civilization in a frontier town. Actually Andover seemed like a civilization in progress. Certainly, the dirt parking areas in front of the general stores and Addie's Cafe and the lack of curbs or sidewalks refreshingly disabused the mind of any notions of civic orderliness.

The old residential area was different altogether. There the houses surrounded by lawns bordered by flowers and bushes looked like the second stage in the civilization of Andover. There were still few sidewalks or curbs to represent the third stage, but I suspected that, in time, they also would come. I certainly preferred the pace of evolution as contrasted to the instant construction resulting from a developer's or a county planning commission's concept of community. The result was a rustic atmosphere that not only was pleasing to the eye but also was reflected by the people. I liked Andover the minute I got off the truck.

There was no mail waiting at the Post Office. Either I had misunderstood Cathy or Cathy had misunderstood me. I gathered up my gear and headed for the home of Mrs. Eva Bodwell who, "The Philosopher's Guide" indicated, often put hikers up for the night. I marched up to the door and rapped loudly. No response. I tried again with the same result. After the third time, the next door neighbor emerged from beneath the hood of his car to tell me that "Eva" had left, "probably gone for a walk." He said she went walking at that time, "most every day," that she would be gone "'bout twenty minutes." He then disappeared beneath the hood again. I leaned my pack and hiking stick against the wall beside the front door and went back to the restaurant I had passed on the way to the Post Office.

On this small trek, I met an elderly lady walking towards me and asked if she might be Ms. Bodwell.

"Heavens, no!" she replied. "Eva's 82 and needs a cane." This woman appeared not to be a day older than 81 and had the use of only one eye. But she wasn't carrying a cane.

Addie's Cafe was a spare, simple, one-room establishment with several small, square tables and a long lunch-counter behind, which lay the grill, oven and the other kitchen paraphernalia on which Addie and her assistants worked their magic. I sat at the counter and ordered a hamburger special and then asked if they had a restroom where I could clean up.

"Nope," said Addie. "Just come around here and wash." She nodded, pointing toward the dishwashing sink behind the counter.

The conversation ebbed when I entered, but then quickly resumed. Everyone knew and was friends with everyone else, especially Addie. The restaurant was a gossip market as well as a diner where people came and went, picking up or dropping bits of gossip along with comments about the weather, jobs and lumbering — and everything else that came to mind.

Addie set a plate with two large hamburgers and a huge heap of french fries in front of me along with a salad, two slices of white bread and a large glass of iced tea. One couple seated next to me began a conversation as I started to eat. In between mouthfuls I talked about my adventure and some Trail experiences and how tough the Trail was, especially in Maine. They asked what I ate on the Trail and how I resupplied, and I explained how that occurred and mentioned that the logistics on the Trail were sometimes difficult. I told them about Mahoosuc Notch and Speck pond and Gentian Pond and the White Mountains and that induced Addie to show them an issue of "National Geographic" magazine which contained a very well done article on the AT. They began reading the article, and I was then able to finish my meal. Addie was only slightly surprised when I ordered another "hamburger special." I was sure similar requests had come from hikers before me.

The second two hamburgers arrived in what seemed like a lot shorter time than the first. I finished them as quickly as the first ones and than topped off the feast with a big helping of blueberry pie ala mode. The bill came to a whopping $6.25.

Mrs. Bodwell was sitting on the front porch of her home awaiting my arrival when I returned. I could see her as I walked up the street and noted that she never took her eyes off me. She said she figured I was a hiker from the way I walked.

She showed me to my room on the second floor, climbing the stairs with exceptional strength and agility for an 82 year old. I asked if there was a laundromat in town, and she replied there wasn't, but for a dollar I could use her washing machine. The dollar included the soap. The machine did the wash in short order and in the process shredded my hat more efficiently that any machine built for that purpose could have done. I went back to town and bought another hat, a dark-brown, crushable, felt model from the general store next to Addie's Cafe. When I returned Mrs. Bodwell was waiting and proudly produced a spanking clean cotton hat she had rescued from a previous guest and offered it to me. It was a light tan color and very similar in design to the one I had shredded; it fit even better than the one I had just purchased. I accepted her offer.

There ensued a very interesting conversation; I learned much about Eva Bodwell and life in rural Maine after the turn of the century. Eva was born in 1906 and raised on a farm about a mile outside of Andover. She had lived there her whole life. She talked about having to walk a mile and a half to school.

"They used to roll the snow back then," she reminisced. "Didn't have plows. Didn't have cars," she added emphatically. "They had these great big log rollers. They were pulled by horses and packed the snow down and that's how we got around. And we walked to school," she recounted, her eyes twinkling with the memories. "Now a bus picks 'em up a block from school," she snorted.

In 1906, Andover must really have been a frontier town, I thought. "You must get downright cold here in the wintertime?" It was a statement, but also a question.

"You get used to it," she replied laconically.

"Does it get real cold early in the fall?" I pressed, perhaps too eagerly.

"Some years we have some frost every month of the year. Been pretty good so far this year, though. Hope it holds. All the tomatoes aren't ripe yet," she said. "It'll turn nippy by the end of next month — September."

I suspected from the gleam in her eye that she was putting on a little for my benefit.

The next morning was Sunday, and Andover was closed down except for the liquor store that also had a sandwich counter; and I went there for breakfast. The only hot food was the coffee. Other than that, the place offered only snack items and cake and doughnuts. I bought a small bottle of orange juice, a container of yogurt and a piece of freshly baked apple cake and sat at the counter to eat.

People came and went the entire time I was there. They were farmers, tradesmen or lumbermen, rough mannered, friendly, uncomplicated men fully at home in the north woods. They talked about pickup trucks and hunting and fishing, asking one another if anyone had seen any moose or moose tracks. They talked about doors for their cabins, and hunting camps and teased the blushing young girl behind the counter about her boyfriend.

On the way back to Mrs. Bodwell's, I stopped at the fire house where all the trucks sat gleaming red in the sunlight out front. The pride of the fleet was the hook and ladder truck — it was a good 20 feet longer than any of the other trucks. It had the rear wheel driver's seat hanging off the back and in front, in the open cab behind the steering wheel, sat a large Dalmatian dog. It was a perfect setting for a Norman Rockwell painting and I didn't even have my camera along.

The general store by the baseball field was open; I bought a pint of ice cream. While I was eating, Craig Upshaw — complete with pack on his back — rode into town on the back of a motor-cycle. He went directly into the general store. I hurried over to see him and ran straight into Bob Guba, Bill McClure and Charlie Smith coming out. They had completed their hike. With them was Ken Patrick, the "Homeless Hiker," who seemed to be the worse for wear.

Bob told me that Louis Lanier was totally recovered and had passed them under full steam headed for Katahdin. While I was talking, Craig Upshaw slipped out of the store, got back on the motorcycle and headed off before I could get to talk with him.

When I mentioned that I was staying at Eva Bodwell's home, Ken's ears perked up. He told me he was feeling poorly and needed a place to stay, until he could recover. It was still early in the afternoon, but I wanted to make some entries in my Trail journal and get my gear ready for the next day, so I said goodbye to everyone and with Ken in tow headed for Mrs. Bodwell's.

Ken went to bed almost immediately upon arrival about 2:00 p. m. When I was putting the finishing touches to my journal notes at 8:00 p. m. I noticed that he was still sound asleep.

Ken struggled to accompany me to Addie's for breakfast. He was still battling whatever bug was after him, suffering from chills, a cold sweat and stomach nausea; he had decided to stay off the Trail for another day. His wife was vacationing in Maine and he planned to have her come pick him up and take him to a doctor.

"Who've you seen on the Trail?" I asked.

He started naming off people he had met or passed on the

Trail, adding that he wondered why many of them were on the Trail at all.

He talked about how much of a contest the hike had become for many thru-hikers and how they raced from shelter to shelter. One specific example, he pointed out, were the two men who decided to hike through the state of Maryland without stopping. They did it, but had to hike the ridges when rain flooded the canal by Harpers Ferry. He said it took them five days to recover from their feat.

I decided to return to the Trail crossing at East B Hill Road and slack pack to South Arm Road, then return to Andover for the night. I would then continue on from South Arm Road the following morning. I informed Eva of my plans, telling her to keep a bed open for me.

CHAPTER 18

We should never so entirely avoid danger as to appear ir-resolute and cowardly; but at the same time, we should avoid unnecessarily exposing ourselves to danger, than which nothing can be more foolish.

— Cicero

Andover, ME to Stratton, ME

It was a beautiful day for a slack pack stroll, but the Trail made the effort anything but a stroll even without a pack. It was a wilderness experience in every sense of the word with a crisp touch of fall air to accentuate the ruggedness of the land-scape. The tree colors were beginning to change, and in the exposed higher elevations, the deep greens were turning pale, and some yellow and red tinges were already showing in the leaves of the birches and alders. The Trail followed a series of climbs and descents through interesting land and rock formations, some with exquisite views of the mountain sides and valleys, and crossed several small, turbulent streams. I made good time without a pack and reached South Arm Road early in the afternoon. A family on the way to town from a nearby lake gave me a ride back to Andover, dropping me off in front of Addie's Cafe where I stopped for another two hamburger special.

When I left for the Trail the next morning after breakfast, it was the last I was to see of Ken. I left notes of encouragement to him in the various shelter journals during the next several weeks, but I suspect he never saw them. I later learned he had con-tracted hepatitis and was forced to come off the Trail for an extended period.

The climb up the initial portion of Blue Mountain was steep and difficult enough to be disagreeable to the point of frustration. After one particularly obnoxious little climb — where I had to pull myself up a small rock face by holding onto some over-hanging tree branches — my frustration turned into dejection. I felt like I was doing gymnastics with a pack on my back. This was supposed to be a foot path, I thought, not an acrobatic exercise course. My stomach felt queasy from the exertion and even lunch seemed tasteless. I forced down a can of oily sardines, thinking as I did, what a great way to treat a temperamental stomach.

After finally reaching the mountain top and resting, the view of the forested valley, vibrant green in sunlight with swaths of gold and red, sweeping down to Andover, acted like a mental balm. The view erased the queasiness and the irritation, not to mention my negative disposition. Then the Trail passed through an impressive stand of magnificent virgin red spruce, some of which the guide indicated, dated back to 1620. A quick calculation told me they were 367 years old. I couldn't tell which were the 367-year-olds, though. They were all stately and each looked like a candidate for Cathy's Grandfather tree. I didn't have any tobacco for an offering and wondered if the trees would look with favor on me anyway.

It was starting to get noticeably colder now. Eva Bodwell had told me the temperature the night before had reached 35 degrees. I slipped on a pair of phosphorescent red wool gloves I had bought in Andover. They not only kept my hands warm, they also provided a degree of color that I hoped would be a signal to hunters; I was not a deer or moose moving down the Trail!

Elephant Mountain shelter faced a broad marsh containing a slow-flowing stream meandering around the few small tree skeletons that remained. It was, in my mind's eye, ideal moose country. That perception was further reinforced by an entry in the shelter journal; someone had written that they had seen a mother moose and two calves directly in front of the shelter. They said they didn't even need to get out of their sleeping bags to watch them.

I didn't see any moose, but the next morning three gray jays, the first I had seen on the Trail, appeared in front of the shelter, probably looking for tidbits. They looked around for only a few minutes, then flew off. A very bold mouse had fared better. It had confiscated a piece of toast from the fire pit and dragged it to its nest, a hole under a tree root just to the right front of the shelter. It had one big problem, though. The toast was too big to fit in the hole. The mouse struggled mightily to drag it into the nest, repositioning it several times in a vain attempt to make it fit. Finally Will McGlaughlin, who had arrived after I went to sleep the night before, broke the toast in half and the two pieces then quickly disappeared beneath the tree root.

The weather during the hike was odd; a mixture of sun, clouds, wind and rain, each taking its place several times on stage for the day. I still saw no moose, but a lot of signs, droppings and hoof prints. Moose hoof prints looked like giant deer hoof prints and one could only imagine the size of the animal that left such a large reminder of its passing.

The Sabbath Day Pond shelter was sited about 30 yards from the water's edge with an expansive view over the lake. Three people had already claimed space in the shelter by the time I arrived. I was very tired and wanted no one to be waking me up — if I snored; I opted to tent camp on a large tent platform just up the hill from the shelter.

One of the three people in the shelter was Craig Upshaw. The other two were a younger couple in their late 30's or early 40's from down state Maine. Will McGlaughlin appeared a short time later and set up this tent on the other half of "my" tent platform.

For some reason, I thought about Anna, my German girl friend. Her birthday would be in another eight days, and I wanted to send a card. It would almost certainly be late; at least a day or more would pass before I could get a card and then one could figure eight day's transit time. I wondered if we would ever be able to overcome our cultural differences — she being too German, me being too American. I was thinking that she would have agreed with me about that, and that was all I remember until I heard someone walking through the woods above the platform.

I unzipped the inner tent liner and as I did the noise stopped. I waited for the noise to resume and it did. I opened up the rain fly and looked out in the direction of the noise. I saw what appeared to be the hind quarters of a bay horse. What the hell is a horse doing up here? I thought. I slid part way out of my sleeping bag and stuck my head out to get a better view. That was when I saw the eyes of a moose staring back at me.

"Will, Will!" I whispered loudly, "There's a moose." I could hear the sound of a zipper; after some commotion, Will's shaggy gray head popped out. He looked around until I pointed in the direction of the moose. "Up there," I called. Just as I did that, the moose headed back up the hill. Will didn't see the moose at first, but he finally caught sight of it moving laterally along the ridge line.

No sooner had the moose disappeared than Craig left the shelter. He had told me about how badly he wanted to see a moose, and I wanted to call and tell him that I just saw one; I restrained myself. He'd surely have other opportunities, I thought.

Craig hadn't been gone for more than five minutes when the man at the shelter came hurrying up the hill. "There's moose in the lake," he called excitedly with a distinct down east accent. "Too bad the other fella missed it," he said gleefully.

Will and I hurried down to the shelter and there they were — three moose, a female dining on lake bottom vegetation and two calves browsing the bushes about 300 yards away on the far shore. We watched the moose for about 15 minutes, then returned to our tents for breakfast.

For all the time I had spent in his company, this was the first chance to talk with Will in private. He was a very quiet, gentle man, never saying very much; he seemed content to remain in the background in any group. But he was also quite articulate with a dry sense of humor and a twinkle of mischief in his eye.

He was on a different journey than the other hikers I had met. An aura of inner peace seemed to surround him and he exuded the self confidence of a man who understood the source of his power and his destiny. And he brought a refreshing and reassuring outlook toward hiking the Trail that uplifted me. He told me he was planning to hike to Katahdin but at a very slow pace. What interested me most about Will was he never talked in terms of I or told me what he did in life, preferring instead to maintain a privacy which one was forced to acknowledge. There was just something about Will that made the past irrelevant.

We went back to take one last look at the moose. The calves had moved down the shoreline away from us and were now standing on some large rocks that jutted out from the shore. The cow had decided to go for a swim and was about a 100 yards out and moving parallel to the shore.

I packed up my gear quickly and departed while Will was still fiddling with his tent. I told him I was going into Rangeley and that I was planning to follow the Houghton Road down the mountain. Will said he was planning to do the same.

I went about 200 yards down the Trail, arriving at the point where a moose had recently left the lake. The ground where the moose had exited the water was still soaking wet and little puddles surrounded the prints. The moose tracks followed the Trail for about 200 yards before turning up the mountain. With so many signs and after seeing the moose by the tent platform and then in the lake, I thought the possibility of seeing a moose on the Trail was very good and walked slowly for a while, peering around every bend, half expecting to see a monster with antlers. No luck.

Houghton Road was an old, severely-deteriorated fire road that led to a long abandoned cabin. Beaver dams had been built near the road, which resulted in water backing up into a small valley; near the center stood a large beaver house. The area remained, for the most part, clear of bushes and trees, but was so wet as to be impassable to everything but the moose. Much of the road now lay under water and those parts that weren't under water were so soft from moisture that my feet got wet from sinking in the marshy grass. Fortunately, remnants of corduroy parts of the road remained and provided convenient stepping logs that helped to keep me somewhat mobile.

Eventually the road climbed the ridge above the beaver pond and over a hill crest where it diverged, one leg heading east, the other north. Will wasn't carrying a map. Therefore, I determined the right road, left a wooden stick arrow pointing toward it, and scratched a message in the dirt, "Will — Go Left." I scratched my head at the thought of navigating off the Trail in Maine without a map, but then thought, if that's the way Will wanted to do it, it was his hike.

The road had been improved at that point and served as a main route for logging operations. The lumbering had scarred large portions of the forest and logging trails crisscrossed the hills. After walking about three miles, I met a man in a pickup headed toward the area from which I had just come.

Sonny Haines was my stereotypical down to earth north woods lumberman. Sitting with his left elbow sticking out the blue pickup window, his smile told me he was eager to talk. He was stocky, not tall, but with a substantial stomach; though he appeared not to be ideally suited for the 100 yard dash, I would never have bet against him in a weight lifting contest. His left forearm looked like a junior-size tree trunk.

I reached Route 4 at about 11:30 a. m. and was picked up about 30 minutes later by two young women in a small hatchback car with Massachusetts license plates. A parking sticker on the lower left side of the rear window indicated it was for an Episcopal Divinity School. I was surprised they stopped for me and asked the appropriate question. They told me they had both hiked parts of the AT, figured I was hiking the Trail and was headed for Rangeley for a mail drop. "Right on both counts," I told them.

I ran into Craig Upshaw in the center of town almost immediately after the women dropped me off. He still had not seen a moose but told me he had been awakened at about 4:00 a. m. by a moose cavorting in the water in front of the shelter. He was crestfallen when I told him about the mother moose and the two calves at Sabbath Day pond and the moose by the tent platform. Craig planned to be in Rangeley for only a short time to get stove fuel and to mail letters, then intended to go right back to the Trail. He wanted to make it to the Piazza Rock lean-to before night fall.

Later, as I was passing a restaurant, I spied Will waving wildly at me from inside. He wanted to thank me for leaving directions in the road. He was staying "a couple of days" in the bunkhouse at the Farm Inn about a mile and a half from town on the road to the Trail.

The following morning was heavily overcast and the air from Rangeley Lake was damp and cold, not the kind of day I would have picked to hike the Trail. I briefly considered staying in Rangeley to wait for a change in the weather. I couldn't justify staying a whole day, however, so after a great breakfast at the restaurant where I had met Will the previous evening, I packed up and started back to the Trail.

The hiking was not nearly as difficult as I had imagined from the Trail profile on the map. The sun soon burned through the mist to reveal an absolutely dazzling blue sky without the hint of a cloud anywhere. I saw several ruffed grouse along the pathway and another bird that looked very much like a ruffed grouse, except it was larger and more colorful with jet black feathers flecked with white and a crimson arc above the eyes. It also was loath to leave the Trail, walking warily ahead of me for about 50 yards, until it sidled off into the bushes. I learned later it was a spruce grouse and remembered Bob Guba mentioning that he had seen one on the Trail around Mahoosuc Notch. At the time, I thought it was just a close variation of a ruffed grouse.

After a couple of hours, the Trail broke out of the forest and climbed above tree line. The scenery was gorgeous and I remembered that I had almost sat out the day. What a mistake that would have been! Saddleback Mountain seemed to go on and on, until I came to the summit where the rusted remains of an old fire tower along with some equally rusted electrical appliances strewn across the ridge top marred the otherwise pristine environment. I crossed over The Horn and Saddleback in short order and headed for the Poplar Ridge lean-to; I planned to spend the night.

The characteristic clump and stumble of hikers walking through the forest announced the impending arrival of company at the shelter. The first to arrive was Heidi Henderson, a young woman with beautiful long legs that even ugly hiking boots could not detract from; she was followed a second later by her friend, Stephen Rogers. Both were Colby College alumni and were now pursuing advanced degrees. Heidi was studying dance, while Stephen was studying architecture.

Both were experienced hikers who had planned in detail the content of all their meals and sorted them in plastic bags along with spices and additives each separately packed and labeled. I expressed an interest in how they prepared their "gourmet" fare along the Trail and received a short course in how to make the normal Trail slop more interesting, if not more edible or nourishing. They had some extra pesto that they donated for a trial run to spice up the noodles in my "Curran Casserole." It worked. Pesto became a staple in my Trail "cupboard."

I slept late and did not get on the Trail until 9:00 a. m., still earlier than Heidi or Stephen; they were still cooking breakfast when I left. I moved rather slowly, and they overtook me about an hour later while I was trying to photograph two very obliging spruce grouse.

The Trail down to boulder-strewn Oberton Creek was well maintained and nicely graded. I descended easily. The climb that followed was both steep and fairly long. At one point, the terrain leveled out slightly and the stream formed a shallow pond. I dropped my pack and undressed, planning to bathe. I stepped into the water; after groping around for a minute, I stepped out. The water was so cold my feet were already numb. I then tried to splash a little on my chest, but it took my breath away.

The Trail up Spaulding Mountain was a recent relocation and the climbing was difficult. Not only that, the relocation by-passed the shelter by about half a mile and the connecting trail was not well marked. Consequently I missed the turn off and walked for about another half a mile before realizing my mistake and backtracking. The day was not with out its rewards, however. Along the way, I stopped at several red raspberry patches loaded with ripe fruit. I wondered if I'd meet a bear; the berry patches were severely torn up and trampled in places and I could not envision hikers causing so much damage. By process of elimination, I figured that bears had to be the culprits.

It was rather late by the time I arrived at the shelter. Stephen said he and Heidi were getting worried, since it had taken me so long to get there. Stephen was getting ready to go back to the cut off to leave a note for me.

The Trail register at the shelter was a literary battlefield containing invective and insults directed toward thru-hikers or local hikers — depending on who was doing the writing. Buckeye had started it off by writing some denigrating comments about all the "——— tourons" he was meeting on the Trail. The register had been divided into sections, one for thru-hikers and another for other hikers; it was easy to tell that Buckeye was a thru-hiker. He was disappointed at not being alone in the wilderness and chose to make his feelings known by his inflammatory rhetoric.

When I reviewed the day's progress before going to sleep, I found that I had made only eight miles for the day, all of them tough. I also noted that I had less than 200 miles to go.

It started to rain as soon as I stepped on the Trail the next morning. I was glad I had not tent camped the previous night as I had considered doing, after realizing that I had missed the shelter trail turnoff . Initially the path was not too tough, and despite the wet and cold conditions, I made good time. I thought I might be hiking above tree line, and I was glad to find that was not the case. The Trail turned off the shoulder of Sugarloaf Mountain about a half mile from the summit and headed down the side ridge toward Caribou Valley. A blue blazed trail led some 400 feet up to the summit of Sugarloaf. Had the weather been nice, I might have climbed it.

When I looked back in the direction from where I had come, it was very clear why the relocation was necessary. Logging operations had denuded large tracts of forest and entire ridge lines and hill tops to the west and southwest were bare.

The weather was now very windy and had turned cold; my hands were cold, though I was wearing my phosphorescent red specials. The water had seeped through the gloves making them virtually useless.

The path down from Sugarloaf was long, steep and treacherous. The mountain side was barren of vegetation, except for patches of very low brush that formed islands of greenery among the massive rock slides. The Trail had been cut on a descending contour across the precipitous mountain side, crossing several sections of the low scrub brush where the vegetation had been uprooted to make the pathway. The exposed earth was a soft, spongy loam type soil that became very slick when wet.

Despite being very cautious, I slipped and fell twice as I descended. The slipping and falling was not as bad as landing on rocks, but the real danger was that after I fell I kept on sliding, pack and all, down the Trail. The first time I fell, I slid for about five feet, until some rocks stopped me from sliding farther. Trying to regain my feet and my balance was tricky, not unlike trying to get up after falling with skis and the pack weight made the problem more difficult. Meanwhile, the weather deteriorated rapidly. The wind became a gale with gusts of up to 40 miles per hour, buffeting me and driving a stinging rain that all but blinded me.

The first fall was bad enough. The second was almost a disaster. I was being very careful to step on places where a rock or a piece of vegetation would provide traction, and it was necessarily slow going. Then I came to a small drop off of about five feet before the Trail leveled out slightly to cross a rock slide area. I used my hiking stick for support by stabbing it into the soil on the Trail in front of me; I wanted to take as much weight as possible off my feet. I then cautiously planted my feet to make sure I had secure footing. It worked pretty well, I thought, until I came to the ledge.

I was about to stab the ground with my hiking stick when my feet shot out from under me and I landed on my side sliding over the ledge and gaining speed as I slid down the Trail like I was on ice. At the bottom of the little incline, the Trail turned to the right across the rock slide, but the direction I was sliding was going to carry me straight over the lip of the Trail and down the shale rock slide.

I tried frantically to grab anything to stop my slide but nothing was reachable. Then just as my feet slid over the side of the precipice, I stopped. In sliding, my pack and clothes had scraped away the slippery, wet topsoil and had come in contact with the dry soil beneath. That and that alone saved me.

I lay there for a moment motionless, not wanting to cause any movement that might set me off again. Then when I looked up the Trail, I realized what had happened. I thanked Providence for my scruffy long pants and good fortune. (I don't know what would have happened had I been wearing the brief nylon shorts most thru-hikers wore.) I rolled over on my stomach and pulled myself into a position, so that I lay parallel to the pathway. The irresistible urge to look over the side revealed a nearly sheer drop of about 50 feet to a jumble of boulders below.

I inched my way on my belly — feet first — to a fairly level place in a rock slide and stood up. My legs were still trembling and my heart was thumping as hard as if I had just finished a mile run. My clothes were caked with mud. I vowed to do the next incline on my hands and knees; and off I went. I didn't fall again, although I did slip a couple of times; when I reached the tree line a couple hundred feet above the valley floor, I took a long break in a sheltered area behind some rocks and trees to collect my wits and my breath.

The Trail down the nose of the ridge in the trees was only slightly less perilous than the stretch across the rock slides had been. The Trail made a number of steep drops, some 15 or 20 feet over sheer ledges of wet and slippery rocks. I negotiated several on my belly to reach foot holds and find another step down. Just when I thought the Trail had reached the bottom, it would take off again to the south, contouring some very steep rock formations that required me to use even greater caution to remain in a vertical position. After it reached the valley floor, the Trail led over a miniature "Devil's Racecourse" of alluvial rock deposits that formed a river bottom.

The stream flowing down Caribou Valley was the south branch of the Carrabassett River. Two 2" by 6" board planks nailed together and stretched between rocks formed the "bridge" that spanned the portion of the river where water flowed in any volume; the remainder of the crossing was accomplished by rock hopping. It was not difficult, just a little precarious in wet conditions.

After the hairy descent from Sugarloaf, I decided I'd had enough mountain climbing for the day and followed a logging road some five miles down to Highway 27. It took about two hours of foot squishing, puddle-hop hiking to reach the highway. I thought how dumb it was, trying to stay dry by hopping across the puddles. My feet couldn't have gotten any wetter had I been walking in the river.

At Highway 27, I headed for Stratton and was immediately picked up by Bob Petrino of Merrimac, Massachusetts; he had come to Stratton to participate in the annual marathon. I was hesitant about getting in the car at first. I looked and felt like a drowned rat, and I was still carrying some of Sugarloaf on my clothes. He told me it was really no problem. To preclude further concern on my part, he hefted my pack through the hatch door of his car. We were in Stratton in no time at all.

CHAPTER 19

The heroic lie is a cowardice. There is only one heroism in the world: to see the world as it is and to love it.
— Romain Rolland

Stratton, ME to Pierce Pond Shelter

I recognized the Widow's Walk immediately. It was like no other house in town, a gingerbread mansion that towered over its neighbors. Its most prominent feature was a three-story sextagonal tower, capped by an elongated bell-shaped cupola that formed the right front corner. The center roof of the main house boasted a classic widow's walk, enclosed by a slat and railing fence. Only a female figure with shawl blowing in the wind was needed to complete the image. Two dormer windows protruded from opposite sides of the roof just above where it joined the house. The other end of the house was a large, square wing capped by a four-sided roof above which rose a square louvered tower. A long one story elevation with two front facing dormer windows connected the two larger sections. The outer walls were faced with an extensive shingle pattern that complemented the gingerbread carving on the gables and dormers. The entire structure was painted white. A man named Blanchard had built it in 1892. Blanchard had amassed a fortune selling supplies to gold miners in the Yukon. The place is now in the national Historic Register.

Even though it was recommended in the "Philosopher's Guide" as a bread and breakfast whose owners catered to hikers, I was more than slightly apprehensive as I approached. It was such a beautiful house, and I was decidedly less than beautiful, soaking wet and still carrying part of Sugarloaf on my pants. But, the sign on the door told guests to come in and register.

I scraped my boots on the mat, screwed up my courage and entered. Inside the intimidation was palpable. It was spotless with wooden floors and stairs polished to a warm glow. It was simply but tastefully furnished and decorated. Unconsciously I held my breath as I heard someone coming, then exhaled when Mary Hopson greeted me warmly.

Mary showed me to my room upstairs, indicating that if another hiker came, I might have to share it. Then she led me to the bathroom and shower and told me I was welcome to use the living room to make myself at home as well.

I was out of my hiking clothes and into the shower before Mary's feet hit the first floor landing. I luxuriated as long as I dared in the hot shower, before soaping down twice to be sure all the accumulated grime was removed.

That evening Mary and Jerry Hopson talked about the thru-hikers who preceded me and related an incident involving Screamin' Night Hog and AT Believer. As Jerry described it, AT Believer became friendly with the Episcopal minister in Rangeley. This led to the minister offering to give him and Screamin' Night Hog a lift to the point where the Trail crossed a dirt road by Oberton Creek. They accepted the offer, leaving their packs with the minister, intending to slack-pack back to Rangeley, spend the night, and then the minister would take them back to the Trail in the morning.

The minister missed the turn off to the dirt road and they ended up instead at the point where the AT crossed Highway 27. They got off there. Mary mentioned that the minister was in a time bind and had to go back for something. The result was that instead of a 13 mile day, as they had planned, they had to hike 30 miles with only a little food and no sleeping gear. They were unable to reach Rangeley before dark and walked for a while by flashlight, which was fine, until one of them dropped it and it broke. They then continued on in the dark, until the Trail dropped off so abruptly they couldn't see the bottom. They stretched their feet down and not being able to feel anything, decided to wait for daylight before continuing. They huddled together to stay warm and at about 4:00 a. m., when it became light enough, they continued on. As is so often the case, they learned they had spent the night only a couple hundred yards from the Piazza Rock lean-to. Mary said that after the minister brought them to Stratton, all they wanted to do was sleep. The Hopson's also mentioned that some of the hikers who were going through that year seemed to be racing from shelter to shelter. I was interested to hear that, since it was made as an after thought, completely without solicitation.

Two thoughts came instantly to mind: when one is as close to his goal as one is in Stratton: One, you don't want to dally. On the other hand, Maine is a paradise of natural beauty and one should really take the time to enjoy it, to "stop and smell the roses," so to speak. I suspected that thought may have occurred to some, but by the time they reached Stratton, they have seen enough vistas, trees and rocks and want only to make the last climb up Katahdin. Certainly some have a few moments for philosophic dalliance, but their goal right then is to finish the Trail.

I awoke in the morning to a strange sound, something I had never heard before, something like a pop gun going off. It kept repeating itself and I couldn't — for the life of me — place it anywhere in my experience of sounds. After a minute, I got out of bed and went to the window to see a group of runners passing the house. Then I realized what I was hearing; plastic cups hitting the ground as the runners discarded them. The marathon was going on. I instantly wondered if Bob Petrino had already gone by.

The Hopson's had set up a water station in front of the house; they and other volunteers were handing full cups of water to the runners who took a swig, poured the rest of the water over their heads and then dropped the empty cup. I got dressed and hurried down stairs. I arrived at the table just in time to see Bob run by. I yelled out to him; he grinned and waved back. He was quite far back but holding up well at that point. After the last of the runners came through, we went inside for a delicious breakfast of bacon and eggs, then loaded into the car and went to Kingfield for the finish.

Jerry carefully wove the car through the field of runners strung out along Route 27. We arrived only a scant 30 minutes before the winner, Bruce Ellis, crossed the finish line. His time was two hours, 22 minutes and 21 seconds, fast enough to qualify him for an Olympic tryout. Ellis was in fantastic shape, not even breathing hard, and looked like he could do another 26 miles. My favorite, Bob Petrino, arrived about two hours later on the verge of collapse. Many of those who finished behind Ellis were ecstatic; their times were fast enough to qualify them for the Boston marathon.

I couldn't imagine running 26 miles, let alone running it in two hours and 22 minutes. But an even greater feat was one I witnessed at the awards ceremony. The race organizers had also included a 15 KM race as part of the marathon course and a 73 -year-old woman received a prize for completing that race in one hour and nine minutes. She received the largest ovation of any of the participants.

We walked around Kingfield for a while after the race and visited the historic hotel. The men's room had the most massive urinals I had ever seen. They looked so large that I thought if they were to be laid out horizontally, they could be used as coffins. After I thought about it, I figured that would be an inappropriate use of a urinal and wondered why it had entered my mind in the first place. Then I thought they could be used for planters. Then I dropped that idea, wondering why I couldn't accept that these were just big urinals. Why did I want them to have another function? Then the bright idea came to me that it would be impossible to miss when standing in front of one of them. Ah, enlightenment!

When we returned from Kingfield, I gathered my gear together along with the Trail notes I wanted to send back to my home in Naples, Florida, and in general got myself ready for an early morning start. That chore done, I crossed the street to the Stratton Historical Society, housed in a former church. The contents of the Society looked like a collection of souvenirs from every attic in town. In addition to a very comprehensive history of the Blanchards and the Widow Walk, there were WWI and WWII military uniforms, and pictures of the local high school basketball teams from the 30's to the 50's, as well as all sorts of antique farming and logging tools and kitchen utensils. It was a treat to be able to browse through the treasures of some long past times and of some long past people.

The Trail dropped down from Route 27 to Stratton Brook, then followed fairly level ground for about a mile across a marshy area created by Jones Pond before starting up Bigelow Mountain. The weather was sunny and cool; the hiking was a pleasure. I was impressed by the immensity of Bigelow and somewhat apprehensive about the climb. Based on my interpretation of the contour lines on the map, the size of the mountain and the trail profile, I had expected the climbing to be tough. I was pleasantly surprised to find it wasn't.

Jim Campbell, a solo hiker from Long Island, New York, caught up to me, and we walked together for a while talking about the Trail and ourselves. I learned he had an MBA degree in Real Estate and had worked for a real estate firm in New York but had become disenchanted with the industry and had quit. I was interested to find out why someone with his credentials would give up such a job. He told me he couldn't deal with the "sleaze factor" but said nothing concrete as to the specifics of his displeasure.

Jim came from a family of hikers. He had learned early that whenever he needed to sort things out in life, the Trail offered an ideal venue for contemplation. And he was doing just that, trying to find a new direction to his life. My pace was too slow for him, and I think he wanted to be alone. Eventually he decided to go ahead, leaving me behind, as he climbed the ledges and inclines seemingly without effort.

The Horne Pond Camp area was a fairly extensive facility with two large wooden lean-to's and several tent platforms. The first lean-to I came to was occupied by two men, a minister about to leave to go back to Stratton and the caretaker; the caretaker lived in a large tent on a platform about 50 yards into the woods from the shelter. Jim Campbell was already at the other shelter so I chose to stay there.

Night had descended by the time I finished cooking dinner and I ate in the dark. Jim and I talked for a while afterward, and just as I was about to crawl into my sleeping bag, a group of about 12 hikers came clumping up the Trail. They were a freshman student orientation group from Colby College. I learned that several of the local colleges used hiking as a vehicle to get incoming students to know one another. The remainder of the group arrived a short time later and they went about trying to set up camp in the dark. They were all very considerate and quiet, congregating around the other shelter and tent platforms. I was appreciative!

It began raining very hard shortly after I got in my sleeping bag; I could hear kids heading for the shelter, but none came to ours. I snuggled a little deeper in my bag and hoped the rain would be gone by morning. Occasionally I could hear a mouse running around the shelter, then it got really noisy with them scampering over the shelter walls and beams and scurrying over clothing and equipment. At one point, the mice became so loud that I thought they were in my pack or someone's pack. I flashed my Mag-Lite beam up toward where I thought the sound was coming. As I did that, a mouse popped its head up from inside Jim's pack that hung by its frame from a nail in the shelter wall. He had left his pack open but had placed his food in a side pocket; and it was closed. The mouse stared back at me without apparent apprehension. It appeared almost insolent. I wondered if it was trying to chew through the pack fabric to get to the food. The same thought had crossed Jim's mind; he got up to check his pack, and as he did so, the mouse hopped down. His pack appeared to be okay.

When I awoke it was the first of September and the rain was pouring down; from experience I knew it was going to be a miserable day. I procrastinated about getting up. I procrastinated about making breakfast. I even procrastinated about packing my equipment. Clearly the prospect of walking in the rain was less than enticing. In the end, however, I knew I couldn't just sit for a day in the shelter and stepped out only to have a torrential cloud burst send me right back to the shelter for another few minutes of procrastination.

After an appropriate amount of time had passed, the rain let up long enough for me to really get started. Jim waved farewell at me from his sleeping bag as I headed for South Horn. The wind was very strong and played tricks with the mist that was fast making me wet. The farther up the mountain I climbed, the brighter and lighter it became with occasional patches of blue peeking through the clouds. By the time I reached the summit, the entire countryside was bathed in sunlight.

The views were spectacular, particularly those of the West Peak of Bigelow Mountain that rose massively above me. So much for my miserable day experience, I thought.

The wind became much stronger as soon as I left the protection of the col between South Horn and the West Peak, and it increased in intensity the farther up I climbed, making it difficult at times to maintain my balance. It was still beautiful, though, and when I arrived at the summit I sat behind some rocks for protection and admired the vastness of the wilderness that stretched before me.

On the descent from the summit, a gray jay flew in level flight from across the valley directly at me, like it was on a strafing run, then climbed slightly to pass about two feet over my head. Several others also flew by, albeit much higher than the first bird. The entire top of the ridge was above the tree line and the temperature dropped with each wind gust. It was becoming much colder than I had anticipated; I wondered if it was going to get any colder in September, forgetting that it was already September. I pulled the hood of my Gor-Tex jacket over my hat to keep it from blowing away and continued on.

The views from Myron H. Avery Peak were even more sweeping and beautiful than the views from West Peak. Jaded as I had become, I was impressed. The Trail description on the back of the map mentioned that the views there were perhaps, "unequaled in the state," and that "on very clear days the Barren Chairback Range and Katahdin" might be seen to the northeast. Unfortunately the day was not that clear, but it was exciting, nonetheless, to know that I was within sight of my goal — even if I couldn't see it. I felt my pulse quicken with anticipation.

I had run out of water and all the springs where I planned to resupply were dry; even the one by the Bigelow Col was dry. The "Philosopher's Guide" was once again right on target. It recommended carrying extra water on Bigelow; the springs were usually dry by mid-summer. I finally took a short side trip down the mountain near the Safford Brook Camping area and found some water under a large rock. It was very clear and cold; and I thought it would be safe to drink but decided to take no chances and dropped a couple of iodine tablets into it. The tablets didn't dissolve, so I ground them up, then waited for 20 minutes before drinking.

The Little Bigelow shelter was to shelters what the Taj Mahal was to residences. It was without a doubt the finest shelter I had seen on the Trail; it had a sky light in the roof, a house like box to protect the spring, and big and little tub bathing areas where hikers could cool off or bathe. I thought seriously about bathing, but the water for the tubs came from a stream flowing through the site; and it was seriously cold. The waist high food preparation area and log benches complemented two beautifully made fire pits complete with grill work. Log steps had been constructed to help people climb over the low wall in front of the sleeping platform and the roof had steel cable reinforcement; I surmised it was built to provide support in the event of heavy accumulations of snow. Those who designed and built the shelter had to be hikers, since they knew exactly what they were doing.

I had the whole place to myself. I couldn't believe it! Finally — a night to myself!! I hadn't realized how much I wanted to have a shelter to myself, a place alone in the woods — a place where it would be just me and the moose and the bears. I cooked dinner and sat contentedly under the skylight writing trail notes quickly against the encroaching darkness.

Shelter journal entries by Granma on the 25th of August and the Jersey Kid and G-Man, dated the 26th, indicated they were not that far ahead. I wondered if they had cherished the solitude as I did now. I reminisced about the previous summer in Georgia and North Carolina and how lonely I felt and how I wished for company. But now — what a treat it was to have the forest all to myself. I had come full circle.

In the morning a red squirrel watched intently as I ate breakfast and screeched every time I moved from the shelter. I got on the Trail at about 7:00 a. m. in cool and breezy weather. The hiking was pleasant and the day quiet, until I neared the summit of a small mountain between Little Bigelow and Roundtop.

I was taking a break, sitting on a flat rock, when I heard animals crashing through the forest. In seconds, two hounds with radio transmitter collars came bounding over the hill to where I sat, circled around me, barking. After a few minutes, they disappeared, then returned. I expected to see a hunter show up and watched intently up the hill in the direction from which the dogs had come, so that I could warn him not to shoot. No one appeared.

In the meantime, the dogs settled down quietly in the woods

about 30 yards away and watched me. When my break ended I shouldered my pack and started up the hill. The dogs went absolutely crazy when I put my pack on. They came racing over, barking and baying, running around me and dashing away at my slightest movement. When I started out they got on the Trail in front of me and every time I approached to within a certain distance, they would run up the Trail at full speed with their tails between their legs — barking with ear splitting intensity. Then they would stop and quiet down, until I eventually caught up to them and the process was repeated.

After gaining the crest of the hill, they ran off to the south, and I thought I was rid of them. But suddenly they appeared behind me. They stayed on the Trail "dogging" me for the next three miles, barking and baying all the way. Annoyance couldn't begin to describe my irritation. I couldn't understand why they had chosen to follow me. I suspected I may have appeared threatening with my pack, but they should have become accustomed to the likes of me. They were definitely on a hunt, but why they kept following me was the mystery. I felt like yelling, "Hey, stupid dogs. You don't hunt people — and I'm a people."

They tried to sneak up on me from behind and whenever they got too close, I would turn and face them. Then they would race off howling with all their might. I tried not to do anything to provoke them; in fact, I to ignore them (which was next to impossible). I only responded when the braver of the two would get too close. I didn't want to get bitten in the behind or in the leg as G-man had been. I had learned that dogs seldom attack from the front; they almost always try to get behind to bite.

I got exasperated to the point that I finally pickled up a rock and threw it at the nearest dog, missing by a mile, but I only succeeded in sending the stupid mutt into another barking frenzy. The dogs followed me until I crossed the Long Falls, Dam Road. They then disappeared. Ah, I thought, they're gone for good. Wrong again.

When I stopped at the Jerome Brook lean-to for a break they reappeared, but this time did not bark. They again disappeared, and I started up Roundtop. Then one of the dogs appeared, coming up from behind again. I was now fit to be tied. I removed my pack, grabbed my hiking stick and raced down the hill screaming after the dog; in turn, it howled its way back toward the shelter and that was the last I saw of them.

Later on, I learned that the dogs were probably hunting bear, that using hounds with radio collars was how many hunters found their prey. The area was full of bear and moose signs, and it looked like a perfect place to be able to see some wildlife. But the dogs had made that impossible.

I arrived at the Pierce Pond shelter at about 5:00 p. m., startling a man absorbed in a book. The shelter was nice, but the "Trail Guide" indicated that just a little farther on was the side trail to the Harrison Camp, formerly the Carrying Place Camp; it offered accommodations and meals to hikers. I chatted with the man for a decent interval, then headed for the camp. I arrived about ten minutes later.

My arrival startled a large black Labrador retriever dozing under the bumper of a jeep- like vehicle; it launched into a frenzy of barking to make up for its lack of vigilance. "Jeez," I said to myself, "Why can't I go someplace with running into some damned mutt?' I eased myself around the dog, keeping one eye on it and the other on the door.

A young woman appeared at the door and told me not to worry, that the dog didn't bite. She looked at me with an expression that asked, "What the hell do you want?" I thought I'd try the bright-faced kid approach and smiled, saying I wanted to contribute to the camp fund by staying over night. The expression went glum. "We're a sportsman's camp. We don't rent to hikers."

"Oh, I didn't realize that," I replied. "I read in the 'Trail Guide' that you offered accommodations to hikers."

"We've asked them to change that."

"Can I get something to eat?" I tried.

"No. We only plan enough food for the people we have staying here."

"What about breakfast? Could I get breakfast in the morning?"

Her expression softened a little; perhaps the old Curran charm was working. "You want breakfast?"

I wanted to say something smart but bit my tongue and kept my cool. I thought I might be able to salvage something from the situation yet; making her mad would not do it. I nodded my head gravely like it was of the utmost importance for me to eat breakfast there. "You all have a great reputation among the thru-hikers for your great breakfasts," I replied brightly.

Her face softened a little more. "Well, okay, you know anybody else that wants to eat?"

"There's another guy at the shelter; I can ask. You sure you don't have a corner somewhere that I could lay out my sleeping bag? It sure would be a lot more convenient."

She thought for a moment. "If you've got $41, I can probably find you a place."

I pressed my luck. "Does that include meals?"

She shook her head. "Nope."

"If I was a hunter, how much would you charge me to stay here?"

"Forty-one dollars," she replied.

"And that would include meals too, right?"

She nodded sheepishly.

"And you want to charge me the same price and not feed me? That hardly seems fair. If you include the meals, I'd consider it."

"There's not enough food. We only carry enough food for the guests we have," she persisted.

"Okay. Then why don't you reduce the price by the cost of the meals and make me an offer?" Now I was getting persistent.

"Sorry," she said, shaking her head, "the price is $41."

I really would like to have stayed, but it had now become a matter of principle. More discussion seemed futile. But I pressed the issue, only to learn that the place I would sleep was in a storage building, that I would have to go to another building for toilet facilities and that I would have to clean up after me. I reluctantly and somewhat wistfully headed back to the Pierce Pond shelter.

CHAPTER 20

Security is mostly superstition. It does not exist in nature, nor do the children of men who experience it. Avoiding danger is no safer in the long run than outright exposure. Life is either a daring adventure or nothing.

— Helen Keller

Pierce Pond Shelter to Monson, ME

When I returned, the man whom I had met earlier had started a fire and was boiling water for his supper. David Christian, "Cave Man Dave," was a psychiatric social worker from Boston with an interesting life's resume. He talked about the Trail quietly but with a voice that suggested extensive knowledge and great deal of self confidence. He had thru-hiked the Trail twice, once from south to north and the second time in the opposite direction. He was now section hiking, and all that remained to complete his third 2,000-mile plus journey was to hike from where were now to Katahdin.

Pierce Pond was the quintessential north woods lake that reflected both the dark green of the spruce wilderness in which it nestled and an essential sense of purity. Dinner was soon ready and we dined in the glow of the sunset, breathing in the serenity and listening with one ear to the plaintive calls of loons echoing across the water.

David and I started off together in the morning. The path from the shelter to the Kennebec River was a relocation that paralleled Pierce Pond Stream and logically led from Pierce Pond down to the Kennebec. It was just plain tough with little climbs and drop-offs as it bobbed up and down over the small shoulders that led from ridge spine down to the stream. The nearer to the river, the more pronounced became the changes in elevation and in some places, because it was so steep, the pathway had been routed up the ridge line to contour across the compartments.

The Trail dropped steeply down from the ridge to the Kennebec. Peering through the trees I got partial glimpses of what seemed to be a very broad river valley. I was surprised when coming closer to the river itself that it seemed wider than any of the other rivers I had crossed. But then I thought about the Connecticut River and had to change that opinion. Actually it was much narrower than I had envisioned from above when first looking at it. It appeared to be shallow and not all that fast flowing. What's more, there were no bridges.

At the point where the Trail approached the river, it appeared quite deep, but farther upstream, the river banks and bottom were gravel and two gravel bars reduced the actual water width into what looked like three fairly easily negotiable sections. "This doesn't look so bad," I said as we approached the river's edge. David didn't say anything that I remembered, or if he did, my attention was so focused on trying to locate the best fording place I didn't hear him.

The river actually flowed a lot faster than appeared from above or in the distance, and my apprehension built as I got closer. I remembered the admonitions in the "Philosopher's Guide" and other publications about the danger in fording the river. Alice Ference, to whom the "Philosopher's Guide" was dedicated, had drowned at this very point trying to cross in 1985. It said not to cross the river unless the two gravel bars were clearly visible. They were. I looked at my watch: 9:00 a. m. "You want to wait until noon for the ferry?" I asked.

"Think we can make it?" he replied.

"Don't see why not. Up by those gravel bars it looks okay. Let's go take a look."

David followed as I started hopping across the rounded boulders along the shore line. The boulders soon gave way to a steep drop off, and we climbed the river bank and bushwhacked across a marshy area where tall, thick grass made progress more difficult than it had looked from above. It took about 20 minutes to reach the place where the gravel shore sloped gently into the river.

Trying to define a clear route took some time. It looked to be about 100 yards to the far bank and would require traversing three separate channels, each about 30 yards wide separated by gravel bars that seemed to be about ten yards wide. The channel nearest us appeared shallow and not to present great difficulty. The second channel appeared slightly wider and deeper. The third channel between the second gravel bar and the far shore appeared to be the deepest and certainly the most difficult.

I studied the river for several more minutes, building up courage. "I'm going to try it," I announced as I dropped my pack. "The only place that looks really hairy is the stretch by the far bank, and if we find it's too tough, we can come back and wait for the ferry." I removed my boots and put on my "river walkers", thick rubber sandals with nylon thongs that resembled shower clogs with straps. I tied my boots and socks to the top of my pack, rolled my pants legs above the knees, shouldered my pack without fastening the waist belt and with a good deal of trepidation entered the water. (The "Philosopher's Guide" recommended not buckling the waist belt. In the event you lost your balance and ended up in the water, you could easily get out of your pack.)

I took a couple of steps into the chilling water and my right pant's leg became unrolled. I returned to shore. This time I rolled my trouser legs much tighter and cleaner than the first time. By that time, David had already entered the water. I plunged toward the first gravel bar, my feet slipping and sliding on the slippery bottom rocks. The rocks were all fairly small and I was able to keep my footing without great difficulty. The water was deeper than I expected, coming up to my knees, but I made it to the gravel bar in short order and surveyed the next stretch.

It all appeared to be basically the same depth and the same bottom. I started first with David right behind. The water was now mid-thigh depth and the current unbelievably strong. The footing was much more treacherous than the first section; I leaned hard against my hiking stick for support and balance.

My feet frequently slid off the rocks. After a couple of slips — where I nearly lost my balance — I adopted the technique of rubbing the rock with my foot to remove the slippery residue before placing my weight on it. That helped most of the time. But at other times, just when I became confident enough of secure footing to put my weight on it, my foot would slide off the rock and I would end up hanging onto my hiking stick to keep from going completely in the drink.

The problem was compounded by not being able to see the bottom clearly enough to judge the shape of the rocks and to know where to step. To counter that problem, I resorted to feeling around the rock with my foot to determine its shape and suitability as a place to step before removing the slippery stuff. Dealing with the current — even with firm footing for both feet — was difficult enough, but trying to maintain my balance on one leg, while feeling around the river bottom with the second, was tricky at best.

I was a lot less confidant now about the last stretch. It was definitely deeper, the water flowing faster and the bottom rocks appeared to be bigger. I thought about going back. David was quiet. Both of us were engrossed in trying to find the right route across. Finally, I yelled, "Screw it! Here goes!" and started across. David did not follow me immediately this time, but went slightly up stream to enter the water.

The current was very strong now and I had to battle with all my strength to move across the flow and maintain my balance. Each time I moved my leg the current would catch it and carry it out from under me; I had to fight to bring it back into position. I was now in water up to my crotch and that would normally have resulted in some vulgar response, but I was too absorbed in the task at hand to even notice the discomfort.

I had gone about a third of the way across when I came to what looked like a dead end with an apparently deep drop off directly in front and also up stream. I went downstream a few yards to where it seemed shallower and started again. The water was now up to my waist. I stopped for a minute and rested against my stick to catch my breath; I wondered if I should go back. I looked upstream to see how David was doing. He was chest deep in the water and the expression on his face was a mixture of terror and determination. I wondered what I should do if he lost his balance and came sailing by; and if he knew how to swim.

I started off again. I was getting scared now. I couldn't see the water bottom at all — and I expected to go deeper. My foot slipped off the rock I wanted to step to, but fortunately, it ended up wedged between that rock and an adjacent rock. When I slipped, I temporarily lost my balance, but thankfully my stick held me up. I thought about David again, then said, "Worry about yourself stupid; what a dumb time to be diverting your concentration." I continued to struggle to control my legs and body, then suddenly I was two-thirds of the way across — and it was shallower. I again surged against the current and in a short time was only a few feet from the shore.

As I waded across the last few rocks, I was startled by a shout that was the release of the enormous build up of tension and a cry of joy from David; he was also sloshing over the last few rocks. Then I shouted too, the emotional release sending my voice several octaves higher than normal. David shouted again and I joined him, both of us shouting like a couple of school kids coming down a roller coaster.

My body trembled all over, my hands nearly uncontrollably. I jumped up and down a couple of times, shouting in a flush of victory and blowing the tension off. We took pictures of each another walking out of the water, then removed our packs and relaxed for a minute.

Another challenge faced us now — that of climbing the cliff-like sand and gravel river bank that loomed in front of us. It was clearly impossible to climb from where we had exited the water, but David found a spot a few yards downstream where the slope was less steep; with the help of some exposed tree roots and overhanging branches we made it to the soft grassy forested area above.

We were just outside of Caratunk, exactly where we did not know, but close. As it turned out we had exited the river directly across from the road that led to the Post Office. We picked a couple of apples from some road side trees and went to the church where we took a real break to rest, and savoring our apples and our victory. "Bet we made it across just in time. What do you think?" I asked David.

"Looked like the water was about ready to cover that second bar. Could be."

"Let's go back and look," I suggested. We went back, crossing an area full of ripe black raspberries where we stopped to gorge ourselves. Much to our disappointment, the gravel bar was still clearly visible.

We road walked out of Caratunk up to the charming community of Pleasant Pond, stopping on the way to eat lunch on the banks of Pleasant Pond Stream. We reached Pleasant Pond lean-to at almost the same time as a couple coming down the road from the opposite direction.

Megin and Jaime Jewett were a bother-sister team from Harvard, Massachusetts. Megin, a recent Harvard graduate, was preparing to enter the Peace Corps, but she wanted to hike the Trail before going on "active duty." They had started from Katahdin together but would part company at Stratton. Megin would continue on to Springer Mountain. Jamie had to return to his job.

David was surprised that Megin was going to be hiking into the winter and questioned the wisdom of hiking the Trail so late in the season. He was of the opinion that it was getting too cold and it could be dangerous in the mountains, particularly if the hiker was not properly equipped to handle something like the White Mountains. Megin indicated she was prepared to handle winter conditions and was not the least dissuaded by David's comments.

The shelter was not far from Pleasant Pond, and David and I decided to go there to bathe. We had to traverse a private road and cross a private camp to reach the water; fortunately the camp was deserted. At first we did not realize we were on private property until we were almost at the lake shore; when we did realize it, we simply walked farther down the shore, until we were off the property. The water was slightly cold, but the sun was warm. After bathing, I even pampered myself with a short swim. The water felt like silk as I moved through it, and after a few minutes I became accustomed to the temperature. It was a strange sensation to be surrounded by wilderness, yet to experience a sense of luxury.

"Doonesbury" hove into sight just as we were finishing supper. He could have been the model for the cartoon character so striking was the likeness. His face was rimmed with a wispy growth of blond beard and a shock of light blond hair peaked from beneath his cap. His skin was very fair and he was rail thin. His gear was an odd assortment of off-the-shelf discount store bargains. He was as he described it, "a slow walker" who wasn't hiking the Trail, just enjoying the outdoors. After reaching Caratunk, he planned to leave the Trail and head west. I sensed he fit the mold of a drifter more than a hiker.

Doonesbury laid his sleeping bag out next to mine that was, from my point of view, unfortunate; he needed a bath badly. He kept me awake half the night moving around and several times calling to Megin — why I don't know — because he didn't respond when she answered. When I returned during the night from going to the bathroom, he mooched some water from me. It irritated me; he'd had the whole evening to get his own damn water and I told him that. Then I felt like a scrooge for refusing and gave him some anyway.

The hike the next day was very tough, starting with a difficult climb up Pleasant Pond Mountain and continuing along a relocation which followed the ridge spine to Middle Mountain, then across a series of small peaks and jump-ups to Baker Siding. It was only three miles, according to the map scale, but it was one of the toughest three miles I had done on the Trail — but still not as tough as Wildcat Ridge in the Whites. That one was in a class by itself. We had expected the Trail to climb over Pleasant Pond Mountain and gradually descend to the east to Moxie Pond as it showed on the map; I didn't realize we were on a relocation until after we crossed Middle Mountain.

At Baker Stream, hikers were offered the option of crossing the 20-foot span of water via two steel cables one above the other stretched from bank to bank or over a rock and timber foot-crossing a couple hundred yards farther on. I passed on the cables as looking too risky as did David who was now far ahead of me. I later talked with some hikers who had tried the cables and who said the idea was to side step across the lower cable while holding onto the upper cable to maintain balance. But what usually happened was that one ended up in a very awkward horizontal position; their packs pulled them to the rear and the lower cable swayed forward.

After Baker Stream, the Trail crossed the shoulder of an unnamed mountain before dropping down to Joe's Hole Brook lean-to and climbing up Moxie Bald Mountain. The climb was fairly long but not difficult by Maine standards. We by-passed the summit, contouring the mountain about 100 feet below the top before turning north to cross a very broad open ridge that reminded me of Bald Pate. From there, it was basically an easy slide down to Moxie Bald lean-to, a cozy little log structure nestled in the woods about 50 yards from the shore of Bald Mountain Pond.

The shelter was vacant when David and I arrived. We dropped our packs and went down to the water to relax and admire the scenery. I stepped onto a rock protruding out into the water and movement to my left caught my eye. I looked up to see the south end of a moose headed north standing in the shallow water about 50 yards away. The moose had swung its head around and was staring back at me.

David was closer to the moose, but trees obstructed his vision. I motioned for him to come over. I went back to the shelter to get my camera, but the moose decided the place was getting too crowded and opted to leave. I last saw him running up the mountain.

Shortly afterward, a man wearing a fanny pack and carrying a ski pole arrived from the south and began searching the shelter register. He mentioned a name but neither David nor I recognized it. Warren Doyle from Clifton, Virginia, introduced himself and volunteered that we would have the place to ourselves for the night. I glanced quickly at my watch. It was 5:00 p. m., rather late to be heading off into the wilderness without sleeping gear or food. I asked the obvious question: "Where do you plan to spend the night?"

Monson was his reply. Then he said he had a head lamp.

I had already checked and knew that Monson was 16 miles from the lean-to. My curiosity was now fully aroused and I asked from where he had started. He said he had started at 11 a. m. at Caratunk. He left a short time later, and I checked the mileage from Caratunk to Monson; Mr. Doyle was planning to hike 35.7 miles for the day. I was later told that Warren Doyle was one of the Trail legends, that he had hiked the entire Trail, albeit with his father following in a support van, in 77 days.

Later, three south bounders from Maryland, young men in their early 20's, came pounding up to the shelter. They quickly took over the place and started their supper. While their food was cooking, they went to the lake and began yelling, so that they could listen to the echoes. A loon called, and they attempted for about five minutes to mimic its call. When they returned to eat they talked with such volume, I thought they were all hard of hearing. The decision to tent camp away from the shelter was easy to make. I selected a spot in a camping area near the water about 50 yards from the shelter, but even there I could hear in detail much of their juvenile conversation.

I wished I had accompanied David; he had left the shelter earlier, planning to tent camp farther down the Trail. Tomorrow was a Saturday and he wanted to get far enough down the Trail, so that he could get to Monson to pick up a mail drop before the Post Office closed. I knew I couldn't make Monson before the Post Office closed and asked him to pick up my mail too — that is, if the Postal Clerk would let him have it.

A moose splashing in the water not far from my tent awoke me in the morning and wondered if it was the same moose I had seen the previous evening. I poked my head out of the tent flap to see a blue, gold sky framing the dark forest to the east. The air was chilly and it was quiet. There was no moose to be seen and I assumed that the splashing I had heard was the moose leaving the water to head up the mountain.

Later, the sun rose over the horizon, bathing the mountains behind the lake in bright sunshine. The leaves were turning color, the maples already red with patches of yellow and orange were splattered across the mountain side — almost like colored polka dots on the dark green background of the spruces. Mists were rising from the water in the shadows of the tree lined banks. The air was crystalline; every view of the mountains, the trees, the cliffs, the lake and the small islands and the far shore were all sharply in focus. The wilderness was pristine, like it had been down the centuries before we arrived to civilize it. A woodpecker rapping on a tree somewhere above me broke the silence, announcing the start of a new day . . . it was time to go.

The Trail followed beside Bald Mountain Stream for a while, then climbed Breakneck Ridge, and the hiking was easy. After Breakneck Ridge, it descended to the road that led to Blanchard and the Greenville Road, heading east again toward Buck Hill and Homer Hill, then on into Monson. I did the 16 miles in good time, arriving in Monson in late afternoon.

I met David almost as soon as I arrived at Shaw's Boarding

House. He had been able to pick up my mail. There was among other things a note from Sally Prestgard, along with a couple of pebbles she had acquired from Springer Mountain to be deposited on the summit of Katahdin. She wrote that if I had made it this far, I was going to make it all the way. (I had met Sally in Woody Gap in Georgia the preceding summer.)

Keith Shaw welcomed me with open arms, saying it wasn't very often that he had "colonels" come for a visit. David had announced my arrival. Keith was a very accommodating and positive person who did a great service for the hikers. He showed me to my room and into the kitchen where he introduced me to Jim Brennan, "JB" from Philadelphia.

JB had already finished the Trail and had come back to Shaw's for a couple of days to meet the thru-hikers behind him. He knew everybody I knew and then some. I talked with him about the Trail and his experiences and particularly about climbing Katahdin. I was trying to glean the last bit of information about the monster before I had to climb it. He told me the initial climb was easy, then it got tough, and then leveled slightly again about a third of the way from the summit. He also volunteered he had seen a lot of hikers "burning their way from shelter to shelter." That was all right, if they wanted to do that, he said, but he didn't want them to B.S. him by telling him they saw anything along the way.

Supper that night was a hiker's dream: fresh squash, baked potatoes, fresh carrots, fried chicken legs, milk by the pitcher, bread and butter, and brownies for dessert. And there was lots of everything. The conversation centered on an incident where a man had been mauled by a bear in Baxter State Park. I had read somewhere in an article about the incident that the bear had collapsed the man's tent, bit him in both legs, then tried to carry him, the tent and all off into the woods. The man escaped from the bear, climbed a tree and called for help, but no one awoke or came to his rescue.

David said the part of the story not told was that the man had been camped next to a dump and had been cleaning fish in his tent earlier in the evening. That had attracted the bear. I thought about a tree I had seen the day before when we were stopped for lunch. It had been scratched at about eye level by a bear. Deep gouges, some appearing to be a quarter inch deep, had been cut into the bark and the wood, indicating the power and the sharpness of the animal's claws. I wondered if the bear was after the man, why it didn't climb after him. Probably because it was interested only in the stuff that smelled of fish.

The next day was spent resting and ferrying cars. We started off, David and I, riding with Daniel O'Connor in his car, to the junction of the Trail and Highway 17, just east of the Bemis Range. Daniel got out there and headed for Caratunk. Then David and I drove Daniel's car to the junction of the Trail and Highway 27, east of Stratton, where David had parked his pick-up truck. Then I drove Daniel's car up to Caratunk, so that it would be waiting for him when he finished his hike. David followed in his pick up.

When we arrived at the Post Office in Caratunk, we found a note on the door left by Megin Jewett. It said she had lost her wallet containing all her money, credit cards, driver's license and travelers' checks somewhere along the Trail.

David and I looked at one another. "Doonesbury," I whispered softly, breathing in as I said it. David nodded; evidently the same thought came to his mind.

CHAPTER 21

I believe that man will not merely endure; he will prevail. He is immortal not because he alone among creatures has an inexhaustible voice, but because he has a soul, a spirit capable of compassion and sacrifice and endurance.

— *William Faulkner*

Monson, ME to the Gulf Hagas Side Trail

During our conversation on the trip from Caratunk back to Monson, David had told me he was a psychiatric social worker. He said he was in private practice in Boston under contract with the VA among others. He had recently submitted a proposal to the State of Massachusetts to work with prison inmates and was awaiting an answer from State officials. David was quite keen about getting a positive response to that proposal, since it would be very rewarding financially. I sensed that he felt he had been out of his business loop too long and needed to get back to work and become more aggressive in following up on his proposal to the State. I was right.

It was 6:15 p. m. when we arrived back at Shaw's Boarding House and everyone was at supper. Keith needed to issue no second invitation to join in the fun. I looked for a place to sit, sweeping my gaze across all the faces at the table. Something was different. Then I noticed the one person more quiet than the rest.

"I was wondering when you were going to say hello." It was Cathy. She slid over to make room for me.

After supper, David announced that, as much as he hated

to, he had decided to cut short his hike and return to work. But he wanted to cover one more short stretch and asked if, in the morning, I would drive him in his pick up to the point where the Trail intersected a logging road in the vicinity of Jo Mary Mountain and Church Pond. He planned to then hike back to Monson, reclaim his pick up and head back to Boston.

I thought it was a great idea; it would give me the chance to leave a food cache at that same location. From Monson to the next point where we could reprovision was over 100 miles and that meant carrying additional food and stove fuel. Putting in a cache would allow me to limit the amount of food I had to carry to about three, at the most four day's supply. That would make the pack weight about the same as for the last several weeks, and I could live with that. Then I had a brainstorm.

No roads, other than two logging roads, provided access to the Trail for the 100 mile stretch of wilderness between Monson and Abol Bridge. They were ideally sited, the first one about 30 miles north of Monson, the other, where David wanted to be dropped off, about 60 miles away. Because I was going to have transportation, I could really go light and put in two caches. I figured I could drop David off, set the far cache and then on the return, detour and put in the near cache, "killing two birds with one stone," so to speak.

One small problem immediately surfaced. We didn't have enough food for both Cathy and me, and everything would be closed until well after we had departed for the drop off point. We decided to put in the far cache, after dropping David off, then put in the nearest cache the following morning, after the stores opened. That would mean starting late, but it was better that than carrying the extra weight.

Cathy and I sorted through our food after supper, preparing a four day inventory, enough to hold us for the fifty or so miles from the drop off point to Abol Bridge Campground where we could resupply if necessary. We wrapped everything in green plastic trash bags, which we sprayed with insect killer to keep the animals away, particularly the bears.

The West Branch Ponds Road, the most northerly access was a toll road and to use it cost us four dollars per person, a total of twelve dollars, (Cathy came with us). We paid weekend rates because it was Labor Day. We dropped David off at 10

a. m., and he immediately headed back toward Monson.

Cathy and I went down the Trail in the opposite direction to find a place for our food cache. Our reference point was the second white blazed tree from the road. About a 100 yards to the north of it and well off the path we found an easily identifiable lone boulder with a small tree growing up its side. We stuffed our food sack into a second plastic bag, which we coated with bug spray . We then placed the bag on top of the rock, covered it with branches and leaves for concealment, and sprayed everything one last time.

That evening Ken Henderson, "Skeeter," arrived alone . Ken had teamed up with Dan Bruce, "Wingfoot," to do an "anniversary thru-hike" of the Trail in commemoration of the 50th Anniversary of the Trail. Bruce had generated a tremendous amount of publicity for the hike, participating in various anniversary celebrations in towns along the Trail. He was carrying a letter from the Governor of the State of Georgia to be delivered to the Governor of the State of Maine and a video camera to record for posterity excerpts from his hike. Some of the media attention he generated had spilled over on other hikers along the Trail like me and Granma.

The following morning, after picking up some mail Cathy had sent, she and I packed another cache and set out for the St. Regis Paper Company Road, the road closest to Monson. The gate keeper cautioned us about the danger of forest fires, indicating there was a good possibility. Because it was so dry and the forest fire danger so high the Rangers might decide to close down the area to campers. I asked how the Rangers notified campers and he said they sent out helicopters or just walked the Trail.

On the way out of the gate keeper's cabin, I noticed a small sign in the door's window advertising for female companionship for the coming winter. We laughed and hurried along.

On our return, we stopped to see a piece of history embodied in the Katahdin Iron Works that dated from the early 1800's. The huge field stone kiln and charcoal furnace had been restored and looked to be in such good condition that they could be used today. With a little imagination, one could picture the place bustling with activity.

Although the cache site was about 30-Trail miles from

Monson, the road miles were double that; by the time we returned to the Shaw's, it was late afternoon — so late we decided to remain the night and start in the morning.

Several new hikers had arrived at the Boarding House Two young women, calling themselves, the "Slugg Sisters," introduced themselves as did David and Karen Flynn from Boston who hiked under the Trail name, "Boston Baked Beans." Dennis Hill, "Hik-A-Holic" and Tom Menzel, "St. Thomas," completed the contingent of newcomers. All were thru-hikers.

Dennis Hill was a gregarious man; he kept everyone entertained with his stories. He had already hiked the Trail end-to-end once and was back for a second helping, doing it as he liked, not serious at all about hiking, but serious about the fun. At dinner he and Tom Menzel, who was just as serious about fun, got into a contest to see who could eat the most. Dennis was a big man, 205-pounds big, with a substantial belly and next to rail-thin Tom Menzel, weighing in at about 160 pounds, he looked positively fat. There was no doubt in my mind that Dennis would bury Tom in an eating contest. It was another case of looks being deceiving.

Tom ate slowly, while Dennis ate fast. Tom was deliberate in the way he took food from the platter and placed it on his plate and about the way in which he cut his meat and vegetables. He savored every bite, eating with great enjoyment. He looked over at Dennis with a big grin as he started his third helping. Dennis smiled weakly and took his third helping. Then when that was finished Tom helped himself to another potato. Dennis did likewise, and when he had finished it, he lay his utensils down as if to say he was satisfied.

Tom looked over at him and with a devilish smile picked up another piece of meat and a potato and began to eat it slowly as if to tantalize Dennis. Dennis then took an equal amount and began to eat — but clearly it was a labor. By mutual consent, they stopped eating and declared the contest a draw. Tom clearly enjoyed the psychological gamesmanship.

It started raining very hard during the night and was still going strong the next morning; we regrettably delayed our departure one more day. I didn't want to spend another day in Monson, but I even more certainly didn't want to go off in a down pour when the weather reports indicated the rain would last the entire day. I thought about David and wondered how he was faring.

Cathy and I were the first down to eat breakfast the next morning and were just getting settled when Keith excitedly called for us to come to the kitchen. We hurried in — expecting disaster. Instead we found him standing over the stove, holding the frying pan in his hand pointing proudly to a three yoke egg. "It's a first!" he exclaimed. He then showed it to everyone who came to breakfast and all were duly impressed until he got to Tom Menzel. "Aw you just set that up," Tom said in his soft devilish way. "You're funnin' me." Keith protested vehemently as to the authenticity of the egg, but Tom continued to feign disbelief. The exchange lasted several minutes until, exasperated at not being able to get Tom to accept that it was a triple yoke egg, Keith went back to the kitchen shaking his head.

At 10:30 a.m. Keith took Tom and Skeeter in his pick up to Long Pond Stream from where they planned to slack pack the 20 miles back to Monson. All were dressed in rain gear, looking like veterans from the arctic but with facial expressions that indicated something less than enjoyment. As they were leaving, I said I admired their fortitude going out in such conditions. Tom replied softly, "No brain, no pain."

Doonesbury put in a surprise appearance at breakfast. He said he had hitched a ride into Monson the previous evening and that he was hiking south. When I had talked with him at Pleasant Pond shelter, some 30 miles to the south the week before, he had told me he was planning to head west; I asked what made him change his plans. He replied curtly that he had "changed his mind." He told Keith he was going over to Dover Foxcroft to find work in the mill there, and Keith said he didn't think they were hiring.

The next day we started on the Trail at 7:15 a.m. in uncertain weather, sometimes sunny, sometimes darkly overcast. At other times the wind blew strongly, carrying with it the hint of rain. Initially the Trail followed the Greenville Road out of Monson, then turned right onto the Bodwell Road. It followed that road for about a mile, until turning onto a dirt road that led past the Mathews House, an old farmhouse from 1824 that is still occupied. From there, the Trail rolled up and down hill on an old logging road, until it headed northeast by Bell Pond and took a relocation to Lily Pond. We wandered past several beautiful tarns and the hiking was fairly easy, until it got to Bear Pond Ledge and turned north. Here it became tough.

We crossed a series of compartments with testy little climbs and descents before reaching Little Wilson Falls, a spectacular but small cataract where the water fell what seemed to be hundreds of feet down to the bottom of a rocky gorge. Actually the drop was probably only 50 to 75 feet, but the narrowness of the gorge created the illusion of great depth. Layers of the earth's crust were encapsulated in the gorge walls, presenting a very interesting picture for geologists and a beautiful set of patterns for a layman like myself.

Shortly afterward, "I is Blue," whose real name is Blue, from Bristol, Tennessee, came striding briskly over a small rise toward us. A mass of long dark brown hair cascaded from beneath a Bristol, Virginia, baseball cap down to his shoulders and mingled with a beard that almost matched it in volume, since it extended some four or five inches below his chin. He was headed for Springer Mountain, and I wondered what his beard would be like when he reached that point. He said he had met Granma while making an experimental hike earlier in Virginia and then two days before at Cooper Pond. She was hiking alone, but G-Man and the Jersey kid were about two hours behind her.

I put on my river walkers to cross the Little Wilson Creek ford, and after getting to the other side, took them off and threw them to Cathy to wear for her crossing. A short distance away, we found a level camping area and decided to stop for the day to set up camp. We had done ten miles. Since it was Cathy's first day back on the Trail, we needed to take a break early. Not only that, I needed the break too. Cathy was really worried about keeping up with me — now that I had come to be such a "power hiker," as she put it.

The Trail had been relocated over many small ridges with tough ledges and rock formations that I thought could have been much easier to hike had they been by-passed. But evidently Warren Doyle enjoyed them; a comment by him in the MATC register box said he "approved" of the relocation and wished it were longer. The relocation had already added another one and half miles to an already tough Trail. Making it longer seemed pointless to me.

I wasn't sure what influence Warren had on Trail siting, but I was sure I didn't want some guy who walked 30 miles with a head lamp in the middle of the night to be selecting Trail locations for me. Then I remembered another comment I had read some place where he said the ATC should keep the "blazes in Monson." There was a plan in the execution phase to route the Trail out of Monson and take it over Buck Hill — some three miles to the northwest of the town. Warren felt as I did, that the Trail should continue through Monson.

During one of our breaks, a red squirrel came over and sat on a log in front of us with his front paws cocked and began chirping at us. It was a humorous to see him chirp; his whole body bounced with the effort, even his tail quivered. I raised my hiking stick like a gun and said, "Bang! Got Ya!"

"Beady eyes," yelled Cathy, reminding me of her concept of judgement day.

"Does that apply to mosquitoes and flies?"

"Not if they're bothering you. You only get the beady eye treatment when you kill an innocent animal."

"What about the pheasants I shot and ate?"

"Beady eyes!"

"Whoa! I'm in big trouble," I replied. "You get into trouble for eating steak or a lamb chop?"

"No, 'cause you didn't kill them. You bought the meat in a store."

I wiped my brow in mock relief. "Whew, I'm glad you told me that. I coulda been in serious big trouble!"

I tried to give the squirrel a piece of cookie as a symbol of atonement for all the beady eyes I'd sent off to judgement day, but the stupid thing ran off into its burrow behind some roots. We left the cookie, figuring he would most likely return after our departure.

The Flynns caught up to and passed us fairly early, then we passed them. We leap frogged one another a couple more times, until they finally left us at Mud Pond. During our passing conversations, we learned that Keith had taken Ken, Tom and Dennis to Long Pond Stream to resume their hikes and that Ken Patrick had come off the Trail in Andover because of his sickness. We also learned they had met Will McGlaughlin in Stratton and that he planned to climb Katahdin on September 24th.

When they mentioned that, my spine tingled at the thought of seeing Katahdin. I had seen pictures of it at Keith's and had been impressed at how imposing it appeared; it was now only 100 miles away. In another ten days, I would be there and the Trail would be history. The excitement was building.

The following day we crossed the ford at Big Wilson Stream fairly early, then Long Pond Stream before stopping for lunch at Barren Slides. The view of the wilderness from Barren Slides was so broad as to be inspiring, but it was at the same time bittersweet; it also included bird's eye views of logging operations and loaded timber rigs hauling trees down the roads. Shortly after leaving the Slides, we entered a band of clouds that cloaked the top of Barren Mountain, and mist and wind replaced the views. A rickety old, abandoned fire tower stood like a derelict near the summit, but it had been there so long that it looked almost like it was a part of the landscape. With the mist reducing our world to about a hundred yards there was not much else to see, except for rocks and trees and signs of moose. The latter tantalized us with the possibility of meeting one; that alone perked our awareness.

The Trail paralleled the edge of a swamp as it approached the Cloud Pond lean-to and the scenery, even in the rain, was absolutely breathtaking. The lean-to was just that, a small log lean-to, more picturesque than functional. The side and rear walls had large gaps between the thin logs, and plastic sheeting had been nailed across them in an attempt to provide weather proofing. It was built on a rock ledge that formed the shore of Cloud Pond and overlooked the swamp leading to Cloud Pond Brook and the lake itself. It was perfect moose country; I ventured out several times during the course of the evening to see if any might be out on the lake or in the marsh but got only wet as a reward for my efforts.

The Flynns were already there when we arrived, and naturally we fell into a discussion of the day's events and the Trail. We talked about how it was going to be before we reached Katahdin. I said that I had heard that, as they approached the end of their journey, may thru-hikers lapsed into nostalgia or began to experience penetrating philosophic episodes and asked If they had yet entered into that phase of their journey or were

experiencing any twinges of emotion. Karen replied she was savoring her last few days on the Trail. David said he was just
interested in getting the thing over. I echoed his sentiments.

Cathy started supper and I started trying to recapture the
day in my Trail notes. I recorded that I had done 12.6 miles for
the day and that I was now a double digit midget (a throw back
to my days in Viet Nam when those who had less than 100 days
to go before rotation "back to the States.")

The night was cold and rainy. Despite the plastic sheeting,
the wind blew the mist and rain through the gaps in the logs.
Water also entered the lean-to from above by way of the nail
holes in the tin sheeting where it was attached to the roof timbers. The result was that our gear got wet, some of it soaked,
like my sleeping bag, while other stuff merely became damp.

I slept well despite the conditions and it was a good thing I
did. The Trail the next day through the Chairback Range was
just plain tough. Fourth and Third Mountains, as well as Co-
lumbus Mountain, although not high, were also difficult with
the pathway leading over every rock ledge imaginable.

It was fairly late in the afternoon when we recovered our
closest cache at the St. Regis Paper Company Road. Nothing
had bothered it, not even the mice. After packing our food, we
continued down the hill to the road where four weary day-hikers were congregated waiting to be picked up. We learned from
them that the weather forecast for the next few days indicated
we could expect more of the same weather. That was not the
kind of news we were hoping to hear. But all was not lost. One
of the men offered to carry my little Ziplock trash bag back to
civilization for civilized disposal.

The place was loaded with hikers. In addition to the four at
the road, we met a young couple at the West Branch of the Pleasant River, then two south bounders, and we could hear others
in the Hermitage. I commented to Cathy that our much anticipated "wilderness experience" reminded me of Grand Central
Station in New York City at rush hour on Friday afternoon.

Signs left no doubt that camping was not allowed. Therefore, we continued on until we saw no more signs and began
looking for a suitable place to set up our tent. We found one at
Gulf Hagas Brook, just north of where the Gulf Hagas Trail joined
the AT, and set up for the night. I was unhappy about the

weather. But I also was somewhat thankful; the rain had ne-
gated the fire danger and obviated the need to close the region
to campers. I learned again that I was responsible for how I
reacted to circumstances beyond my control and how even sometimes inclement events produce positive results.

The hike over the Chairback Range had exhausted us, particularly Cathy. We went to sleep directly after eating supper. I
tried to write a few entries in my journal, but fatigue so overwhelmed me that I put the paper aside after only a couple of
entries; and the next I knew — it was morning.

CHAPTER 22

Although men are accused of not knowing their own weaknesses, yet perhaps a few know their own strength. It is in men as in soils, where sometimes there is a vein of gold which the owner knows not of.

— *Jonathan Swift*

Gulf Hagas Side Trail to Wadleigh Stream Lean-To

It rained heavily during the night and was still coming down hard in the morning when we awoke. I felt around to see if any rain had leaked into the tent. Since I could find no wet spots, I concluded that my tent repair efforts were successful. I was pleased about that, although if one were to hear my remarks about the Trail and the weather as I was preparing for the day's hike, they would surely have thought otherwise.

I was not in a great mood when we started out. But the relocation along Gulf Hagas Brook was moderately graded and led past several cascades with marvelous rock formations, through picturesque stands of spruce and several small glades with alders and birch; my disposition improved with beauty. The relocation was six-tenths of a mile longer than the original Trail site, but the scenic beauty and the decent Trail siting more than made up for the extra distance.

We soon reached the point where the Trail crossed a brook by a tarn with its associated marshy area and the path was littered with sharply defined moose tracks. The ground was soft and wet from the rain and the mist heavy. I whispered to Cathy that we might see a moose.

We walked as quickly and as noiselessly as possible, until movement off to my right front caught my attention. I froze. A large mink was hunting, and so intent was it on the trying to find prey, it didn't notice us. Its long slender body seemed to flow over the rocks and logs and it stopped every so often to put its nose in the air and sniff. It came to within about ten feet of us, then turned in another direction, continuing its same pace, stopping and sniffing and moving on in such a manner as to suggest it had not even seen us.

After the mink passed, we continued our moose "hunt." So absorbed was I in looking for antlers that I wasn't paying much attention to the Trail. Actually the Trail was easy here; I could afford the luxury of surveying the surroundings — or so I thought. I slipped off the side of a wet rock and went down with a thud; the clang from my cook pot signaled every animal for miles around that I had arrived. Needless to say, we saw no moose!

The climb up Gulf Hagas Mountain was steep but not difficult; however, the wind and rain on the summit were more than uncomfortable. We were semi-exposed and the temperature had dropped to the point where my hands were raw cold. I had become completely soaked and the wind pressed my wet trousers against my legs making them colder. Even my Gor-Tex jacket seemed to offer no protection from the penetrating wind.

At the Sidney Tappan Campsite we sat on a log behind some bushes to eat lunch. I couldn't imagine what I looked like, but I could see Cathy was cold and bedraggled. Despite her outward appearance, she still retained a refreshingly positive outlook. I had had my fill of wet weather, cold and wind, and I was just contrary enough to look for a way to express my displeasure. "Ask me if I like hiking," I told Cathy. She didn't.

The climb up West Peak and to the summit of White Cap was a battle in which we fought not only the roots and rocks along the Trail but also numerous blowdowns. It was time consuming and exhausting as well, as we navigated our way over trees and limbs lying across the Trail. Since there was no way around them, we just had to climb over them or shinny under them, pushing through branches that caught at our packs and clothes. It seemed like we were on a giant obstacle course.

The summit on White Cap was completely above tree line

and had the weather been clear, the views would surely have been dazzling. But The mist was thick and allowed only a vague twilight through its veil that compressed our world to about 30 feet; all that could be seen were the nearest few steps across what was certainly a vast expanse of rocks. It even obscured the blazes and the cairns that marked the Trail. The higher we climbed, the thicker the mist became. Finding our way became a game of trying to anticipate the direction of the next blaze. There was no defined path among the rocks as there is in the forest or in grass; we relied on dead reckoning. Sometimes we were right; sometimes we had to detour a little to find a blaze.

The wind could only be described as vicious. I was staggered time and again by the freezing gusts. I almost went down twice when the wind caught my pack from the side and the thrust of the weight pulled me off balance. One gust knocked Cathy down. I didn't see it happen, but she told me about it, while we were walking down the other side of the mountain. It took the better part of an hour to cross the summit. We were overjoyed to leave the ravages of the wind and get back to the protection of the trees at a lower level.

We staggered into the clearing at the Logan Brook shelter, soaked, cold and exhausted beyond belief and were warmly welcomed by the Flynns who quickly gathered up their gear to make room for us. They were a down to earth couple, and so very positive in outlook that both Cathy and I enjoyed their company. They were, as so many other hikers, at a juncture in their lives. Karen had been a nurse in an intensive care unit in a hospital and had become, in her own words, "burned out." She was looking for a new direction in her life. David worked as a computer analyst, as I recall.

We hung our clothes out to dry and Cathy started supper. I was now beginning to think terms of the "lasts" — the last 4,000-foot mountain, the last hitch hiking, the last river ford, and now the last 3,000-foot mountain. In fact, I had just about finished all the mountains now. All that remained, according to the map, were a couple of small hills. The rest of the landscape appeared to be quite level.

The shelter register contained a number of stinging comments by hikers as they complained about the lack of Trail maintenance. I found the comments to be a bit tiring. I could understand the hikers' frustrations, but I could only applaud the efforts of the Trail maintainers in Maine. They had a huge number of miles of Trail to cover, and there weren't exactly hordes of people knocking down the door to volunteer to help. Not only did they have a shortage of people, but they also had to constantly relocate the pathway to accommodate the timbering operations of the paper companies. My entry suggested that those who chose to complain should see fit to volunteer to help remove some of the blowdowns.

The weather was not through with us. A storm raged across the landscape the whole night and ended only towards morning. The lean-to was tucked into a ravine just upstream from a beautiful small cascade of Logan Brook and the shelter provided by the ridges and forest greatly reduced the effects of the storm. Still the roar from the torrent of rain crashing on the tin shelter roof made conversation impossible. Not only that, but the sound of the wind screaming at the higher elevations and down the ridges and across the tree tops was psychologically unsettling. I could only imagine what the conditions on the summit of White Cap might have been like.

The Trail the next day, despite my expectations to the contrary, was in very good shape. I had expected to see small streams running down the pathway, quagmires and washouts, but the Trail was not damaged; it was in very good condition.

The weather was still cool, partly cloudy and windy when we started off, but the wind died later in the morning and it began to warm up. We still encountered a number of blowdowns, but they were much fewer than the previous day and were concentrated in smaller stretches; and we were able pass without great difficulty. The East Branch of the Pleasant River had become a real obstacle. The Trail Guide indicated the crossing was a snap, but that did not take into account the deluge from the night's storm. The normally placid little stream was now a raging little river; crossing it would require some thought and planning.

The Flynns had already crossed the stream and stopped for a snack. They knew we would be along momentarily and waited at the fording point to see how we would handle the crossing, standing by in case we needed help. Getting to the other bank was going to be tough. We scrambled and thrashed our way through the thickets, arriving at a place where some rocks jut-ted out into the stream; other rocks, slightly under water, looked like they could be used as stepping stones. The growth on the far side of the river resembled a jungle full of fallen trees, thick brush, dead bushes and tall marsh grass. I kept my boots on, mostly because there was no convenient place to sit to remove them. Anyway the far bank looked so formidable that I didn't want to be fooling around in my bare feet, trying to get to a place to put them back on. In truth, it made no difference; my boots were still wet from the previous day.

"Looks like this is the place, kiddo," I said to Cathy who was hanging on right behind me.

She responded with a squeaky, "Eeek."

Cathy stayed right behind me, determined not to let me get so far ahead that she couldn't see where I had stepped. The only problem was that she was too close, and once when I felt I was losing my balance and needed to step back to regain con-trol, I found she was already occupying the rock I wanted to step back to. Fortunately I was able, with the help of my hiking stick, to retain my balance on the rock where I was, but the incident served as an opportunity to give her a gentle reminder, "Hey! Leave me some damned room!"

We made it to the far shore without further difficulty; that may have disappointed David Flynn; he was out on a rock in the river filming our crossing.

The water crossing might have been tough, but it was the easy part. Now we had to break through the tangle of under-growth for about 75 yards to make it back to the Trail. I plunged on, breaking sticks and branches as I went, stepping on dead tree limbs and climbing over or sliding under dead falls, until at last we came to the Trail. The Flynn's congratulated us for our fortitude and moved on, while we took a short break to savor our success and most importantly reward ourselves with lunch.

The Trail now turned delightful, skirting Boardman Moun-tain and Mountain View Lake, a beautiful tarn nestled in the hills between Boardman and Little Boardman Mountain. The climb up Little Boardman was steep, though not long, and when we reached the summit, the sun was shining brightly. We stopped for a while to admire the views and to dry our equipment by spreading out on the short grass. The view of White Cap looming impressively over the smaller mountains was magnificent.

After descending from Little Boardman, we came to Crawford Pond. The warm water, a soft sand beach and rows of low bushes along the forest's edge were ideal for hanging clothes; it was also inviting us to take an afternoon swim. We luxuriated in the water, admiring the red and yellow colors of early fall and the expanse of spruce that remained eternally green along the hill sides and the forests that lined the far shore.

Heading for Cooper Brook shelter, we picked up the pace. There we again met the Flynns and also a young man from Walden, Georgia, a small town about 70 miles northwest of Atlanta. Phil was sitting on the shelter floor with his bare feet resting on the low wall in front of the sleeping platform. When asked about his being alone, he replied in a pronounced drawl that he had "two blow outs." He had been hiking with a group including his brother that was headed for Katahdin. However, because of his foot problems, he was forced to drop out of the hike. The others continued on and planned, after climbing Katahdin, to return to pick Phil up where the Trail crossed the logging road some four miles farther to the north.

Phil's feet were in terrible shape. Both had large blisters and one foot had a particularly ugly looking sore that I was sure was very painful and which I thought needed medical attention. He had some first aid equipment, but it wasn't the right kind. I offered him some of my bandages and Karen, being a nurse, volunteered to help clean the wounds and apply ointment and gauze, binding everything with adhesive bandages. Phil became more talkative as he became more comfortable with us, and I got the impression he was enjoying the attention, even if he didn't enjoy the circumstances.

Cathy started a wood fire that produced more smoke than fire. But it did heat water for supper. Phil asked if we could spare some hot water; his brother had taken their camp stove and also half of the tent. The question of how his feet came to be in such bad condition needed asking, so I did. His boots "didn't fit properly," was the reply. He said he had complained about his feet hurting, but the others in his group accused him of being a "cry baby." A pair of jogging shoes lay beside his pack.

I asked why he hadn't worn them instead of the boots. He had no answer, and I thought back to Nick Sprague and his hunter's specials at Low Gap shelter in Georgia, (who had the same difficulty). Nick followed my suggestion to hike in jogging shoes and made it from there to Big Meadow in the Shenandoah National Park in Virginia.

Phil then informed us that he had spent the previous night alone on the summit of White Cap Mountain. Both David and I were incredulous. He told us his flashlight gave out, and he found the fire tower had been removed. He subsequently got lost in the mist, and eventually had pulled into a small depression, got into his sleeping bag and covered himself with his shelter half and spent the night. I thought back to the previous night and the sound of the wind screaming through the trees. I concluded that Phil was one very plucky guy.

Cooper Brook shelter was located in a small level area in the forest just above where the brook formed two large, very inviting pools. I really would have liked to go for another swim, but the temperature was less inviting than the scenery suggested. I was glad I had bathed at Crawford Pond.

I was handling the physical challenges of the Trail very well now. I experienced almost no episodes of extended palpitations or arrhythmia, though I did notice a few isolated palpitations while climbing Little Boardman, but they stopped as soon as I slowed. We had covered 11.6 miles for the day and by my calculations that meant it was another 58.6 miles to the top of Katahdin.

The weather was beautiful the next day and the Trail easy for the most part, passing several small, picturesque north country lakes, Cooper Pond, Mud Pond and Church Pond, all of which looked like perfect spots to see moose. Unfortunately none were to be seen.

We picked up our undisturbed cache before noon and the added weight of the food made our packs uncomfortably heavy, but that would only last a day or two. I never ceased to be surprised at how much two days' supply of food weighed.

We walked along the edge of Jo Mary Lake; several beautiful sand beaches tempted us to go swimming, but the weather was turning cloudy and we wanted to keep on moving. The Potaywadjo Spring was the largest I had seen on the Trail. It was about 20 feet in diameter and looked to be about two feet deep. Had it been earlier in the season, I was sure the spring would have been even larger and deeper, judging from the way the ground was formed at the water's edge. The water was crystal clear and cold, and I drank several cups before filling my water bottle.

The shelter register contained a number of entries, but by far the best was one by Hik-A-Holic: "Last night about midnight a moose decided to help me take down camp. He got real close to my hammock and tarp so I made noise. He proceeded to run away. There was only one problem — he wrapped his feet into my guy lines on my tarp and proceeded to take it south! I recovered the tarp but lost some stakes and in the meantime I got my hammock, bag and pack wet. Well you know the old saying: SHIT HAPPENS. Onward thru the mud."

The weather the next morning was beautiful and the wilderness a picture book of color and raw beauty — the kind that can only be found in nature. The point where the Trail paralleled Namakahanta Stream was fairly difficult, but the magnificent scenery was worth every bit of effort.

We initially planned to go to Crescent Lake and tent camp for the night, but because the weather was so beautiful and the scenery so magnificent, we decided to stay at the Wadleigh Stream shelter. There we could swim in Namakahanta Lake and dig for fresh water clams. Gathering the clams was a delight. The water was not too cold, and we went in waist and chest deep, squishing in the muddy bottom as we pulled the clams from their beds.

At first, it was difficult to find the clams; then as we became more proficient, we were able to easily spot where the tell-tale edges of the clams peeked above the mud. They generally congregated in little groups, and where you found one, you were likely to find more.

Cathy filled her pot with clams close to shore, but I ventured farther out to find bigger, juicier specimens. I filled my pot too, but kept on hunting. Cathy called to me several times to stop, that we already had more than enough of the little critters. I agreed that we had enough, but continued to pluck clams out of the water — because they were there. Then a couple of rain drops hit and I quit. I dropped about half my load back into the lake and headed back to shore.

We found the spring mentioned in the Trail Guide and filled

our water bags. Now the problem was to get ourselves, our clams, our water bags, our swimming gear and our clothes back to the shelter. I passed my hiking stick through the hand straps on the water bags and the handles on the cook pots containing the clams, and we then carried the stick on our shoulders in the two-man carry mode. With Cathy leading, we walked in step to keep everything in balance. The water bags and pots swayed in unison with our gait, and it took some practice until we got it right. I joked that the Indians who carried deer tied to poles that way made it look so easy.

Another couple, Bill and Wanda arrived while we were searching for fire wood. We gave Bill directions to the lake and described where the spring was; he left to get water. Wanda was quiet during the discussion, but after Bill left, I started talking with her. I asked her how much of the Trail she had walked. She said, "About 700 miles;" She described the places she had hiked, and it was clear to me that she had walked well in excess of 700 miles and said something to that effect, meaning it as a compliment.

That comment caused Wanda to go into a tirade about everyone on the Trail wanting to talk about how far they had walked. The explosion continued with her saying she didn't care how many miles she had covered and asking me if this was a "20 questions routine."

Cathy told her to take it easy, and I tried to explain that I was only trying to make light conversation. Wanda would not be soothed and refused my offers of conciliation. Finally, I said that if I was upsetting her, I wouldn't pursue the conversation any further, and she replied that suited her fine. She then went into the shelter to the very far corner and sat facing the corner with her back to the front and to us, and began to busy herself with her pack. She did not turn around or talk until Cathy and I were in our sleeping bags some three hours afterwards.

Later in the evening, Robb Mann arrived at the shelter. He was not a thru-hiker, just a guy who liked the wilderness and was taking the opportunity to do some hiking before going to work at L.L. Bean. I had met him earlier on the Trail at the Moxie Bald shelter, and he told me then about his interview with L. L. Bean and how excited he was to be going for a second interview with the company. He had since completed the second interview, had been accepted into their training program and would be starting to work in the customer relations department on the coming Monday.

Cathy cooked the clams and we ate several before she added the remainder to our casserole. They were very bland, not at all like I expected which was something like salt water clams or mussels. David Christian had told me that the clams had a delicate flavor; I decided then that the word "delicate" was a euphemism for "tasteless." We gave Bill and Robb some to try. In fact, we gave Robb a bunch so he could make a meal out of them as we had. We also gave one to Bill for Wanda; she certainly would not have taken one from us. After some coaxing, he persuaded her to try it. I was not surprised that she didn't like it. (She sat facing the corner during the entire meal.)

As we were stirring in the morning, Wanda packed her gear and departed the shelter without comment — except to tell Bill she would see him at the lake. I assumed, as did Bill, she meant Lake Namakahanta. The atmosphere around the shelter brightened immediately with her departure.

Bill obviously knew that Wanda was upset the previous evening but didn't know why, so I told him. He mentioned that, as she was leaving, Wanda had asked him in an accusatory way, "How can you talk with people like that?" evidently meaning Cathy and me.

Wanda's speech was staccato in nature coming out in bursts like she couldn't get the words out fast enough. "You hear the way she talked?" Cathy asked.

"Yeah, she was pretty fast, wasn't she?" I replied.

"She's tight as a bowstring. She's got a mental problem. Definitely got a screw loose."

"How do you know that?"

"Trust me. Anyone who talks the way she does is extremely upset, up tight, tense to the point where she can break at any time. Maybe that's why she's on the Trail. She needs to be by herself and away from people."

The explanation made sense.

CHAPTER 23

Man can never come up to his ideal standard — it is the nature of the immortal spirit to raise that standard higher and higher, still upward and onward.

— S. M. F. Ossoli

Wadleigh Stream Shelter to Daicey Pond Campground

Almost as soon as we departed from the shelter, the Trail began ascending Nesuntabunt Mountain. The climb was longer and more difficult than I anticipated, but then eased along some fairly level stretches between some cliffs with varied and unusual ledges and rock formations. A side trail led to the summit that offered magnificent views of the surrounding lakes below and the forest stretching for as far as the eye could see. Once again, however, I was thwarted from seeing my goal. Clouds — the lower layers of which reached almost down to the valley floor, covered the whole of Katahdin.

We hiked a logging road to Rainbow Stream, then followed the stream up through the forest in bright sunshine. It was a warm, colorful day full with the aroma of autumn in the air. The smell of wet leaves, the earth fresh and damp from the evening's rain and now sunny in spots and dappled with shade in others tantalized our senses with reminders of similar days in our youth.

We stopped at the Rainbow Stream lean-to for lunch and Cathy remarked that she thought she recognized the stream and shelter and the little log bridge as the subject of a picture from the article about the Trail in "National Geographic." The entries in the shelter journal were especially interesting because most of the writers were nearing the end of their adventure, which set in motion some very penetrating philosophic observations. Almost all the entries mentioned the difficulty of the Trail and that the writers' were proud of having finished it. Most also expressed some apprehension about the future. Their goals in life while on the Trail were quite clear and required little mental effort to define and attain them. Now, for many, those goals had been achieved and new goals were in the process of being formulated. None would be so definite and concrete as walking the AT and it would require some time and psychological turbulence to make the transition. Again, one's basic outlook on life and the power of faith would be crucial to those making fundamental decisions about the direction their lives would take. The AT Believer said it best when he mentioned that he was ready for the next great challenge and that the "Challenges ahead of us are never so great as the Power behind us." The Happy Feet mentioned going back and facing "withdrawal shock."

I remembered some of the conversation I had had the previous evening with Bill when he said he had seen a number of thru-hikers coming off the mountain. He was surprised at how wasted, or exhausted some looked, with gaunt faces and hollow expressions. I imagined that for some, finishing the Trail might be one huge shock. After all, they had invested a tremendous amount of dedication and effort into their adventure. Some, too, had come on the Trail looking for answers and meaning for their lives and now they were finished and they had no answers and no meaning had shot out of the blue and that was a severe blow.

We followed Rainbow Stream for a short distance to the point where it widened into a marsh pond with slow moving water and a huge concentration of lily pads. We finally saw one, when we were least expecting it. A bull moose stood out in the water about 10 yards from a stand of spruce enjoying the sunshine and aquatic vegetation.

He was about 300 yards away at that point. Fortunately, the Trail stayed inside the trees as it contoured the lake edge. I immediately stopped as soon as I spied him and pointed him out to Cathy. We wanted to get closer for some pictures so we went sneaking down the Trail being very careful not to make any noise. The wind was blowing toward us from his direction, which worked to our advantage to help get closer without being detected. The Trail swung around and passed directly behind the spruce stand, which screened our movements and allowed us to get even closer. The moose was out in the bright sunshine and we were in the shadows, which made it even more difficult for the moose to see us, and we were able to get to within about 20 yards. We both took several pictures and as we did the camera noise alerted the moose. It peered back toward us and we froze. It tried to look into the shadows giving us a great opportunity to see its face fairly close up. It was very large but capped with only a small rack of antlers. His coat looked sleek and very dark and the sun shimmered with the movement of his muscles. He continued to look toward us for a very long time, then apparently satisfied that no danger was present, began feeding again. We moved closer to the water's edge and took more pictures, then moved back. Again the moose became suspicious. He looked toward us for another extended interval, then sensing no danger, resumed feeding. Cathy then tried to move to a vantage point between two trees for a better shot and in the process slipped and banged her pack against the tree. That really did it. The moose headed out across the lake, walking rapidly in water up to his flanks until the water deepened and then swimming the remainder of the way to the far shore about 75 yards away and disappeared into the forest.

The Trail continued to parallel Rainbow Stream and the dead waters of Rainbow lake until it reached the western end of the lake itself. The pathway climbed a slight incline, then dropped down to the water's edge where two boats had been pulled up on the grassy bank. I couldn't believe it. Out across the water, there in the near distance, Katahdin, my elusive mountain appeared almost like an apparition. It was larger than life, larger than I had imagined dominating its harem of lesser hills in a style of the grandest of potentates.

I had finally seen my goal and it was truly awesome. I had a strange feeling of fulfillment, and at the same time a disquieting feeling that I was still to be tested. Cathy stood as motionless and awe struck as I, mesmerized by the beauty and the enormity and trying to bring it into calculable dimensions which the mind could comprehend.

We decided to tent camp at the eastern end of the lake and

pressed on, each lost in our thoughts and trying to pay attention to the pathway and absorb the beauty around us. The Trail
continued to contour the lake, sometimes skirting the shore line,
and, at other times, climbing the ridges that fell sharply down
to the lake from the various hills to the south. We soon passed
the blue blazed side trail that led to the summit of Rainbow
Mountain and began looking for a suitable tent site. We found
none until we came to the extreme eastern end of the lake near
Little Beaver Pond where soft, level tent sites, a fire pit and some
sitting logs beckoned us to spend the night.

We set up the tent on a site about 20 feet from the lake
shore behind some large boulders that screened us from wind
crossing the water. After dinner, we sat contentedly on the shore
looking out over the lake contemplating its beauty and the day's
experiences. A sense of serenity pervaded my mood as well as
gratitude for the good fortune I had thus far enjoyed. As the
darkness descended the loons began their plaintive cry and from
far in the distance calls of coyotes could be heard.

I don't think I had ever felt so far from civilization. I was
flushed with pride at having come so far, and knowing that I
had really won the battle against my physical frailties and inner
demons. Yet it was tempered by a measure of humility — the
kind that comes from recognizing that I was witness to grandeur and power to which I could only marvel. I realized how
insignificant I would be without the power which instills the
spark of life that made it all possible; and that all I was or saw
or had was in the final analysis the ultimate gift of God.

I also thought about Katahdin; my mountain. It had become more than the end of a journey. It had become my personal mountain, a symbol of the quest of a lifetime, a place that
can be "owned" only in the sense that I joined to it in a sort of
spiritual matrimony. It was not something I could possess but I
could behold its beauty and view it from another level as a celebration of life.

Katahdin, although majestic and awesome to the point of
intimidation, had become a symbol in that it was a goal and a
quest both at the same time. When I reflected on it, I realized
that we all have an allegorical component whether we acknowledge it or not. We all have a "Katahdin" lurking somewhere in
the mists of our future. We cannot select it, because it is al-

ready there. It just is. Perhaps it is selected for us. But we can select the route we will take to climb it and that is where the differences among us lay. We can select the route of pessimism and negativism, a route that is safe and predictable, one that is comfortable or self indulgent. Or we can take a hard and risky path that requires optimism and a positive outlook, one that offers challenges, or visions, and rewards those who succeed with beauty and spiritual growth. There are many paths, and some are a mixture of all of the above. But the final result is that the rewards are always commensurate with the effort.

We started to climb Rainbow Ledges almost as soon as we left the campsite the next morning. Initially we skirted the northern shore of Little Beaver Pond, negotiated a small hill climbing about 400 feet, and then dropped down into a marshy valley before beginning the ascent for real. Although it looked quite steep from the map, the Trail was relatively easy and on the summit were some good views of the lake country we had just come through and a view of the bottom half of Katahdin. Clouds again covered the top half.

After leaving the ledges, the Trail headed down the other side and became much tougher. Three very large grouse and several red squirrels, two of which were carrying pine cones as large as they were, greeted us along the pathway. The Hurd Stream lean-to was our lunch stop and I read the register as I munched on my sardines and crackers. It seemed that the thru-hikers had become philosophers writing quite eloquent comments about the Trail and the views and the scenery and Katahdin and wondering what life now had in store for them. It was an entirely different tone than the usual vulgar and sarcastic notes in earlier registers. The Trail did have an ennobling quality and it was now time to recognize that.

We walked for another three and a half miles after lunch before arriving at the Abol Bridge over the West Branch of the Penobscot River. The camp store there had a variety of snacks and souvenirs but after browsing a while and checking prices, we decided to call it a day and head into Millinocket. Our plan was to get a room, stay the night, then rent a car and return the next day to do the stretch between Abol Bridge and Katahdin Stream Campground. We wanted to take it easy for the last two days so as to be fresh for our climb on the 20th.

We eventually got a lift from a man in a pickup. He removed a pistol from the seat as we climbed in which sort of unnerved me, but he was really a pleasant guy. He dropped us at a car dealership that also rented cars and waited until he was sure that we were able to rent a car and then departed. We had done 7.7 miles for the day, not a world record, but we were both tired from the previous days' hikes and it was a welcome respite to come off the Trail a little early and sleep in a real bed in a real house.

The hike along the Penobscot River the next day started off in cloudy, damp weather. But that didn't detract from the beauty of the river, which at that point was flowing swiftly and smoothly, and the scenery along the banks was idyllic. In my imagination I could almost hear a lute player serenading his love under the branches of the sycamores that lined the bank.

The weather cleared as we began the gradual climb that followed Nesowadnehunk stream. The beauty of the stream was as changeable as it was inspiring. In places it was untamed wild water roaring in a frenzy of white froth as it crashed down a boulder strewn course. In other places it flowed placidly, pausing to eddy in small pools before pouring smoothly over a narrow ledge then resuming its headlong rush to the river. Crossing the boundary of Baxter State Park, the home of Katahdin, was cause for a mild celebration. Each time I passed a land mark now it became a miniature event to be recorded and savored as another milestone in my soon to be concluded Odyssey.

Then came Windy Pitch, a tough little climb up stream banks and Big Niagara Falls which was a series of spectacular cascades over massive boulders and broad rock ledges. It was a small Mahoosuc Notch with water.

Further on the log ruins of an old toll dam provided a perfect setting for lunch. Behind the dam was a large Lilly covered pond where the sun sparkled from the water and where the dam was breached, a stream of water flowed toward Big Niagara Falls. The logs that had formed the dam had been thrown about in different directions like the remnants of a great explosion, but more probably had been savaged by an uncontrollable flood and lay about in strange positions. The logs were massive — four or five feet in diameter and about 15 feet long — and we sat in the sun with the pond to our backs on one of the logs that was still in place. We watched the water wend its way through the rocks on its journey to the Penobscot.

We arrived at Daicey Pond Campground early in the afternoon and I went directly to the Ranger's office to get information on the Trail conditions on Katahdin, the weather forecast and to ascertain what bureaucratic obstacles I might have to face the next day. A sign on the door indicated that no one was home and that if you wanted to rent a canoe, it cost so much per paddle.

The campground library/reading room was housed in a beautiful rustic log building almost on the shore of the pond. It also had a hikers' register which contained entries by just about everybody I had met on the Trail. Again I was struck by the poetic and philosophic content of the comments. The Happy Feet had taken the opportunity to record for posterity all the verses they had made up to their Trail song. There must have been ten verses, all quite long and some very good. Granma Soule had made an entry as had The Jersey Kid and G-Man.

On the way out of the campground the Trail passed a shelter which also had a register. It contained many thoughtful comments, but the one I remembered most was one by Jeff Garrison that read: "If you think you're finished when you have done Katahdin — you shouldn't have started."

CHAPTER 24

What we truly and earnestly desire to be, that in some sense we are. The mere aspiration, by changing the frame of mind, for the moment realizes itself.

— *Anna Jameson*

Daicey Pond Campground to Katahdin!

We followed the Grassy Pond Trail from Daicey Pond to Katahdin Stream Campground, arriving there about 3:00 p. m. Much of the area through which the Trail passed was a fragile marsh; an extensive pathway of log puncheons had been constructed to protect the environment. Initially the walking was quite easy. But after skirting Grassy Pond to the east, we came to a massive log jam where the pond outlet led to Katahdin Stream. The logs lay in all different positions and directions; this meant that to cross one had to select stepping points carefully, thinking four or five steps ahead to be sure not to end up at place where the distance to the next log was too great or a dead end.

I hopped from log to log and crossed without too much difficulty. But Cathy's "short Polish legs" wouldn't allow her to step the distances between some of the logs as easily as I had. She had to search for a different route, taking her time and often resorting to tightrope walking the length of some logs that formed bridges across sections of the stream.

I went quickly ahead, then stopped to observe as she crossed. Her face was a study in grit and determination, screwed together by concentration braced by more than a little apprehension. My watching and some off hand suggestions disturbed her concentration, and she yelled sharply a couple of times for me to go on ahead and mind my own business. I did as she said.

The Ranger station at Katahdin Stream Campground was closed when we arrived, but a weather board that contained information about conditions on Katahdin and forecasts for the coming day was posted close by. The weather was now clouding up and the forecast for climbing Katahdin the next day was listed as "Class 2" — meaning wind and rain at higher elevations and climbing not recommended.

Beside the weather bulletin board stood a small podium with a log sheet on which people planning to climb to the summit of Katahdin were supposed to register. The station also had a Trail register and it contained entries by most all of the thru-hikers I knew, but by this time their eloquence had waned. I thought that the anticipation of the climb had reduced their enthusiasm for thoughts of a grander scale — either that, or they had run out of their basic inventory of creative comments.

Although the Trail distance from Abol Bridge to Katahdin Stream Campground was only 9.3 miles, the road mileage was more like 25 miles. Therefore, returning to Abol Bridge was a challenge. Not only that, but the weather had turned much colder and the wind had picked up, adding a wind chill factor to the situation. Initially we were picked up by a bear hunter from the Shenandoah Valley area of Virginia who offered to let us ride in the bed of his open pickup. We hunkered down as close to the cab as we could to escape the wind, but despite our efforts, when I got out I was so cold my hands were stiff and slightly unresponsive. Cathy said she had no problem with her hands, but that the rest of her was damned cold. It took one and a half hours and four rides to make it back to Abol Bridge and our car.

As we returned, I reflected on the day and realized that I now had only 5.2 miles to go — and my hike would be history. I don't really know why, but I had trouble comprehending that I had actually completed a walk of some 2,100 miles. I guessed I had been at it for so long and had always thought in terms of miles to go, that when I finally was in a position to realize that there really was no more to it, my mind couldn't get my emotions to accept the fact. It also occurred to me that barring some unforeseen circumstances, I had just hitched my last ride on the Trail. I had thought that back in Stratton, but now it was the last for sure. Here was reason enough for celebration.

It was now the 20th of September. The day to climb the last five miles had arrived, or better yet, I had arrived to climb the last five miles. There was one slight problem, though. The weather reports indicated rain. It also forecast rain for the next several days.

Cathy and I discussed the options. Should we go now and hope for the best? Should we wait for one more day and see if the forecasts improved? Should we wait out the bad weather, until it passed? It was a tough decision to make.

I desperately wanted a "Class I" day where I could savor a beauty fitting the magnitude of the achievement. Finally I came to a decision. I would accept what I could not control, adapt to it and find or create the beauty and meaning from within.

We departed for Katahdin Stream Campground at 7:00 a. m. under leaden skies. At the entrance to Baxter State Park an elderly couple stood by the entrance booth looking for a ride to Katahdin Stream Campground. The Rangerette on duty asked if we might have room to take them with us, and I responded that we would be honored to have their company. They had fallen victim to the bureaucracy. Their pickup camper, because its shell exceeded the park rules on oversized vehicles, was not allowed on the roads in the park.

The couple, Dr. Glen and Enid Bolton from College Place, Washington, had come east to hike some of the Appalachian Trail. They initially planned to climb the mountain over the Abol Trail that started from Abol Campground about two miles south of Katahdin Stream campground. They changed their minds during the ride and decided to climb the Hunt Spur (The AT), as we planned. It was about 8:00 a. m. when we finally arrived at the campground. After signing the log book and giving everyone the opportunity to visit the facilities, we started up the trail to end the Trail.

The sky was a monotonous gray blanket that stretched from horizon to horizon, broken only where it was stabbed by occasional mountain tops. Katahdin looked like it had lost its top, like it had been sheared off about the 3000-foot level. The Trail was quite easy. During my first break after 30 minutes on the Trail, the Boltons passed us with the Mrs. leading. "Damn, they're fast for 70 year olds," I said to Cathy.

The Trail was beautiful despite the weather, and as if to brighten the day, a spruce grouse hopped onto the trail, walked cautiously ahead of us for a few minutes, then hopped onto a low branch beside the path and watched us pass. We stopped for a minute to admire a small waterfall in Katahdin Stream, then crossed the stream on a bridge made of cables with boards attached. After swaying across the bridge, we started up Hunt Spur and the path became progressively more difficult. I was psyched for the climb and started to gather momentum.

"Hey, slow down. We got all day to do this," Cathy called.

She really didn't need to waste her breath. The Trail had steepened considerably, and I had slowed to accommodate the effort, especially when climbing up a couple of small ledges. We soon came to the tree line. There a wall of boulders rose up vertically before us. "Surely they can't be serious," I said. "The Trail must go around this stuff somehow."

I walked to the right, looking for a blaze, then came back and went to the left and still could find no blazes. I also could find no path. Then I looked up and there on a boulder the size of a car directly in front of us was a white blaze. On top of that boulder was another huge boulder, and it also had a white blaze. As I gazed up the mountain I could see a series of white blazes rising vertically into the mist. "I don't believe it," I called out to Cathy, pointing to the blazes.

Cathy came up beside me and looked up the vertical pile of rocks at the blazes. "Oh, no! Eeek!" she whimpered. "They can't be serious."

I found a hand hold and foot hold and clambered over the first rock, then looked back for Cathy. She was within inches of me. "Don't get so close," I reminded her. You have to leave me some space so I can come back — if I lose my balance."

"Okay! But slow down. I need to see where you put your feet."

"Okay, I'll slow down. Just make sure you leave me enough room."

As soon as we left the protection of the tree line, the wind attacked us, pulling at our clothes and bodies as we struggled over the boulders. Thankfully we had left our heavy packs at the motel and were carrying only a small nylon day pack with lunch and water. We wriggled over several rocks on our bellies, holding our breath, trying to find hand holds and foot holds, then exhaling with each success. As we conquered each little challenge, we'd breathe a sigh of relief — only to look up and see another set of boulders the size of small trucks all marked with a neat row of blazes indicating that they were indeed the Trail. I stopped occasionally to wait for Cathy and looked down the jumble of rocks I had just climbed. I was becoming light headed from acrophobia. My heart skipped a beat from the tension and anxiety.

The tree line looked to be hundreds of feet directly below me. From there, the tops of the trees fell sharply away, until beginning a broad sweep away from the mountain base, gradually subsiding in altitude to the Penobscot. The peak of the Owl, one of the lower peaks of Katahdin, seemed to be about the same elevation as I was, and I could look across the top of it to Barren Mountain. Everything at my elevation was cold, stark rock that impressed me as completely inhospitable, even for a visit. The desolation induced a sense of loneliness, that even with Cathy there, was overwhelming. The mist was becoming heavier and the wind more penetrating. Even with a sweater and my windbreaker, I was getting cold.

On the other side I could see the scar of Abol Trail climbing up the mountain, until it disappeared behind some rocks and the ridge well before reaching the summit. Some of the more impossible to climb boulders had steel bars imbedded to provide hand and foot holds; they were a huge aid. However, in places one or two of the rods had been broken off at critical points, leaving the hiker stranded, and it was difficult and slightly dangerous trying to overcome those little sections. But we did it. It was a real challenge for me, and I simply don't know how Cathy managed it.

Eventually, after about an hour of almost vertical boulder climbing, the Trail became slightly less steep for about 200 yards, then started to ascend sharply. The mist closed in, making it difficult to see the next blaze. The second stretch of boulders, piled one on top of the other, formed an incline about as vertical as the initial stretch had been. It took only about half as long to traverse the second boulder field and reach the Gateway, the point where the Trail began a moderate approach through the

Table Land. The higher we climbed, the thicker the clouds and mist. By the time we reached Thoreau Spring, I was soaked through. (Thoreau Spring received its name in honor of Henry David Thoreau, the author of "Walden Pond" who stopped there for a drink while climbing the mountain in 1846.)

We met a couple coming from the direction of the summit and stopped to exchange greetings. They indicated that because the weather was so miserable, they had stopped short of the summit and decided to head back to camp. They said they had climbed to the summit several times before; it was no great disappointment. They were quite interesting, and Cathy talked for a few more minutes and would have talked even longer, if I had not pulled her away.

In my reveries I wondered how I would approach my climb up this last mountain on the Trail, how I would react emotionally, how I would handle the intellectual and psychological dimensions of the experience. I had visions of myself clawing the last few feet on hands and knees, blinded from tears streaming down my face. In other reveries I saw myself being born across the rocks as Jean Christophe was borne across the river during the final moments of his life, experiencing the ultimate of his emotions.

I was surprised at how emotionally detached I felt. Here I was one mile from victory, from fulfillment, I thought, and I had no damn feeling whatsoever. I knew only that I was damned cold, and I wanted to keep moving. As I thought about that, I realized the climb had demanded so much emotional energy that I had none left to devote to the ending of the adventure. I had expended so much concentration climbing the boulders and containing my anxiety that I was arriving on empty when it counted most. I plunged on toward the summit.

"Slow down, damn it!" came the voice behind me.

I slowed down and Cathy caught up. I tried to contain my speed. It was no use. I would be lost in thought and begin again to race up the mountain — and Cathy would call out again.

No more wet hikes. No more wet feet and miserable days, I thought as I stumbled on. I supposed that had it been a "Class 1" day, I would have been awestruck by the beauty of the panorama, but all I could see now was a few yards ahead and some more damned rocks. I thought of my son smiling and shaking his head when he dropped me off at Nimblewill Gap some 2148 miles ago. It seemed so far in the past. But it was the same lousy weather as when I had started off from Springer.

Several times I could make out the outlines of a fold in the ridge above. Thinking we had reached the summit, I'd call to Cathy that we had arrived at the summit, only to find it was just another pile of rocks and the Trail continued.

I remembered — back at the beginning — how I had waited until my son had driven off before I stopped and took off my pack, barely 200 yards up the mountain; a surge of panic hit me when I realized I was alone in the mountains with 2,000 miles to go. Then . . .

Suddenly, there it was. I could make out the summit sign. I ran up the last few yards and grabbed the sign like I wanted to make sure it wasn't an apparition, that it was real. I read it again and again:

KATAHDIN

Baxter Peak

Elev — 5267

northern terminus of the

Appalachian Trail

I shouted a couple of times in exultation and congratulated Cathy. Then Cathy congratulated me.

We took several photographs of each other, trying to shield the lens from the mist. I wanted to savor the last few moments, but the wind and the mist were just miserable, and we were too cold to think of much more than getting back down.

We opted to take the Abol Trail as we retreated from the ultimate goal. Actually, it was Cathy's decision; after thinking about negotiating the boulders again, I didn't even consider disagreeing.

It was with a sense of pride and quiet satisfaction that we said goodbye to Katahdin.

Epilogue

Faith is to believe on the word of God what we do not see, and its reward is to see and enjoy what we believe.
— *Saint Augustine*

The trail down was just as cold, just as wet and windy as the Trail up had been, but there were dramatic differences. It was no longer an adventure, no longer a challenge. There was no longer the sense of anticipation, the heightened awareness of my surroundings, the concern with failure. To be sure, I wanted off that mountain, but there was not the sense of urgency that had accompanied my climb. I didn't have to get up the next morning and be ready to hike ten to 15 miles. In a sense, I was free now. I had found what I had wanted and would carry it with me for the rest of my life. I would always cherish my memories of the Trail, the good and the bad. The sharp aggravations and small failures would be smoothed and softened by time, and I would eventually come to look on the Trail as an old friend who had tested me in just the right way.

But more than that, I had found a treasure for which no riches could be bartered. I had reached within and for the first time in my life come face to face with my innate spirituality. I had achieved the spiritual confidence that I had longed for at the beginning of my spiritual awakening. There was no cataclysmic event to which I could point and say, "That experience achieved spiritual confidence." It was more the result of constant exposure to all the forces that impacted me during my journey. Probably the most profitable were those times that I most detested, when the romance of the Trail was put into perspective, when the psychological stresses and the physical pain and discomfort were the most acute. It was the sum total of the experiences. I had "paid my dues." I now had come home.

In a way, the spiritual path is like that, like a search, or an adventure that ultimately leads home. We all long for fulfillment of dreams, to be strong and capable, to come into our own. Some of us are successful, some less than successful. We learn that it is not the goals that symbolize success or failure, but the processes or the journey that lead us to what is essential. And as we progress in our journey, we find what we knew all along — that the answers and the strengths ultimately lay within us. It was simply a matter of recognizing that we were really coming home. And that, as Robert Frost once wrote, "has made all the difference."

I was astounded at the way reflections and recollections tumbled into focus as I climbed down. Scenes from hundreds of shelters and faces and places flashed into my mind. I thought about Granma and her crew, Carleton and G-Man, and most recently, the Hopsons and Addie, and Eva Bodwell and David Christian. I also thought back to the previous year and Nick Sprague at Plum Orchard Gap in Georgia, and Dr. Luck in Damascus, Virginia, and Buddy and Jensine Crossman, Sutton Brown and Mike Joslin . Levi and Jan Long and Kate Childress and the Blessings in Bastion, Virginia, also came to mind as did Dr. Jim Laidlaw in Winchester, Virginia. They were the people who helped me succeed, the people who, when I needed help or support, offered their support with a generosity that came from the soul.

I also thought about the mountain people. They were a microcosm of the strength of America, the character of its people. They were people filled with empathy who found helping others as natural as getting up in the morning. Their honesty could be traced through their genes to those generations that created the tradition of a man's word being his bond. There were no qualifications in their friendship, only that you be a fellow human being. And, of course, they all had that streak of independence that I found to be particularly endearing. They were great people in the very essence of the word.

On the other hand, the Trail did not turn out to be a Garden of Eden where people came to be cleansed of their sins to live in idyllic bliss forever after. It was rather a microcosm of our society where the basic strengths and weaknesses, the noble and petty, and the psychological power or psychological deformities of many on the Trail became even more pronounced. Those who came with positive attitudes strengthened their outlooks, and those who saw things in negative terms tended to remain so. They acted for the most part as they would have had they not been on the Trail. They came with their hostilities and jealousies and egos, and the Trail seemed to accentuate those weaknesses. Others, more inclined to be accepting of the world and the Trail, departed stronger. Those who looked for good in their neighbor found good. Those who were tolerant of others found even more reason for tolerance. Those who exhibited spiritual awareness improved their spirituality.

Many had come at critical junctures in their lives, at times when they needed to escape the pressures of life to find peace and solitude in order to sort out the directions they wanted to take. The Trail would do for them whatever they wanted it to do. They had only to be open enough to allow it to work, to be positive and receptive to what it taught. If they did that, they would leave with the answers they were seeking.

I thought about all the thru-hikers who had been racing from shelter to shelter, who cut short their conversations with others for fear of losing too much time, who were more interested in racking up 25-mile days. Who was to say they were wrong? They were doing the Trail "their way." I had to learn and relearn that lesson, that I could only hike the Trail in my way. When I finally learned that and uncoupled from the "Granma express" it made a complete difference, not only in my appreciation for the Trail but also enhanced my entire outlook toward the Trail.

That is not to say that I agreed with the way "power hikers" were racing between shelters. I could not have obtained what I wanted from the Trail had I adopted their approach. Of course, I physically could not have succeeded in doing that anyway. But because of their obsession with speed, they were limited in the range of experiences. I personally found a great deal of interest and enjoyment in talking with the great variety of people I had met. I found that they helped expand my focus, which I surely would have missed had I been concerned only with being the first 53-year-old up Katahdin that year.

In a way, I was greatly impressed by the "power hikers," much as marathon runners impressed me. I was impressed by their dedication to their goal and their total concentration on that effort. They also seemed unperturbed by the physical difficulty of the Trail. They could go up hill or down hill at the same speed — and it was always fast. They also seemed oblivious to the weather. They appeared to assume the worst and were determined not to let the worst affect them. Their determination could only be described as awesome.

I had come on the Trail with a slightly romantic picture of hiking, of the Trail and the mountains. My imagination had been captured by the descriptions of the great natural beauty I had read about in various books and periodicals. It was different now. I was an authority. No one would ever be able to tell me about the Appalachian Trail without me being able to compare it with my own certain, personal perspective. I had walked that "sucker" and knew the AT was no "foot path" — as it was so often described. I knew that the words "foot path" were a euphemism for "rock scramble" and that the Trail was a very physically demanding, a constant series of climbs or descents of varying degrees of steepness over very trying terrain consisting of boulders, ledges, roots and rocks. But that was tempered to a degree by more than a few welcome respites along the logging trails and roads and abandoned railroad beds and in occasional valleys and towns through which the "foot path" passed.

For me, hiking the Trail had become a study in contrasts that played out in my mind according to the circumstances of the path and my particular mood at the moment. And one influenced the other. After the first few weeks, the natural beauty had lost its allure, and the bone and muscle-grinding rock inclines became the dominant reality. The hike became an endurance contest, and it was matter of gritting my teeth and refusing to give in. At other times, the Trail would come to a beautiful place, a mountain, a stream, a gorge or a spruce forest, a hemlock stand or a tarn, and these broke the tedium of rocks, trees and roots — and then it was a matter of savoring the time and the beauty.

But for the most part, the Trail led through forests, and it was impossible to see more than a 100 yards in any direction.

The mind can only appreciate so much beauty before what was once exciting becomes tedious. And after time, the succession of rocks, roots and trees became tedium requiring me to search for the positive aspects of hiking, of looking at the landscape with a fresh approach to maintain interest. And that was not always easy, particularly when faced with tough trail conditions or bad weather, or both at the same time.

Many of the people I met would ask how I could stay on the Trail for such a long period. For me, it was three months at a time. For most thru-hikers it was a six-month challenge. I always replied that if I were ever to hike the Trail again, I would break the hike into smaller segments spending not more than a month on the Trail in any one stretch. In doing this, I might maintain a fresh perspective about my hike and why I was on it.

Finally, as I was walking into Katahdin Stream Campground, it occurred to me how fortunate I was to have had the opportunity to walk the Trail. Despite its difficulty, its misery, its aggravation the Trail had been more than matched by its beauty, its exaltations and its victories. It had been one great, once-in-a-lifetime experience.

I had started out with two things in mind primarily, and that was to make the transition from being an Army Officer to becoming a private citizen and to explore in my mind the possibilities for a second career. What I received, when I let myself be receptive to it, was a complete reordering of the priorities that governed my life up till then, even to the most basic outlook towards my existence. That was absolutely phenomenal — when I reflected on it.

I was proud of myself. I was also confident about the future. I now knew who I was and what I was about. I also knew I was involved in a new beginning and was anxious to get started. The comment in the shelter register by Jeff Garrison flashed before my eyes:

"If you think you're finished when you've done Katahdin — you shouldn't have started."

Index